OBJECT ORIENTATION

WILEY SERIES IN SOFTWARE ENGINEERING PRACTICE

Series Editors:

Patrick A.V. Hall, *The Open University, UK*
Martyn A. Ould, *Praxis Systems plc, UK*
William E. Riddle, *Software Design & Analysis, Inc., USA*

Aims and Scope

The focus of this series is the software creation and evolution processes and related organisational and automated systems necessary to support them. The aim is to produce books dealing with all aspects of software engineering, particularly the practical exploitation of the best methods and tools for the development process.

The series covers the following topics:

- process models and software lifecycle
- project management, quality assurance, configuration management, process and product standards
- the external business environment and legal constraints
- computer aided software engineering (CASE) and integrated project support environments (IPSES)
- requirements analysis, specification and validation
- architectural design techniques, software components and re-use
- system design methods and verification
- system implementation, build and test
- maintenance and enhancement

For a full list of titles in this series, see back pages.

OBJECT ORIENTATION

TECHNOLOGY, TECHNIQUES, MANAGEMENT AND MIGRATION

John S. Hares

Object Technology Associates, UK

and

John D. Smart

BAeSEMA

JOHN WILEY & SONS

Chichester • New York • Brisbane • Toronto • Singapore

Other Wiley Editorial Offices

John Wiley & Sons, Inc., 605 Third Avenue,
New York, NY 10158-0012, USA

Jacaranda Wiley Ltd, 33 Park Road, Milton,
Queensland 4064, Australia

John Wiley & Sons (Canada) Ltd, 22 Worcester Road,
Rexdale, Ontario M9W 1L1, Canada

John Wiley & Sons (SEA) Pte Ltd, 37 Jalan Pemimpin #05-04,
Block B, Union Industrial Building, Singapore 2057

Library of Congress Cataloging-in-Publication Data

Hares, John S.
    Object orientation : technology, techniques, management, and
  migration / John S. Hares and John D. Smart
      p.   cm. — (Wiley series in software engineering practice)
    Includes bibliographical references and index.
    ISBN 0 471 94124 7
    1. Object-oriented programming (Computer science)   I. Smart, John
  D.   II. Title.   III. Series.
  QA76.64.H358   1993
  005.1'1—dc20   93–30490
                                                            CIP

British Library Cataloguing in Publication Data

A catalogue record for this book is available from the British Library

ISBN 0-471-94124-7

Typeset in 10/12pt Palatino from authors' disks by Text Processing Department,
John Wiley & Sons Ltd, Chichester
Printed and bound in Great Britain by
Biddles Ltd, Guildford and King's Lynn

To my family
and the memory of my first grandchild,
Alice Ruby, whose short but happy life,
whilst this book was in preparation,
was a joy to us all.

John Smart

CONTENTS

PREFACE

This book is the amalgam of the ideas and experiences of two very different authors, one having a database background and the other a programming background. Each started out with very different views of object orientation, to the extent that discussions on what makes object orientation "tick" were quite strongly expressed. By the time that the book was written the differences of view were minimal to the point of invisibility.

The ideas in the book on how to design and implement object oriented application systems are those of the authors. There is very little dependence on the ideas of previous authors on the subject. That is why there is none of the usual thanks to hosts of participants in the preparation of this book.

All that is described is based on practical experience. None of the book is theory. If the reader follows the advice he/she will find that the designed and implemented system will work.

1

THE INFORMATION DESIGN AND SOFTWARE DEVELOPMENT ENVIRONMENT FOR THE 1990s

This chapter starts by describing the purpose of the book, the concepts underlying object orientation and the fact that relational technology has hit the technical buffers and is quite unable to satisfy the requirements of software development in the 1990s. This is followed by an explanation of why object orientation is the answer to those requirements, along with a detailed description of the many benefits to be obtained from the use of object orientation.

1.1 THE BASIS AND PURPOSE OF THIS BOOK

This book describes and considers object orientation.

Object orientation is the technology that is replacing today's database and programming technology for the design and development of computerised application systems, the technology that some regard as the ultimate paradigm for the modelling of information, be that information data or logic.

The book is general on the subject of object orientation rather than focusing on a particular part of what is a huge field. All the facilities of object orientation are addressed. No particular object oriented technology, no particular object oriented technique and no particular object oriented product is considered.

The book addresses:

- *The Features of Object Orientation*
  This describes the concepts underlying object orientation, why object orientation is different from the current IT implementation technologies and logical and physical design techniques, and the whys and wherefores of the need to, the benefits of and the business case for adopting object orientation. This is addresed in Chapter 1.

- *The Technical Facilities of Object Orientation*
  This describes those technologies that enable the concepts of object orientation to be supported. The general facilities for modelling information[1] in an object oriented way are identified, described and explained, and are then put in the context of object oriented file handlers and programming languages for the implementation of object oriented application systems. This is covered in Chapters 2–4.

- *The Evolution of Object Oriented Technology*
  This first describes how object oriented programming languages evolved and the different approaches to the provision of object oriented facilities which the various languages have adopted. A review of the leading object oriented programming languages is considered, with worked examples of how the object oriented facilities are supported. The more recent development of object oriented file handlers is also discussed. A general consideration of the market place for object oriented technology is then given. This is covered in Chapter 5.

- *The Design Techniques of Object Orientation*
  This starts by describing the various "battles" underway over how to model information in an object oriented way, followed by an assessment of the new structured methods specifically developed for object oriented information modelling. The chapter then describes the requirements of the three main design techniques for object oriented information modelling, and shows how easily the long established "traditional" structured methods, such as SSADM, Information Engineering and MERISE can be made object oriented. This is addressed in Chapter 6.

- *The Management of Object Orientation*
  This describes the increased role that prototyping can play in the design and development of object oriented application systems, the different structure of the information life cycle with object oriented projects, and the different roles, responsibiliies and management issues that an object oriented project requires. This is covered in Chapter 7.

---

[1]   In the context of this book, information is defined as both data and logic.

- *The Migration to Object Orientation*
  This chapter describes the various strategies for migrating existing applications to an object oriented design, their strengths, weaknesses and applicability. This is addressed in Chapter 8.

The book is therefore targeted at both practitioners of information technology in general, and more specifically at:

- anyone who wishes to know what object orientation is and why it is so powerful as compared with today's other software development technologies;

- a general audience of IT practitioners who are familiar with current file handler and programming technology and the design techniques of current structured design methods, and who wish to understand how to adopt object orientation within this framework. As will be seen, object orientation does not require experienced practitioners to unlearn their knowledge and their expertise of existing technology and techniques and "start again". *Object orientation is an extension, a significant extension but an extension, nevertheless, of today's application systems development technology.*

- the managers of IT departments and IT projects who need to know the migration management and organisational issues that object orientation creates.

It is assumed that the reader has a good understanding of database technology, particularly in relational database technology, and of structured methods for batch and online processing. Such readers would have a minimum of five years' practical experience.

The basic thrust of the book is that the IT industry is moving into an era of post-relational technology, particularly in the way that we design information, both as regards the data component and, above all, the logic component. We are also seeing the probable introduction of a further set of information in that knowledge can now also be used alongside the traditional data and logic. Although object orientation is able to model information in the form of knowledge, the technology of object orientation, of itself, is not able to use the knowledge. This requires an inference engine, the technology of an expert system. However, the important point is that object oriented design is already an excellent basis for an expert system as far as the application information is concerned. Information redesign for the support of knowledge is not required.

1.2 THE SCOPE OF OBJECT ORIENTATION

The scope of object oriented design techniques and implementation technologies is exactly the same as for today's database and programming technology, namely the design and development of computerised application systems.

Where object orientation is compared against database technology that is assumed to be relational. Most database users are now relational, and relational technology is an almost universally understood standard. In addition, relational technology is the third generation of database technology[1], as well as being the generation that object orientation is replacing.

Relational technology is composed of the following main facilities:

- a file handler for the storage and access of data;

- a data definition language (DDL)[2] for description of the database tables and their data properties;

- a command-based data manipulation (DML) language (universally SQL) for access to the tables of data;

- a 4GL procedural programming language[3] for specifying processing logic for the manipulation of data, once accessed;

- a cursor-based screen painter for easy formatting of input and output screens and the definition of appropriate built-in functions for screen presentation and data editing[4];

- a report writer for rapid definition of the formatting and logic requirements of batch reports.

These facilities provide all the functionality required for designing and developing an application system.

So it is with object orientation. Object orientation contains the equivalent of a file handler, a programming language and a report writer. As described in Chapter 3, almost all object orientation products are currently restricted to a file handler and a programming language. When the relational vendors

---

[1]   The first generation is hierarchical database file handlers, such as IMS from IBM; the second generation is the Codasyl standard, such as IDMS from vendors such as ICL and the erstwhile Cullinet

[2]   This language is used for defining the structure of the data tables and their data properties of both relational and pre-relational databases. The definition of the data is therefore taken from the programmer and transferred to the database administrator.

[3]   This contains the sequence, selection and iteration facilities of the traditional programming language for the writing of process logic.

[4]   Quite a few relational products combine the 4GL programming language and the screen painter. A leading example of this is ORACLE with SQL*FORMS and PL*SQL.

respond with their own enhancements to their relational products with object oriented facilities, then the full set of relational-type facilities for the object oriented development of software applications will be available.

1.3 DATA PROCESSING ENVIRONMENTS: CONCEPTS, TECHNOLOGIES AND TECHNIQUES

Seven data processing environments can be identified. Two of these—centralised and realtime processing—have long been established, and are well recognised and identified by widely used and understood terms. A further four—distributed, expert system, neural and object oriented—have only recently been recognised, but will become established during the 1990s. The final environment, that of conversational processing, has long been established but is seldom appreciated and seemingly little used in its original form. It has recently been enhanced with new technology and will, as represented in the new windows technology, become a standard for the man/machine interface. The environments are diagrammatically represented in figure 1.1.

Centralised processing occurs where all data processing is to be executed on a single processor, with remote dumb terminals linked to the processor. The terminals are dumb because they contain no data processing facilities, and they may be spread over a large geographical area, even at multiple sites.

The centralised environment is generic, with its technologies being used by the

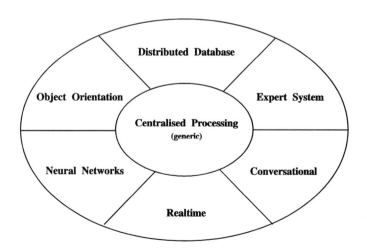

Figure 1.1 Data processing environments

other data processing environments. Facilities such as the file handler, screen painter, query language and the report writer are all used by the other environments. All these environments contain batch and online processing, and function within a centralised environment. *They are, in fact, nothing more than centralised processing "plus a little bit".* This is because the vendors of the technology for these other environments have followed a policy of *using the existing technology of centralised processing without change and adding additional software facilities on top.*

Distributed processing occurs where multiple processors support a set of multi-site application systems, each with a local database. The processors are widely distributed geographically, one to each site, and are linked dynamically so that the applications and their databases function as a synchronised whole.

Much confusion exists as to the difference between realtime and online processing. The Yourdon definition of realtime best identifies the difference; it is defined as "immediate output of current input". This means that as an input message is received it is immediately processed in a processor, and the output from that process is immediately displayed.

For example, a radar aerial monitoring the movement of aircraft through the sky records the electrical signals received and passes the information to the processor, which then immediately displays the information on a visual display unit (VDU). The process may access a standard database to retrieve user data to ascertain, for example, the type of aircraft which matches the signal received. This part is online and not realtime processing. Much realtime data has a limited life-span, even as little as a few seconds. The radar system can discard the signal received after a few revolutions of the aerial if the system's task is merely to monitor the flight movement of aircraft.

With online processing the output is not the result of immediate input. Modifying Yourdon's quotation, "Online processing is immediate processing of previous input". For example, the data for an online request to display a customer's orders may well have been stored in the database for some considerable time. Online processing produces immediate output, but not on the basis of immediate input.

Expert systems have the ability to store and access knowledge as well as data, which means they can represent expertise regarding a particular application domain, for example how to service a car engine or diagnose an illness. Expert systems can therefore be relevant for different types of computer applications to those which have traditionally been developed. They are particularly suited to those applications requiring expertise to solve problems. Traditionally, data processing has been for those applications where dumb data is presented to users for them as homo sapiens to interpret. Expert systems, by contrast, can offer advice as well as merely present data. They can thus "assist" and "advise" in such expertise-based tasks as diagnosis, planning, design and interpretation.

The neural network environment is not addressed in this book as the authors have no experience of it. It is the ability of computers to learn from the information they are processing. The environment is not considered further here.

Conversational processing is the least clear cut environment. It is an extension of online processing, where a user is requesting an immediate response to database access requests. The difference is that the user is having a dialogue with the processor at a terminal, and thus needs to monitor previous iterations of the conversation. For example, a user may wish to terminate a conversation but record the state of the conversation, typically as represented by the data currently displayed at the terminal at the point of termination, for subsequent recall. When the conversation is renewed at a later point in time, the user wishes to recall the state of the conversation, which may have been forgotten, by retrieving the relevant information from the last screen. The application program/system software therefore needs to recognise explicitly that the user requires continuous running iterations of online interactions with the application system, each iteration being represented by one or more screens. An early form of conversational processing was that used in IMS/DC teleprocessing with the scratchpad facility for recording information from one conversation to another. The most widely used form of conversational processing today is windows technology, with each window acting as a scratchpad. This is different from online processing, where the application program switches itself off between output and input screens and the data from the previous screen is lost.

The object oriented environment is a "modernised" version of centralised processing. Until recently, all application systems were designed and developed on the basis that:

- data and logic are kept separate—the data in the database and the logic in the application programs. It is now realised that this separation is illogical (after all, both data and logic are information) and inefficient (data has to be moved to the logic), with a raft of other inadequacies and inconsistencies. Object oriented technology has been developed in database file handlers and application programming languages to bring both types of information together.

- key-based data and event based logic. There are two information modelling paradigms here—the data on keys for the identification of "things" of interest to the user, and the events as business requirements being supported by the logic of an application program. These two paradigms have, as suggested above, generated two sets of technologies and ultimately two sets of data processing skills and careers. The authors represent this dichotomy—one specialising in the design of data and the other in the writing of logic.

These two paradigms are perfectly valid—they are what the user thinks in terms of. For example, the user thinks in terms of customers and orders, and customer 123 being a different customer from customer 321, and that customers place orders and pay invoices. Given that is how the user thinks it is not surprising that current information design techniques and implementation technologies reflect this fact, and have therefore separated the definition, storage and access of data (the customers, orders and products) from the specification and writing of logic (the placing of orders and the payment of invoices). This technical separation reflects users' thinking, and the adoption of object orientation will not alter the way users operate or managers run their business. *It therefore means that object oriented technology will continue to use key based data and event based logic.*

But it is now realised that these two paradigms are merely the visible representations of the users/view of the world. There are, in fact, other information modelling paradigms that the user is not aware of, but which are nevertheless present and offer a much more powerful way of information modelling. There are such paradigms as behaviour—different key-based "objects"/tables can have the same behaviour—employee and pensioners are different objects/tables, yet both have a common behaviour of being persons. There is also the fact that objects can be complex—object A is composed of objects B, C and D. This can and should be modelled. Object orientation provides this facility for a more powerful information modelling of behaviour and complexity on top of key-based data and event-based logic.

Given that object orientation is another form of centralised processing, why has it been treated as another data processing environment? The reason is that, of all the other environments, it is the one that is more than centralised processing plus a little bit. There is some modification. There are, as described throughout this book, some differences in the design techniques and implementation technologies for those parts which overlap centralised processing.

It has been suggested to the authors that the word "technology" be used rather than environment. In fact there are three points to consider—concepts, implementation technologies and design techniques—and the points need to be considered in that order. The authors prefer to use the word "environment" because the data processing environments *are each based on their own different set of underlying concepts*. The concepts characterise the environments. And it is physical technology that supports the concepts.

For example, to support the concept of location transparency, distributed databases need to provide various database access mechanisms that can access the appropriate data stored at various locations without the user knowing this. The fact that the data is distributed is transparent to the user: the concepts drive the technologies, not the other way around. The physical hardware/software technologies are merely tools to do the job which the environments seek to provide.

The techniques, in turn, have been designed on the basis of the technologies. The reason for the relationship dependency of the design techniques on the implementation technologies is easy to explain. Throughout the history of computing, technologies have preceded techniques. The reason is simple: There is no point in developing a structured method containing a set of logical and physical design techniques if there is no physical technology to implement the logical and physical design specifications.

There has been technology to support batch and online processing for the last three decades or more, but structured methods with design techniques have only gained wide acceptance in the last 15 years. The time gap between technology and techniques is the same for the other environments; And so it is with object orientation. Object oriented implementation technology has been available for the last five or more years, but the design techniques are only now appearing.

There is a cascading relationship. The concepts are the basis of the environments and drive the technologies, and the technologies drive the techniques. *These relationships of the concepts to the technologies and the technologies to the techniques are rarely recognised—yet they are the basis of this book.*

It is important to realise that if the technology has not been developed to support the concepts then the technology is unstable. The technology for centralised, realtime and expert system processing is fully developed. The authors believe that there is thus little technical improvement to be found in these environments. The technology will remain stable. Neither of the concepts of distributed database are fully supported, for example there is no fully automatic synchronisation of recovery for hardware across locations. The concept of update synchronisation is therefore not fully supported for hardware; it is for database update and software recovery, but not for hardware. Distributed database technology is therefore unstable, because basic improvements, not just the fine tuning of what is there, are still required.

This book will show that the concepts underlying object orientation are also fully supported by object oriented technology. The technology is therefore also stable.

What is true of the technology is true of the structured methods containing the design techniques. Consider the Yourdon method. It is specifically targeted at realtime processing, and explicitly recognises the concepts on which this data processing environment is based. The method was developed in its initial form by Ed Yourdon, and has been further

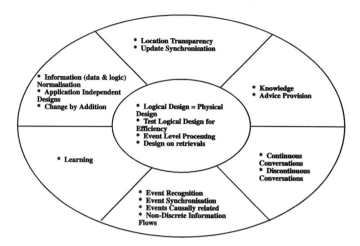

Figure 1.2   Data processing environment concepts

upgraded by others, such as Ward and Mellor. The authors find the method a delight to apply, with the techniques directly reflecting the concepts underlying realtime systems, and hence relating to each other most attractively and producing a set of excellent integrated deliverables. Yet the method does not support many of the concepts of centralised batch and online processing.

The book will show that the current structured methods for object

Figure 1.3   Data processing environment technologies

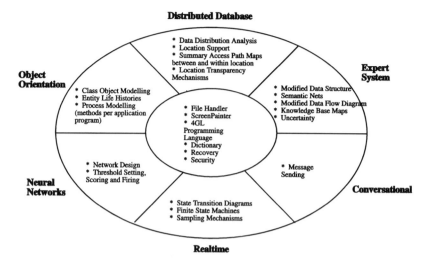

Figure 1.4 Data processing environment techniques

oriented information modelling fall far short of supporting the concepts of object orientation.

The concepts for each of the data processing environments, the related technologies and the appropriate techniques are illustrated in figures 1.2–1.4. Given the purpose of this book, only the concepts underlying object orientation are described.

1.4 THE CONCEPTS OF OBJECT ORIENTATION

Three concepts or principles underpin object orientation:

1.4.1 The normalisation of information

Dr Codd of relational fame[1] developed rules for ensuring that the data properties were correctly placed to the tables of data to which they "belong", Customer Name "belonging to" the Customer table. But these normalisation rules only relate to data. It is now possible to apply these normalisation rules to logic. It is now appreciated that some 80% of logic relates not to the

---

[1] Dr. E. Codd defined a set of 12 rules that became the foundation of relational technology. The basis of the rules is that data is defined as flat records/tables containing data attributes/properties that described the objects the tables represented. There could be a Customer table with data properties that describe the customer. Backing these rules was a further set of rules for "normalising" data so that the properties would correctly describe the table. The data property Customer Name would normalise to the Customer table on the basis that Customer Name "belongs to" Customer.

event/business requirements but to the objects/tables. Virtually all information, be it 100% of the data or 80% of the logic, can be normalised to objects. The 20% of logic that remains at the event level is typically the initialisation of the variables, sending messages to processes to access the data properties in the relevant tables/objects, input and output formatting and any pre- and post-processing prior to and following the data access. This concept of normalising information of either type is appropriate given that an object in object orientation can support, unlike relational tables of data, both data *and* logic within objects.

A formal definition of an object is that "it is an entity that exists uniquely and distinctly in time and space, *containing both data and logic about itself within itself*".

The first part of the definition is not particularly significant: today's database technology supports it. Logical entities and physical tables of data describes "things" of interest to an application about which data, and only data, can be recorded. But objects are more than entities. Objects describe "things" of interest to an application about which data *and/or* logic can be recorded. *It is the logic component which primarily distinguishes objects from records/tables of database file handlers, which only contain data.* There are other facilities, as will be ascertained, but it is the logic that is the prime distinguishing feature.

The significant point here is that information, be it data or logic, is defined *within* the object to which it logically relates. It is well known that the customer name data attribute normalises to the customer entity. Why shouldn't the logic "All customers with red hair receive a lump sum of £100" also be normalised to the customer entity? The answer is that it can be—it is not logic that relates to any particular event. The logic, like the data, is normalised to the object Customer. *The first concept of object oriented design is therefore the normalisation of information.*

1.4.2   Application independent designs

The normalisation of information leads to the second concept, *the creation of application independent information designs*, that is the design of information which is generic to a corporation. To date, the only part of information that is corporate is data, hence the creation of corporate databases. The reason for this is that the data has been normalised to the appropriate entity/object and not to a business requirement/event of a functional area of an application. Customer Name is a data property describing Customer, not a business requirement. The data is therefore not specific to an application and its constituent business requirements. The same data objects can be "accessed" by multiple functionally based applications.

The same is true when the logic information is normalised to an object. If the logic is "All Customers with red hair receive a lump sum of £100" then it, like the data, has nothing to do with a particular business requirement/event but with the Customer object, in the same way as Customer Name. The logic is a logic property describing Customer, not a business requirement. It is therefore likewise normalised to the Customer object. When logic is normalised like data it has the same corporate characteristics as data in that it too is application independent—but in this case the logic can be "re-used" (a word much used by object oriented devotees) by multiple applications. *Only the 20% of logic that remains at the event/business requirement level is application dependent.*

1.4.3 Change by addition

There is a third concept, which is perhaps the most significant in that it most distinguishes object orientation from pre object oriented technology. The concept is that *enhancements made to application systems are through addition rather than through modification.*

There are two ways in which enhancements to an existing application system can be made—by modification or by addition. Of the two, addition is by far the better approach as the existing information is untouched and therefore remains stable.

Pre-object oriented technology enhanced an existing application through the process of modification. The user requests an enhancement to an existing business requirement in the application system. The code of the supporting application program would be modified, recompiled, retested and run. Modification would be the approach adopted for supporting the changed situation. The problem with this approach is that the stability of the existing application program is lost, hence the need for retesting the modification.

Object orientation adopts the strategy of supporting enhancement through the process of addition: there is no modification. When a change is required to the design of the data or the logic, it is not a case of altering the existing design but of using the existing information as much as possible, and adding data or logic properties to the existing information only if it is unable to support the new requirements. The new is added to the old. This process of addition is mainly supported by the creation of a specialised sub class to the existing object class, with the new sub class inheriting the data and logic properties of the existing and now super class.

One can also create generalised super classes of the existing information. As new properties are added to the class model, new commonality of now common properties between the classes can be ascertained. These common properties are abstracted as super classes to the existing base classes.

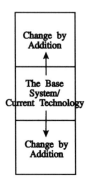

Beneficial Result

Existing information becomes increasingly reused and stable

Figure 1.5   Object oriented business enhancement by addition

This change, by addition to the existing information of the base application, is illustrated in figure 1.5.

This change by addition is also true of the technology used by object orientation. Object orientation uses the same technology as that long used by current file handlers and programming languages. For example, the object oriented file handlers continue to use keys for concrete objects and procedural code for processing the data properties of the objects. Additional facilities *have been added* to today's technology to support the additional requirements of object oriented information modelling, for example the use of property inheritance and polymorphism.

The concepts underlying the other data processing environments and relevant to object orientation are described in Appendix 1.

1.5   DOES OBJECT ORIENTATION REQUIRE A NEW WAY OF THINKING?

In discussion with vendors of object oriented products, the authors have been consistently advised that a new way of thinking is required: "You need to throw away much of what you have learnt before about systems design and development and apply new ways of thinking".

It is argued by some (B. Meyer, *op cit*) that object oriented design is the antithesis of the traditional analysis and design structured methods, such as SSADM and Information Engineering. These methods typically use the top-down approach of taking a high level process and decomposing it down to its constituent sub-processes. This approach is good at ensuring that the design will meet the initial user requirements, but it does not promote reuseability—the sub-processes may overlap. Reuseable software requires that systems are designed by combining existing elements as much as possible, which is the definition of bottom-up design.

The authors are not so sure. Why can't one add the additional data and functionality of the new application system after applying the top-down approach to identifying what the new information requirements are. Add bottom-up design to the results of top-down analysis. It was also stated earlier that centralised processing is generic, because the facilities of batch and online data processing supporting the centralised environment are common to the other and more recent data processing environments such as expert systems and object orientation. Why should object oriented systems be fundamentally different from the generic facilities of centralised processing when the other distributed, realtime and conversational data processing environments are nothing more than centralised plus a little bit?

Based on initial practical experiences, a picture of reality as opposed to opinion is emerging. The logical/physical component parts of a computer system are:

Logical		*Physical*
data structure	)	database/file
data access	)	application programs
data process	)	

As already mentioned, there are two ways in which existing software implementation technology and design techniques can be enhanced—by addition or by modification. The former is much to be preferred, if possible, because it preserves investment in existing computer systems. *What is becoming clear is that the traditional technologies and techniques for data structure require addition to become object oriented, while those for access and process logic require modification to become object oriented.* Given that data is normalised, all that is required is to build a traditional logical data model and then to add the object oriented facilities, such as data abstraction of common data properties, to convert the logical data model into a class-based object model.

But even for the part requiring modification there is a position of comfort. The technique for normalising logic is, as we shall see, the same as that for data. This, of course, results in modification as the logic design paradigm for today's application programs is event-based logic. But only some 20% of logic is event-based. There is therefore modification to some 80% of the logic—it is logic that can be normalised to object classes. This 80% of logic is redesigned to be object- rather than event-based. *But we are using the technique for the design of data to the technique for the design of logic.* It is therefore not a case of unlearning the skills we have, but of applying one of the techniques, the technique of data normalisation, in another context.

It is therefore more a situation of using existing technologies and techniques and enhancing them by addition. The authors cannot think of anything that requires a practitioner of the current structured design methods and relational and other database file handlers and programming languages to unlearn his/her skills. Apply it differently in some parts, yes, but unlearn, no.

Object orientation is a major subject, with a substantial array of additional technical facilities not found in traditional processing. These facilities need to be reflected in the design techniques. They include class and aggregation object abstraction in the class model, property inheritance in the class model, encapsulation, property instantiation at the class level, polymorphism of processes that have a common name but different functionality for its achievement depending on the object instances being accessed, function name overloading, where a process of the same name can support different functionality depending on system circumstances, logic normalisation and message passing between object classes. But none of these facilities negates the pre-object oriented skills.

1.6   THE PROBLEM OF TERMINOLOGY

Object oriented technology has evolved from two independent paths—the programming and database paths.

The programming path evolved first, with the earliest object oriented products being object oriented programming languages. The OO languages like C++ and SMALLTALK contain not only the DML facilities for accessing and processing data in an object oriented-like way, but also the data definition facilities for modelling the data and logic in an object oriented like way. The programmer has to define the class model of objects and send messages to the appropriate classes to access the object instances to obtain the benefits of object orientation. Object orientation is DIY[1] in the DML of the object oriented programming language.

Object oriented file handlers evolved only in the last few years, and in most cases these are object oriented file handlers tied to specific object oriented programming languages. The Objectstore file handler, for example, is specifically based on the C++ language. Object orientation is therefore still largely a matter of do it yourself. The OO file handler is typically able to support the definition of the class model and is therefore able to support some object orientation in the DDL, but the support for the OO processing, such as property inheritance of object oriented processes, is still in the associated OO programming language.

This two part history has spawned its own object oriented terminology for the definition of objects and their occurrences. Given that most readers of this book will have used relational technology the base terms about to be described will be related to relational terminology. Relational technology

---

[1]   "Do it yourself".

uses the terms tables and table rows to identify "things" of interest to the application and their occurrences. Tables of data would be identified for such "things" as customers, orders and products, and there would be a table row record for each occurrence of the customers, orders and products. If the business had 100 customers, 1000 orders and 50 products there would be 100 rows of the table Customer, 1000 rows of the table Order and 50 rows of the table Product.

Those from the OO programming fraternity use the equivalent terms of class and objects, and those from the database fraternity use the terms class objects and instances of the class objects. This book reflects this dichotomy in that one of the authors is from the programming school and the other from the database school.

The terms class, objects, class objects and instances of the class are therefore used interchangeably. There should be no difficulty in understanding the meaning, as the context in which the terms are used makes the meaning clear.

The structure of the terminology is:

Relational	*OO Database*	*OO Programming*
Table	Class Object	Class
Row	Instance Object	Object

What is becoming clear is that the terminology used by the object oriented programming fraternity seems to be winning the day. Indeed, in a recent assignment with one of the relational vendors on reviewing their product from an object oriented perspective, equivalent object oriented programming terms were used rather than "OO relational terms". This book reflects the "winning side".

1.7 THE REQUIREMENTS OF APPLICATION SOFTWARE IN THE 1990s

This is addressed from the point of view of the developer and the user. The attractiveness of object orientation would be much reduced if it was applicable to only a single interest group. Unfortunately this is the case.

Object orientation is targeted at the software developer and not the user. The user gains little to no benefit from object orientation. What is true, however, is that object orientation has a high degree of technical overlap with expert systems[1] and is therefore an excellent basis for "intelligent" query

---

[1]   Object orientation is able to model knowledge data through the facility of the class model, which is also a semantic net. The semantic net is one of the two facilities for modelling knowledge, the other being rules. Object orientation is therefore an excellent basis from which "intelligent" query languages can be supported. The languages are intelligent in that they can provide advice to queries from knowledge modelled in the knowledge base of semantic nets and rules. This is fully discussed in a book authored by John Hares, *SSADM version* 4 (John Wiley & Sons, 1993).

languages, this being one of the major user tools yet to be widely used. It is through this technical relationship that object orientation can offer long term benefits to the user.

1.7.1   Requirements of the software developer

Software development is now characterised by some serious problems. If there were no problems there would be no need to adopt new technologies and techniques. The current leading application software development technology of relational file handlers and 4GL programming languages is now recognised as being inadequate for providing good solutions. As described in Section 1.10, relational technology has hit the technical buffers due to inherent design faults.

The two prime requirements for software development are that there is a need to support:

● complex business situations that are

● forever changing.

Facilities for complexity and change are the most urgent requirement for object orientation.

But this is not the end of the shopping list. Additional requirements include:

● *The need to handle all information, whether it is data or logic, in exactly the same way.* After all, both are just information. This will mean a common technology for the software developers and a single common modelling technique for the information designers.

● *The ability to model information at its appropriate level of relevance.* One of the problems with current design techniques and implementation technologies is that there is no recognition of or facilities for the fact that information is not all of the same degree of applicability—"abstraction" to use the object oriented buzzword. Some information is general and some is specialised. The ultimate general information is that which is universally true (the world is round, for example) while other information is highly particular (both authors are approaching the "nifty fifty" years of the life). The general information is more applicable (everybody wants to know the world is round) than the specialised information (who cares about ageing authors?). The more particular information should be subordinate to the more general information.

● *The ability to write software and store data only once.* This can only be done if the software and data is held where it sensibly belongs, that is it is normalised. Currently, some 80% of all application code is held in the wrong place, at the event level, and it is thus not surprising that there is much duplication and hence wasted maintenance effort. There is probably logic written in the correct place as well the same logic written in the wrong place—the same code being duplicated. From a design point of view, if code is duplicated something is wrong.

- *The ability to support the enhancement of a business application by the process of addition rather than modification.* This is the ability to reuse the existing information in the application as far as possible and then only adding the required additional functionality.

- *The ability to write declarative code.* Until recently, all application code was written in a procedural manner. A new and very powerful way of writing code is now available—what is called declarative code. Both forms of logic have their strengths and weaknesses, and it is important that both types of logic can be used where most appropriate, even within the same application program.

- *The ability to model information according to class/behaviour and aggregation/complexity and not just by key.* Relational technology can only relate tables of data together by foreign keys. The technology is designed for key-based data. Employees have a key of Employee Number and pensioners have a key of Pensioner Number, the keys being required to identify each occurrence of employee and pensioner. But this use of keys takes no account of the fact that tables of information can also be related together because they have a common behaviour, a common class. An employee has the same behaviour as a pensioner in that they may have common features, such as birthdays. These common features, as modelled by their data attributes, can be abstracted to another class that reflects this common behaviour, to an object of person. Persons have birthdays and employees and pensioners are persons.

    There is an associated need to move away from key- and table-based data access languages, languages such as SQL, to what are class/behaviour based languages. The current key-based languages are fine for hard numeric type questions such as "How much money was paid to the company employees last month?". But there is a need for softer behaviourally based questions: "Get me all the information about persons". The enquirer does not know that person includes employees and pensioners and all other objects that have similar behaviour to persons, brokers, sports persons, politicians and law officers, to name but a few. Person is a class, not a key.

- *The ability to obtain "assistance/advice" from the computer in the man/machine interface.* At the moment the data displayed on a screen is dumb, and is for us, as *homo sapiens*, to interpret. Many of the more powerful types of query languages that can access by class as well as by key are able to explain what the information is and provide advice.

Object orientation provides technical answers to all but the last of these requirements, but even here there is an excellent basis for the provision of advice. There are some 14 technical facilities used by object orientation to provide technical solutions to the above. Some of the facilities, such as function name overloading, are used in a narrow and limited programming context, providing only part of a solution to one of the requirements, while others, such as class and property inheritance, are general and used for information modelling and hence applicable to the solution of many of the requirements.

1.7.2   Requirements of the user

The user has been restricted to accessing data on the basis of key-based technology used by current database technology. This means that the type of access to queries of the type "How much/how many" is merely the presentation of the information about a specific set of tables rows. "How many customers have red hair?" would be one such typical access query, and the answer would be, for example, "10". The answer is dumb in that it is up to the user to ascertain the significance of the data presented. What is needed is new types of query language that are:

- "intelligent," in that they can provide advice with the information presented.
  10 is significant because there are only 11 customers.

- able to access information on the basis of behaviour.
  "List all information about animals". There is an invisible addition to the query of "whatever they are". Unlike traditional query languages the user does not have to know or specify the full scope of the query. Wherever there is information about animals of whatever type it is accessed and presented. The structural and hence procedural queries of the relational type access would be abandoned.

- able to access data in a non-procedural way.
  All that should need to be specified in a query for data is "Get me such and such data where the following values are true". Where the data is, within which tables and what the relationships are between the tables is a matter of total indifference to the user.

1.8   SOLUTIONS TO THE DEVELOPER'S REQUIREMENTS

The solutions to the developers requirements are supported by object orientation.

1.8.1   The need to support complexity and change

The issues of complexity and change are addressed together because their technical solutions are based on the use of a common facility. The solutions are therefore intertwined. This can be seen in figure 1.6. The object oriented facilities for the management of information complexity are as follows.

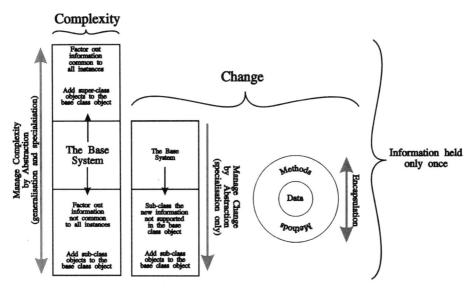

Figure 1.6 Managing complexity and change

1.8.1.1 Class abstraction[1]

This is the placement of information in the class object model according to its appropriate level of "relevance".

If the information is of more general relevance then it is abstracted and put higher up the class object information model—more generalisation—whereas if it is more particular then it is abstracted and put further down the information model—more specialisation. If the information is universally true then it is put at the top of the model—maximum generalisation. If it is incredibly particular then it is put at the bottom of the model—maximum specialisation.

The solution to complex situations is to simplify each situation as much as possible by identifying common features/behaviour, and generalise and specialise the result as appropriate.

If the properties of the class objects are common to each other and to all instances, then factor them out through generalisation, moving the factored out information further up the object class model by creating one or more super-class objects to the existing base class objects. This can be seen in figure 1.7. The data properties of Date of Birth are common to both the

---

[1] Within object orientation the term class has two meanings. The first is class as a template definition of the properties of an object—the object is composed of a set of data and logic properties that require definition to the objectbase, just as the data attributes of data tables require definition of the database. Class also means objects with common properties having a common behaviour and belonging to a class hierarchy. This latter meaning is explained in this section.

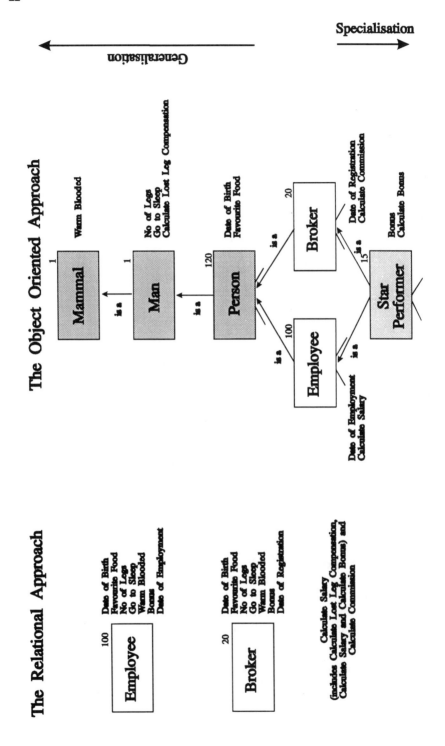

Employee and Broker class objects, so that there is common behaviour. Since the common properties are applicable to all the instances of Employee and Broker they can be generalised/abstracted to a super class of Person.

If the properties of a class are not common to all instances then factor them out through specialisation, moving the factored out information further down the class object model by creating sub classes to the existing base classes. This is illustrated with the data property of bonus. Not all the employees and the brokers (12 out of 100 and 3 out of 20) are star performers. This information can be specialised/abstracted as a sub class of Star Performer.

Consider figure 1.7 more closely for the handling of complexity. There are two classes, Employee and Broker, each of which has an array of data properties as listed. There are 100 employees and 20 brokers. Some of the data properties are common to both classes, this commonality being the hallmark of complexity. The duplication of the properties adds to the complexity. What needs to be done is to assess the degree to which abstraction of the common properties can be done. Close analysis of the data properties shows that the following properties are common to all instances of both class objects and can therefore be generalised:

- Warm Blooded
- No. of Legs
- Go to Sleep
- Date of Birth
- Favourite Food.

The question arises "To which super class is the abstracted information to be generalised?" *A new feature of object orientation needs to be introduced—the role of information.* There is no hard rule for the role of information, it being up to *homo sapiens* to ascertain to which of the super classes the abstracted properties should be allocated. Education indicates that Warm Blooded is a property that relates to Mammal, No. of Legs and Go to Sleep are properties of Man and Date of Birth and Favourite Food are properties of Person.

It has been argued by some who have seen figure 1.7 that Date of Birth and Favourite Food can be generalised to Man. But consider this. No. of Legs and Go to Sleep are properties that are generic to Man in that all sub-class objects such as Person, Employee and Broker all have legs and go to sleep—there is no choice in the matter. They are also all generically warm blooded and warm blooded is a feature of Mammals. As regards the classes

---

Figure 1.7 The handling of complexity through abstraction

Man and Mammal, there are no instances of these classes, there are just classes describing only the general features of these things called mammals and man. The data properties therefore have a value that is generic to all instances of the sub class. All instances of Persons, be they employees or brokers, have a warm blooded indicator of yes, have two legs and always go to sleep. This allocation of a generic value to a data property is called "instantiation". There is one instance of this class, the class itself.

Date of Birth and Favourite Food are properties which must have a value specific to the individual instances of the classes. Everybody has a date of birth and a favourite food, but each employee and broker can have a different birthday and different favourite food, so there can be different values for the two data properties for each instance. Date of Birth and Favourite Food are applicable to all instances of Employee and Brokers, and therefore need to be generalised, but the properties do not have a common generic value for all the instances of Employee and Broker. There is, in fact, a total of 120 Person class object instances, this being made up of the 100 employees and the 20 brokers. There are therefore potentially 120 values for Date of Birth and Favourite Food as the instances of the abstracted Person class object. There is no generic instantiation.

Further analysis of the properties shows that bonus is common, but that not all instances of Employee and Broker have bonuses. This property can therefore be specialised, with the creation of a sub class of Star Performer to the existing base classes of Employee and Broker. There are 12 employees and three brokers who are star performers, so the number of Star Performer class instances is 15. There are therefore 15 potential values for Bonus as the instances of the Star Performer class. Again, no instantiation.

There are two properties remaining—Date of Employment in Employee and Date of Registration with Broker. These properties are not common to both classes and therefore should not be abstracted. They are correctly unique to the existing base class objects. There are 100 values of Date of Employment as the instances of the Employee class and 15 values of the Date of Registration for the instances of the Broker class.

The feature of role can now be seen. Date of Employment is relevant to the role of Employee, having nothing to do with broking, and Date of Registration is relevant to the role of broking, having nothing to do with employment. Date of Birth is a feature of both employees and broker, and is therefore not relevant to the role of employment and broking. It is relevant to the role of being a person. And being warm blooded is relevant to the role of being mammalian. And so on.

And what is true of the data properties is also true of the logic. The Salary process is composed of sub processes for the calculation of compensation for losing a leg (the process reads the No of Legs data property to see if there is a value less than "2"), for the calculation of the basic salary of an employee, and for calculating the bonus for Star Employees. Using the same rules as for the data, the processes of Calculate Salary are allocated, as illustrated in figure 1.7.

Chapter 6 discusses the feature of the role of information in the context of the normalisation of information.

1.8.1.2 Aggregation abstraction

This occurs where objects are composed of other objects. An engine is composed of an engine shell, a carburettor, pistons, and so on. The component objects (like engine shell, the carburettor and the piston) are abstracted from the source object class (the engine) and made super classes.

1.8.1.3 Property inheritance

This is the ability to access the general information higher up the class model from the specialised information lower down the class model. Abstraction, either for class or aggregation, requires inheritance.

What this means is that Employee and Broker can inherit the properties of the super class, that is the properties of Person, Man and Mammal. The concatenation of the super-class properties means that each employee still has the properties as defined in the relational design but, in this case, most of the properties are inherited. And if the employee is a star performer he/she will also have the property of a bonus.

This concatenation of the class inheritance hierarchy to form the full structure of the instances of the class is illustrated in figure 1.8. Each class is a union of all the information of the class and its super class in the class hierarchy. It shows the inheritance of the properties of the super class, both Employee and Broker inheriting the properties of Person, Man and Mammal. If an employee and broker is a star performer then bonus is added as a property. The result is that all the properties higher up the class hierarchy are contained in the class object instances lower down the class hierarchy.

The object oriented facilities for the management of information change are:

● *encapsulation*
   This is the ability to ensure that the information contents of an object are hidden from the outside world—object A does not know what object B contains, and *vice versa*. Encapsulation is often known as information hiding.

   A problem long faced by the developers of current applications is that a change in one application program has a "ripple effect" in other application programs. For example, a range check in one module will cause problems if another module is innocently recording "out of range" data.

26

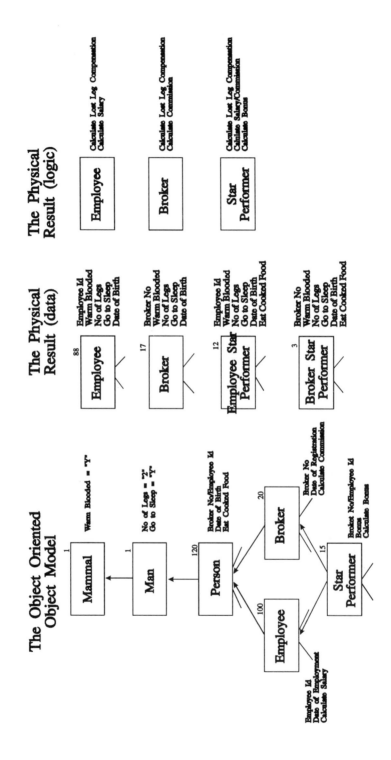

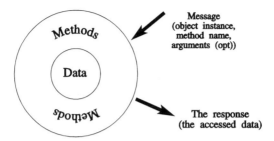

Data cannot be accessed other than via the methods, so its structure and contents are hidden
Location and logic of the methods is not known, only the response to the message

Result

There is no ripple effect of change

Figure 1.9 OO support for change—specialisation

The size of the ripple is aggravated by the fact that much code is written in the wrong place, being at the event level, and not normalised to the class object. The same code is often found in many application programs.

The solution to this is not merely to make sure that code is placed correctly to the objects it describes, but to surround the object code with an interface layer, such that those wishing to access the code do not need to know what the code is. All they need to do is send a message that invokes the appropriate code and know the form of the response to the message. The code can access the data properties in the object class, and processes the data into an appropriate response. What the data and processing of the object that received the message is is irrelevant to the object that sent the message. Encapsulation is modelled in figure 1.9.

- *the addition of sub-classes*
This is the ability to reuse the existing information as much as possible so that only new unsupported information needs to be added to the information already available.

  If the data and code of the existing application is unable to support the requirements of the change, the object oriented solution is to reuse the existing information to a maximum degree, and where there is a deficiency, to add to the existing information through specialisation, that is the adding of sub classes to the existing classes and inheriting the existing information that can be reused.

  The mechanism of sub-classing change can be seen in figure 1.10. This shows a base situation of a class of Employee. At point in time 2 there is a

Figure 1.8 Sub-class object concatenation

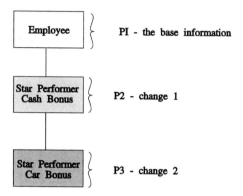

The previously created information remains unchanged

Figure 1.10   OO support for change—specialisation

need to reflect the fact that some employees can now be classified as Star Employees because a new cash bonus scheme has been introduced. A Star Performer Cash Bonus sub class to the base class Employee is created. However, the scheme has not proved to be totally satisfactory, so that at point in time 3 an addition to the cash bonus is a car bonus. A further sub class of Star Performer Car Bonus is created.

Notice the use of addition and not modification to support the changes. The existing information is not modified but reused, and only added to where the existing information is inadequate. *Indeed, the existing information is the basis of the enhancement.* A very different design approach from today's software development technology. Current technology would require two program modifications to the base logic for handling employee remuneration.

- *polymorphism*
This is the ability to add additional functionality to a process without requiring one to write a differently named program, the creation of derived processes from the existing system. As shown in section 4.9, polymorphism is a powerful facility for handling change.

One therefore has the elegant situation where object orientation can support both complexity through generalisation/simplification of the information already existing, and change through the encapsulation and specialisation of/adding to the information already existing. Either way, the approach is through the addition of new super and sub classes of objects rather than through the modification of the existing objects.

1.8.2 The need to handle all information the same way *and* the writing and storage of information only once

With today's database and programming technology there is a clear separation of data and logic, the data in the database and the logic in the application programs. This separation is illogical—after all both data and logic are information.

It is also inefficient. The policy has always been to move the data to the logic. The data is accessed on the storage medium, brought into the buffer pool, and from there into the application program's working storage, all involving expensive physical and logical I/O. Merging logic and data would eliminate some of this inefficiency.

In addition, information design techniques have also been developed to reflect this physical separation: there are distinct techniques for the modelling of the data and for the modelling of logic. There are thus two sets of techniques and two sets of technologies for what at the end of the day is merely information. Why? Why is it not possible to have one common information modelling technique and one set of information implementation technologies?

Possibly without realising it, the developers of object oriented products have developed a set of technical facilities for the treatment of data and logic in a much more unified way. The gap between data and logic is narrowing. Given that the data is a passive component and logic is an active component acting on the data, there is inevitably some difference in the technical facilities, but the facilities merely reflect the different roles of data and logic. From a modelling and storage point of view, object orientation treats 100% of the data and 80% of the logic in the same way—both merely properties that describe the state (the data) and the behaviour (the methods) of an object class—the data properties holding the values for an object instance at a point in time and the logic representing the way the values can change. How this is done is described in Chapter 2.

The design techniques for information modelling are even further down the road of treating all information in the same way as the implementation technology. The similar treatment of all information, data and logic is through the common mechanism of normalising both types of information. It will be seen that the rules for data normalisation can be applied to logic, suitably rephrased, in exactly the same way as for data. There is a rule of logic first normal form, of logic second normal form and of logic third normal form. By applying these rules it will be found that some 80% of logic will be normalisable to the classes that contain the normalised user data. Even the 20% of logic that does not relate to the classes containing user data can be normalised, if one regards the events/business requirements as another type of class. How this is done is described in Chapter 6.

The immediate benefit of information normalisation is that the information is defined and stored only once. This automatically addresses one of the other requirements for the software developer in the 1990s.

1.8.3   Modelling information to its appropriate level of abstraction

Examples of the abstraction of information to its appropriate level of "relevance" have been given in Section 1.8.1. This ability to place general information higher up an information model than particular information is a unique feature of object orientation, and is based on the class facility. With traditional data modelling all the entities are based on keys, so all the entities are of equal "relevance". The generalisation and specialisation of information is achieved by applying the rules for information abstraction and the role of the information. These rules and the role are described in Chapter 6.

1.8.4   The use of different forms of logic

The writing of application program code with the 3GL and 4GL programming languages is procedural. The program starts with a BEGIN statement and n lines of code later finishes with the END statement. Each line of code is a single statement of some action that has no value in its own right. The line of code is only of value in the context of what precedes it and what succeeds it. The line of code is therefore in a fixed position within the application program. If a line is moved or removed then the carefully constructed flow of control will fail. It is not surprising that conventional procedural application programs require the skill of professional coders.

The alternative form of logic is declarative rules. Each rule is a declarative statement of some universal or application domain truth. *Each rule therefore has value in its own right. A rule can therefore be standalone.* The rule structure is usually in the form of "If condition(s) then conclusion(s)". The principle of rules states that when A is known to be true and if a rule states "If A then B" it is valid to conclude that B is also true. Stated differently, when we discover that the conditions of a rule are true we are entitled to believe the conclusions. An example could be if you know "If today is Monday then tomorrow is Tuesday" and today is Monday, then you can conclude tomorrow is Tuesday. This rule is a standalone piece of declarative logic.

The rules can be chained together by the conclusion(s) of one rule pattern matching the condition(s) of another rule, such as "If condition A then conclusion B" and "If condition B then conclusion C". The important point here is that not only are rules standalone statements of truth which can be chained to form groups of logic, but crucially, since they are symbolically linked through pattern matching of the conclusions of one rule matching the conditions of another rule, the logic does not have to be positionally and hence procedurally written. The related rules can be written in any order and the logic will still work.

Object orientation is not specifically designed to use procedural or declarative code, but it is noticeable that a trend is emerging. The logic that is normalised to the classes to which it relates are stored in what are called methods. A class can have n methods that define its behaviour. What is occurring is that the process logic for the manipulation of the data access in the class is written with a procedural object oriented programming language, but that the pre- and post-conditions that define the state of the object instances before and after the execution of the process logic are increasingly written as declarative rules. The pre- and post-conditions are rules which state that an object must be in such and such a state for a specified method to execute, and when the method completes the object must be in such and such a state. There is a procedural method for a class of aeroplane for the handling of the Take-Off function. The pre-condition rule is that the aeroplane must be moving at n miles per hour and ... . If these conditions are true then one can conclude that the method Take-Off can proceed. When the method completes the post-condition of the aeroplane class is that the height must be greater than 500 feet, the flaps should be retracted, etc. If these conditions are true then one can conclude that the method Take-Off completed successfully and method close down can proceed.

The attractive feature of declarative logic for object oriented methods is that a single standalone rule can be used for both the pre-conditions and the post-conditions. A rule for condition testing can be composed on n conditions and one conclusion.

The use of declarative logic is a very nice and easy way of ensuring that the procedural logic in the methods is provably correct.

1.8.5   Support for class/behaviour

Once data abstraction has been done there must be support for property inheritance so that the sub class can inherit the properties of the super classes.

1.9   SOLUTIONS TO USERS' REQUIREMENTS

The requirement for intelligent query languages is supported by expert systems. This is outside the scope of this book and is not addressed further.

Object orientation is able to support non-procedural data access through the message facility, where the message merely contains information that says "Get me these object instances and do this named process to them".

1.10   THE PROBLEMS WITH RELATIONAL TECHNOLOGY

This section only considers the deficiencies of relational technology from an object oriented point of view.

Relational technology has hit the technical buffers—it can go no further from an information modelling and access point of view. An explicit recognition of this is the announcement by several leading relational vendors that their products are moving to the object oriented information modelling paradigm. Oracle Inc. has announced that they will be object oriented by 1993/94. The INGRES and SYBASE products already have several object oriented facilities, such as the ability to define stored procedures, triggers and rules attached to the database tables, and INFORMIX will be object oriented in the near future.

Relational technology is based on:

- the premise of key-based data and event-based logic. This leads to the problems of
    — distinct technologies and techniques for data and logic;
    — inability to support the modelling of information on the basis of class and aggregation;
    — a failure to recognise that some 80% of logic has nothing to do with events.

    It all leads to the conclusion that the *relational information modelling paradigm is deficient, both for data and logic*.

- the 12 relational rules developed by Dr. Codd in the 1970s.

These underlying features are now recognised, with the usual benefit of hindsight, to be open to criticism.

As already explained, the separation of data and logic and their distinct design techniques and implementation technologies is illogical—data and logic are just different forms of information and can be subject to the same design techniques—the normalisation of information—and a common technology—object orientation. The normalisation of information is also the solution to the problem of 80% of logic being in the wrong place. Normalising the logic to the object classes ensures that object based logic is exactly that: object- and not event-based.

The prime features that are entirely new are those of class, the identification of properties that are common to many entities/objects and their abstraction into super or sub classes, as appropriate, of the original base entities/classes and aggregation, where an object class is composed of other object classes.

Dr. Codd has done much for the computer industry, increasing our understanding of the structure of data and from this improving the technology of file handlers for the storage and access of data. For this he deserves much credit, and any comments in this book must be set in the context that the authors accepted the relational rules when they were developed. But time moves on, and the understanding of the weaknesses of the rules as well as their strengths has become apparent.

The problem with relational technology is the concept of tables and the relationships between the tables, explicitly defined in Dr. Codd's rules 1 and 2. Rule 1, the information rule, states that data is to be viewed in the form of tables. Rule 1 is fine and remains true for object orientation—tables of data replaced by objects of data. Rule 2, the guaranteed access rule, states that the data attributes in the tables to be accessed and, when accessing multiple tables, the relationships between the tables must be defined. This rule is the problem area.

Dr. Codd's rules are heavily reflected in SQL, the standard data definition and data manipulation language for relational technology. The SQL data manipulation language constructs are typically in the form of SELECT some data attributes FROM specified table(s) WHERE certain attribute values(s) are met and (where relationship joins on multi-table access are required) common between tables.

The first problem is the FROM construct. Users still have to specify which tables of data need to be accessed to retrieve the data required. This means that the user must know the distribution of data attributes across the tables, as well as the names of the tables. The second problem is that users must also understand and specify the relationships between the tables in the WHERE construct. The much vaunted claims of relational database vendors to provide non-procedural data access cannot be supported. SQL does not provide fully non-procedural data access. SQL does not provide join-free access to data.

Certainly, relational data sub-languages (and hereafter it is assumed to be SQL) provide some features of non-procedural data access in that the *access logic* appropriate to the access commands is automatically and implicitly generated. For example, should SQL select all customers with red hair, the application programmer is not concerned with accessing each table row in turn and ascertaining whether the row is representing a customer with red hair or not. Each row is implicitly accessed by the relational software and presented to the program as appropriate, which merely proceeds with process logic execution on the basis that each table row presented is for a customer with red hair.

All in all, users still have to be aware of the tables in the database, the names of the tables, which data attributes are in which tables, and the relationship between the tables. This is decidedly not non-procedural data access. There is no information hiding, and no encapsulation.

Relational technology has created the facility of the view so as to hide the underlying data structure of the base tables. The great advantage of the view is that if one is accessing the information specified in the view then all one has to do is to specify the view name rather than the underlying base table(s) in the FROM construct. However, the benefit is more apparent than real. The idea that the view facility hides tables and the relationships between them is not totally correct! The problem is that the view itself is a table, albeit a conceptual or virtual table. A user can have many views and therefore must still understand what data is in what view table. The user might have one view as a storekeeper, one as a packaging engineer, one as a despatcher and one as a manager. In short there might be a view per user role. There is therefore still a need to understand the concept of tables and which data is accessible from which view table. In short, the user must still think in terms of a logical data model, even with views. And views are restricted to a single table/class for updates. There is therefore no value in views for updates.

It will be seen that object orientation provides non-procedural data access. There is complete data hiding[1]; you do not know what the data is in the objects—indeed, the object you are "accessing" may not even contain the data you are requesting. It does not matter; object oriented software will do the data searching for you.

There is a further problem. Dr. Codd's rules relate only to data. What a pity he didn't realise the full potential of the rules and that, suitably modified to reflect that the normalisation is being applied to logic, they can also be applied to logic. *Dr. Codd's legacy to computing is more significant than at first realised. His legacy for data was to the benefit of relational technology. His legacy for logic, albeit unwittingly, is to the benefit of object orientation.*

The benefit of technology being based on a set of standards, on a set of rules, is that there is a common understanding of what is required. Standards are being increasingly used for the development of computer technology, such as the 7 layer ISO model for telecommunications, the slowly emerging standards for information repositories for CASE tools, and the standards for the SQL relational data sub-language. This is fine provided that the standards and rules have two features—they must be accepted as being valid as universally true, and they must be without time limit. The most perfect example of universally accepted standards without a time limit are the Ten Commandments. There is no need for the benefit of hindsight. The standards were well thought out from the beginning. But this is not the situation with relational rules: hindsight has shown that they are not watertight or flexible—they only relate to data, and the structure of the data is not hidden from the user. They fail the test of the two features.

---

[1]   If a data property is being added to or deleted from the objectbase there is not, and cannot be, any data hiding. All application program processing of a deleted data property has to know it has been deleted. Information hiding relates to modification of existing data and logic properties.

Object orientation provides a solution to both of the above problems:

● The principle of the normalisation of data and logic, of information no matter what form it is in, is applied in the technology. Both data and logic are normalised to the classes they "sensibly belong to".

   Access to the application information is totally non-procedural. All the user has to specify is "Get me this instance(s) of this object and do this to it" in the message to the objectbase[1]. Where the data and the supporting "do this" method logic to access the data are is unknown to the user.

Unlike relational technology, the basis of object oriented technology is not based on rules and is therefore not based on a fixed modelling paradigm. If improvements are required then there is no fixed basis that prevents it. Standards for object orientation have not been defined—requirements yes, but standards, no. The object oriented paradigm is flexible.

1.11 THE BENEFITS OF OBJECT ORIENTED DESIGN

Object orientation provides all the facilities required by the systems developer, and most of the identified facilities required by the user.

   Added to the above functional requirements and the technological capabilities there are additional issues such as software quality, application independent designs, maintainability, robustness, extensibility and reuseability.

   Object orientation is about all of these, but particularly software maintainability, extensibility and reuseability. There are other software quality features such as portability and efficiency, but these do not benefit from the adoption of object orientation.

   It has been seen that object oriented information:

● adds the facility of class and aggregation abstraction to the key-based data of a logical data model, thus converting the logical data model into an object class model;

● normalises logic to the object classes so constructed from the data abstractions so as to match the role of the object class.

The results of this enhanced information model is a set of significant benefits in the design and generation of application program code. The benefits are:

---

[1] The authors suggest that the term objectbase will become as widely used as the term database. An objectbase contains 100% of the corporate data and some 80% of the logic of the corporate processing. This is the application independent part of the total corporate information system. Some 20% of the logic remaining at the event/business requirement level is not application independent.

- *Application Independent Designs*
  This is achieved through the normalisation of information.

  The normalisation of all information is the feature that enables the creation of application independent information designs, that is the design of information that is generic to a corporation, not to a particular application or event/business requirement.

  To date, the only part of information that has been corporate and therefore application independent is data. The reason for this is that the data has been normalised to the appropriate entity/object class and not to a business requirement/event of a functional area/an application of the business. Customer Name is an attribute describing Customer, not a business requirement. It is therefore not specific to an application. The database is corporate. The same data objects can thereby be "accessed" by multiple applications.

  The same is true when the logic information is normalised to an object. If the logic is "All Customers with red hair get a bonus of £100" then it, like the data, has nothing to do with a particular event/business requirement but with the Customer class, in the same way as Customer Name data. It is therefore also normalised to the Customer class. When logic is normalised like data, it has the same corporate and application independent characteristics as data—but in this case the logic can be "re-used" by multiple applications.

  The residue of logic from the business requirement in the event objects will be all that is dependent upon the applications. The logic is relevant/unique to the business requirement. Such logic could be the initialisation of the program variables, the formatting of the input and output data on the screen and the final processing of some data accessed from the information-base, such as the calculation of the bonus of the salesman for this month. This logic is the residue of logic that remains in the conventional application program, where logic has always been processed at the event, the business requirement, level. And it is the business requirements, by their very nature, that are application dependent.

  The more the logic can be moved away from event level processing and "normalised" to the business objects of the object class model, the greater the independence of the computer system from the application. The designs will be as corporate as possible.

  The additional benefit of this is that the corporate information in the business classes is much more stable, being subject to change only when the corporation as a whole changes its business. And being more stable and subject to increasing reuse it becomes more robust.

  The need to change the information at the traditional business requirement level will be restricted to the application-specific parts in the event objects. As has been already described, this is limited to only some 20% of application code.

Application independent designs therefore offer reusable and robust logic and stable information. These are significant benefits.

- *The Minimisation of Code*
This is achieved through the normalisation of information.

Normalised logic is entered/written and stored only once. Code minimisation is maximised—there is thus minimum logic/software maintenance, and the minimum code is therefore more easily maintained.

- *Easier Management of Complexity and Change*
This is achieved through information abstraction.

By defining logic at the class level, the overall complexity of a total application is broken down in a way that accurately reflects the real world, in that objects are "things" in the real world. Instead of an enormous mass of code that is traditionally pitched at the business requirements/event level, most logic (80%) is now produced at the object level.

With logic at the business requirement level it is often necessary to access *n* data tables, such that the logic code supporting these *n* tables can potentially be interwoven in a difficult to fathom sequence of statements. With the object oriented approach the business requirement invokes the appropriate class based logic by sending messages rather than data access calls to the appropriate classes, each of which contains the appropriate data and logic. The instances of the object class are only accessed via the normalised logic stored in the methods, which themselves are defined within the classes. It is therefore impossible to interweave logic in an unnormalised manner.

Since each class is a self-contained unit containing all its own data and logic with no interest in what the other classes are or what they contain, classes can be defined and constructed on a standalone basis. As each class is standalone and self-contained, one can now develop an application incrementally one class at a time, the ultimate "mechano", piece-by-piece, style construction process for the building of application systems. Object orientation is the ultimate form of modular system construction.

But this is not the only way in which object orientation handles complexity and change. There are specific facilities as described in Sections 1.8.1 for supporting complexity and change. Object orientation is tailor-made for supporting large volatile business applications. With database technology there are no facilities, so it is a case of DIY, and since change requires modification the existing application systems lack robustness.

- *Software Maintainability and Reuse*
This is achieved through information abstraction, property inheritance and encapsulation.

Object orientation takes the idea of software reuse much further than the current capability of common program modules. An object oriented system is already installed, and there is a need to increase the functionality of the system. This can now be done through the process of enhancing the design by addition through information abstraction, primarily though specialisation, and not modification. New sub classes containing the new and additional functionality can be added to the existing application, to the existing class model. And through property inheritance the existing information is reusable by the new sub classes.

A general situation of great flexibility therefore exists. A library of business and system classes might contain a class that has most but not all of the properties needed for the new application. A new sub class can be derived from the original super class which has the base properties required. This entails writing only the code to support the added features of the new sub class. The rest of the code needed to implement the new class is simply inherited from the super-class definitions.

The encapsulation facility provides the ability to change the data and the logic properties in a class without any ripple effect from the change. Since the only communication between classes is via the message and response interface, what occurs in one class is immaterial to the other classes.

- *Reliability/Robustness and Security*
  This is achieved through information reuse (see above) and encapsulation.

Traditional procedural programming systems have the data and logic portions of application programs separated. This can lead to a number of problems, especially where more than one programmer is working on the same system. For example, it is relatively easy for one programmer to write a module that relies on side effects generated by code in another module. If this second module is changed, all the modules that relied on the side effect it produced are likely to fail. Change the one module can have an adverse affect on other modules. Change control is much more difficult to manage.

Encapsulation eliminates these problems by hiding the form and content of the information stored within a class to the outside world. With object orientation the only information available to the programmer about a class is the list of messages to which the class will respond and the responses that such messages will generate. It is not necessary to make assumptions as to how to access a class and the data within the class. All that is required is to issue the message that corresponds to the response desired. This message and response interface is the only view that the outside world has of the class. One can thus change the logic in the methods in an object without any fear of a ripple effect to the logic in other classes.

Abuse of the data in an object and illegal access is also prevented since it is only possible to access the data in the classes through messages.

- *Software Building Blocks.*
  The way that object oriented technology will evolve is illustrated in figure 7.6 . The event objects will act as the "glue" that links the business classes and the system classes. This is because it is the event classes that initiate the messages to the business and system object classes in the objectbase and ultimately synchronise the responses.

  All that the event classes will need to do is the normal event level logic as already described, and the selection of the classes appropriate to the business equivalents. One will eventually only need to write the logic that is unique to a company's business, and the rest will largely be logic for the "cherry picking and glueing" of the business and system class libraries.

- *Natural "English" command-based query languages.*
  Semantics have the benefit that a query language can be made much more user friendly and non-procedural in that the relationships between the classes to be accessed in a query can be specified using the semantics that describe the relationships. The query can therefore be more in the form of a natural language and not in the form of a procedural join, as in relational query languages. One could say "select the information in the commission <u>earned by</u> broker 123" (the semantic is underlined) rather than "select the information from broker 123 and commission where commission.broker_number = broker.broker_number".

- *Substantial increases in software development and maintenance.*
  This is the cumulative result of the above benefits. As shown in section 7.6 these benefits are of the order of between 30 and 40%.

The facilities of object orientation can be achieved with an object oriented programming language, but much needs to be "do it yourself". Property inheritance requires to be defined explicitly in the program language data definition declarations. But the full benefits of the object oriented approach can best be achieved with an object oriented database linked to an object oriented programming language. The language can be specific to the database, such as with GENERIS and its Intelligent Query Language, and ONTOS, which requires one of the traditional languages, such as C++.

A number of object oriented databases and programming languages are now available which support object oriented design. One such product has already been identified as GOLDWORKS. GENERIS has been upgraded to support object orientation. Another is from an American company, Ontologic, with their object database OB2 (formerly called VBASE) and Servio Logic with GEMSTONE. The leading object oriented programming languages are C++, SIMULA (one of the first), EIFFEL and SMALLTALK.

As usual, the technology is ahead of the techniques. None of the leading structured design methods, such as Information Engineering and SSADM, explicitly support the concepts and techniques for object oriented design. However, methods specifically developed for object oriented design are already appearing, the prime example being HOOD (Hierarchical Object Oriented Design) from the European Space Agency, designed specifically for the Ada programming language, and other more recent products from Coad/Yourdon, Shlaer/Mellor, Booch and Rumbaugh *et al*. As described in chapter 6 all these methods are significantly deficient.

1.12   SUMMARY

The chapter shows that:

- there are three concepts underlying object orientation—the normalisation of all information, including logic, application independent systems and system enhancement by addition rather than modification;

- object orientation does not require a new way of thinking. Any changes in the way that information is modelled is based on extensions to the existing information modelling techniques;

- object orientation is uniquely capable of supporting complex and changing business applications through the main facilities of abstraction (generalisation and specialisation) and encapsulation;

- relational technology has many deficiencies, the main ones being procedural data access, the separation of data and logic, and the inability to distinguish between general and specialised information;

- object orientation provides many benefits for the software developer.

2

OBJECTBASE MODELLING TECHNOLOGY

This chapter is presented in two parts, the first describing object oriented facilities for modelling information (information is both data and logic). These facilities include:

- class objects
- aggregation objects
- encapsulation
- messages
- private and public methods
- polymorphism
- property inheritance.

The second part describes the structure of an object class model in terms of the different types of class and composition objects, and their roles and relationships with each other

Object orientation is a data processing environment that will have a leading and increasing impact on IT application system design and development. Many leading industry thinkers believe that object orientation is the next "leap forward" for the 1990s as relational technology was for the 1980s.

The authors are convinced that the future of object orientation will be more significant, more beneficial and longer lasting than the relational database. For reasons explained in Chapter 1, relational technology is based on separated key-based data and event-based logic with procedural data access, each of these being serious limitations to the effectiveness of the technology. Object orientation suffers from none of these and other deficiencies.

By convention, people have been talking of object oriented databases and object oriented programming languages. This obviously reflects traditional thinking, but also the fact that they have evolved separately, the object oriented languages preceding the arrival of object oriented databases, as well as being developed and marketed by different companies. Notwithstanding this, the two subjects are effectively one: if you describe one you in large measure describe the other.

Nevertheless, the traditional separation is preserved in this book, as there are certain aspects of object oriented design that a data administrator needs to know which are different from what an application programmer needs to know. The technology of object orientation is therefore considered under the traditional data and programming headings.

2.1 An Object—What is it?

An object is the unit of object oriented application system design. It identifies something of interest to a business application or a system process about which information needs to be modelled and stored. An object could thus be an order in a purchasing application, a policy in an insurance application, a robot in a manufacturing application, a container crane in a container port application, and a print routine in a system process. The object contains all the information, both data *and* logic, that describes the object.

An object oriented application system is a network of intercommunicating objects—each object in itself being totally self-contained with all its information, but functioning as part of a total application system. The application system is the total of all the objects and their relationships with each other, plus the application program events, one for each event/business requirement. Many, quite correctly, regard the business requirements as event objects.

An object is, in simple terms, composed of two types of information (as illustrated in figure 2.1), the data and logic information components. An object does not have to have both types of information simultaneously, and can contain data and logic or just logic. The object must contain logic, because, as we shall see, the data component cannot be accessed except via the logic component. The data component is optional.

The data component has been described as the attributes and the logic component described as the services provided by the object. Another

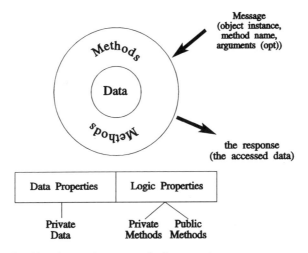

An object does not have to contain data properties

Figure 2.1   The structure of an object class

term for services is methods. This is the term more usually used in this book. The attributes and their values describe the state of the object at any point in time, and the services/methods define what can be done to the attributes of the object, the behaviour[1] of the object class.

The data and logic components both describe the object and are defined in the dictionary schema definition of the object. Unlike the standard schema definitions of relational and earlier database file handler types, the object class definitions of the properties can contain values of information. In the case of the methods, the value is the logic. Both components can have many properties (object oriented buzzword for data attributes and methods), which correspond to the fields of a file handler record/table. Thus a method is classed as a property just as a data item. An object can have many data and logic properties.

The methods are of two types—public and private, with the former being user triggered and the latter system triggered. Methods are described in more detail in Section 2.2.7. It suffices at this stage to say that the public methods are invoked by an explicit message from the user triggering an event/business requirement, while the private methods are invoked automatically by the application when specified conditions occur. All objects

---

[1]   There are two meanings to behaviour: where there are common properties between objects and which require abstraction to four class hierarchies, and the methods that process the data properties of an object class.

must have at least one public method: they do not have to have a private method[1].

There is, in fact, an invisible third component, the interface layer, composed of messages to the objects and responses to the messages from the classes. Through the encapsulation facility, object oriented technology does not allow objects to know information stored in any other classes. Indeed, these other classes do not need to know and do not care what the information is. *The interface layer provides encapsulation to the methods and the methods provide encapsulation to the data.* The only thing that the users/other objects need to know is the interface message to send to the object to invoke a named method and the response that is sent in return. This interface layer is the component that is referenced by the messages passed between objects.

It is now feasible to consider objects as abstract, in that the user of the object does not know the data and logic contents/properties of the object. An object is a "thing of interest" about which information, all information, can be recorded, but what that information is is unknown, is abstract, to the outside world[2].

2.2   OBJECT ORIENTED TECHNICAL FACILITIES

The full array of technical facilities that a product claiming to be object oriented requires are detailed in Table 1.1.

Some of the facilities are common to both the objectbase and the programming sides of object orientation. Those facilities that are specifically concerned with modelling information, and therefore more oriented to objectbase technology, are highlighted. These are also the facilities that the information modelling design techniques of the emerging object oriented structured methods will need to support. This chapter only addresses the facilties that model information in an object oriented way.

The facilities that are specific to object oriented programming are about the functionality aspects of object orientation and not about object oriented information modelling (see Chapters 4 and 5).

---

[1]   In C++ there is a three part distinction—private, which declares that the properties are visible only to the class itself, protected, which declares that the properties are visible only to the class itself and its sub classes, and public, which declares that the properties are visible to all other objects that message the class.

[2]   There are two definitions of abstract objects, one of which is defined above. The other is of classes with no instances. An example would be the class Man, there being no instances of Man, just a generic description of the class, such as having a data property of the Number of Legs. These classes are merely definitions of the data and logic properties the class "contains".

Table 1.1 Technical facilities of object oriented products.

The Facilities		OO Objectbases	OO Programs
Class Objects Aggregation	)	*	*
Aggregation Objects	)	*	*
Business Objects		*	*
Concrete Objects		*	*
Abstract Objects		*	*
Property Inheritance (class & aggregation)	)	*	*
Semantics (class, aggr' & business)	)Information	*	*
Methods (private & public))	) Modelling	*	*
Encapsulation	)	*	*
Polymorphism	)		*
Message Passing	)		*
Dynamic Binding			*
Function Name Overloading			*
Operator Name Overloading			*
Genericity			*

2.2.1 Object definitions

Database technology has made a clear distinction between information that is static in structure and passive and that which is dynamic and active. The static and passive information is the database data and the active and dynamic information is the program logic. The static information has always been defined in a database data definition language (DDL), with the definitions being stored as templates of the tables of data in a schema (pre-relational database term) or repository/encyclopdia (relational term). With database technology the structure model of the data is DDL defined in the schema.

With non-database technology the structure model of the data is DML defined in the application program. The DML templates are accessed by the application programs and compiled into the programs as definitions of the table formats. This DML information definition approach is used by the C++ object oriented programming language.

This "placement" of the definition of the structure of object oriented information, either in the database schema or program templates, might seem a minor matter. At the end of the day, the result is the same—the definition of the structure of the object class both in their properties and relationships to each other is obtained by the application programs. It is not a minor issue.

The application programmer should only be concerned with the writing of logic for support of the functionality of the business. In the past this has been through the traditionally event-based application program, with the definition of the tables to be accessed being referenced in the source code and then compiled into the runtime code. But the definition of the table properties still has to be done by application programmers, who happen to put the DML definitions into a table library. It is the programmers who are the custodians of the physical definition of the modelled data.

One of the purposes of database technology is to take the role and responsibility for the definition of the structure of data away from the application programmer to the database designer/administrator and store the DDL definitions in a database schema. The programmer should not need to understand the structure of the data, thus enabling the database administrator to change the design of the data without needing to modify the application programs that access the "affected part". The view facility of relational technology was the beginning of hiding information.

Object orientation provides total information hiding through encapsulation of the data via the methods and the messaging of the methods. Yet object oriented programming languages need the definitions of the class properties to be DML defined in the code of the programming language. We are back to pre-database technology! OK, the application programmer sends messages to the methods that contain the logic and therefore does not know what the logic is, only the response. But the definition of the object classes and their properties is still with the programmer, not the objectbase designer. The responsibility of object oriented information definition is in the wrong area.

It is pleasing to note that the DDL component of the relational SQL database sub-language is being enhanced with object oriented facilities. Object SQL is beginning to emerge, with the ability to define such facilities as sub-typing and database procedures and rules associated with tables. *The definition of object oriented physical design is moving from the programming to the objectbase fraternity.*

There is a claimed performance overhead associated with the move towards defining the objectbase in the DDL (see Section 3.5).

2.2.2   Class, composition/aggregation, property inheritance and relationship semantics → information abstraction

These four facilities are unique to object orientation. They each require the other, class and composition (increasingly called aggregation) being unsupportable without property inheritance, property inheritance having no purpose without class and aggregation, the different relationships between the different types of objects, and from this the property inheritance paths, being defined by specific kinds of semantic descriptions. Each without the other would not function—that is why they are described together.

Class, aggregation, property inheritance and relationship semantics together provide information abstraction, this being the single most important feature of object orientation.

2.2.2.1 Class

Class is the facility that models common behaviour between objects. Sets of objects with a common behaviour have a common class. As described in Chapter 1 (figure 1.7), common behaviour is identified as data or logic properties that are common to more than one object. Figure 1.7 showed that the two objects Employee and Broker had common data and logic properties, and that both the objects therefore have the common behaviour of being Persons.

Man has long classified information into classes—and the classification goes from the most general to breakdowns of the general class into sub-classes of increasing specialisation—a hierarchy of generalisation to specialisation. For example, a very general classification of animals could be into those that are warm blooded and those that are not. The warm blooded animals can be further sub-classified into those that are herbivores and those that are carnivores, and the carnivores into those, let's say, that hunt as packs and those that hunt alone to form what are known as class hierarchies. Warm blooded animals could be lions, cheetahs and eagles. The eagles would fall into the classification of animals that fly, the lions into those that walk and hunt as packs, and the cheetahs into those that walk and hunt alone. And there are many other animals that fall into the same classification categories. All these classifications are based on the fact that there are groupings of animals that have common characteristics, common data and common operations that describe their state and behaviour.

Figure 2.2 is a variation and extension of figure 1.7, and shows a model of classes with the Mammal object at the top and the Star Performer at the bottom. The class structure represents a fully abstracted class model of the base class Employee, in that the base class properties, including logic properties, have been generalised and specialised as appropriate. This facility of a class behaviour relationship is supported by the semantic description of the relationship as being of the "is a" type.

The objects higher up a class model are more abstract/general in the information they contain than the classes lower down the class model, which are more particular/specialised. The Mammal is a more general case of Species, which is in turn is a more general case of Person, which is in turn a more general case of .... and so on down the class model. All the classes in figure 2.2 are related by class in that they are all mammalian—they all have a common mammalian class behaviour, the properties of a super class being relevant to all instances of the sub classes. Warm Blooded is thus relevant to the sub-class object instances of Man down to Star Performer, Date of Birth being relevant to the sub-class object instances of Employee and Star Performer.

The mammal class is relevant to all the sub classes of the application

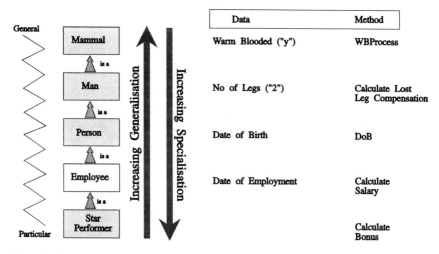

Data	Method
Warm Blooded ("y")	WBProcess
No of Legs ("2")	Calculate Lost Leg Compensation
Date of Birth	DoB
Date of Employment	Calculate Salary
	Calculate Bonus

Instantiated class information is generic (ie, applicable) to all instances of the class

Figure 2.2   Abstraction generalisation and specialisation

model illustrated. The sub classes of Man, Person, Employee and Star Performer are all mammalian in the mammalian class hierarchy. The Man object is relevant to all the classes of the model except the Mammal. Person, Employee and Star Performer are therefore all within the class hierarchy model of Man, and Employee and Star Performer are also within the class hierarchy model of Person. And so on, becoming progressively more restrictive as one progresses down the class hierarchy model.

There needs to be an understanding of the difference between class and class hierarchy. All objects in an application system are class objects because they each have a class template definition of their data and logic properties, but not all objects belong to a class hierarchy.

Consider figure 2.3. The objects Customer, Order and Product are class objects, each in their own right, but there is no class hierarchy. This is because there is no common behaviour—it would not make sense to say that an Order "is a" Customer and an Order "is a" Product. And there are no common properties between the classes: the data property of Customer Name is not common to all instances of Order—indeed, the data property is not to be found within Order. Orders are not a sub-class specialisation of Customers or of Products, and therefore do not inherit the Customer's and Product's properties. Nevertheless, Customer, Order and Product are each classes with their own template definitions in the objectbase schema. The fact that there is no class hierarchy, no common behaviour, is modelled by the fact that the semantic description of the relationship between the classes

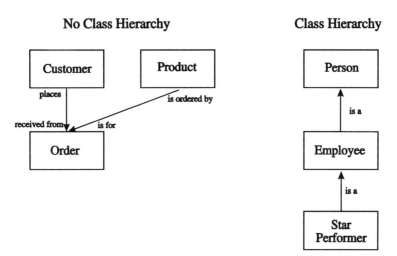

Figure 2.3 Class and class hierarchy

is of the free form type describing the business role of the relationship between the classes, as shown in the figure.

The fact that objects are currently only classes and not part of a class hierarchy does not mean that they can never be within a class hierarchy. At some point in time someone might ascertain that it is possible to generalise and specialise any one of the classes into a class hierarchy. There could be a later business need to specialise the Customer class into those that are credit-worthy and those that are not credit-worthy, and thus create behaviourally related sub classes of the base class Customer and a class hierarchy of Customer. By contrast, the classes of Person, Employee and Star Performer are very much within a class hierarchy, that of Person. There is a common behaviour of employees and star performers of both being persons. And the class hierarchy is modelled with the "is a" semantic of the class relationships.

As described so far, the increasing specialisation as one descends the model is only at the class level. However, the specialisation can go further — to the instances of the class. In the case of being warm blooded, all the instances of the classes that can inherit from Mammal can only be warm blooded—they would die if they were not. An instance of Person would be dead if his/her blood was cold. However, this total applicability of class information does not have to be relevant to all the classes. Consider the Man class. Not all instances of Man will necessarily have two legs. It could be that a particular Man has lost a leg. The instance (Henry has lost a leg) would be a specialisation of the class *at the instance level*, Henry having only one leg.

2.2.2.2   Aggregation

This is a data modelling facility that is not used by database technology. It occurs where an object class is composed of other object classes. A Car class is composed of the classes Engine and Carburettor. It is the ability to take each data property of a class and generalise them into super classes of the base class. This is shown in figure 2.4, where the base class Customer has two data properties of Name and Address which have been generalised into two super classes.

The relationship that is established is of the data properties to the prime key of the base class. The "has a" description is that the prime key, Customer Number, "has a" Address and "has a" Name, is "composed of" Address and Name. It would be nonsensical to have a "has a" relationship between the non-key properties of Address and Name. There are no other relationships between the data properties, otherwise the class would not be in third normal form (it would be in second normal form).

The composition facility is particularly useful if there is a method that processes a specific data property of a class. With the ability of object orientation to support the normalisation of logic, it is reasonable to take the normalisation to third normal form and see if there is logic dependency on a non-key data property, if there is a dependent relationship between a data property and a method. The first two rules of normalisation test the data and logic properties against the prime key and therefore

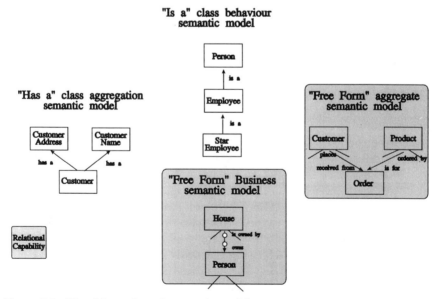

Figure 2.4   The object oriented semantic models

against the class object as a whole. The rule of data third normal form tests a non-key data property against a non-key data property, inter data dependence, and therefore against part of the entity. And so it is for the normalisation of logic—is a piece of logic dependent on a non-prime key data property.

In the example in figure 2.4 there could be a method to check that the Customer Names are within a certain value range (the business is in the marketing of named shirts and sends sample shirts out to lists of customers on the basis of named selections: once the selection has been made there is some additional processing regarding the marketing of the shirts). While this logic is still generally relevant to the Customer class, it would be more true to say that the logic, the method, is specifically relevant to the Customer Name property, which thus needs to be abstracted as a class in its own right. One is correctly normalising the method to the specific property of the new base class, abstracting it and creating a new class of a single non-key data property and one or more associated methods. One is in fact testing inter data/inter logic dependence, the rule of third normal form for logic. The piece of logic (the method) is dependent on a data property of the class and not the class as a whole. This being the case abstract it with generalisation (remove it in normalisation terms). The role of the method has been correctly related to the role of the data property.

Without this facility of decomposition of a complex object of n data properties it is not possible to take the normalisation of information to the ultimate form. The first two rules of data and logic normalisation have been based on relating the dependence of the values of the data properties and the role of the logic against the prime key of the object class/relation.

The logic that remains as methods in the base class is that which needs to process the key data property of Customer No as well as other non-key data properties or, and this suggestion is controversial in that the method logic is not being properly normalised, to process several non-key data properties. Again, using the Customer example of figure 2.4, the selection process for the shirts is for specified names and addresses. In this case, the logic is appropriate to several non-key data properties. This method, while functionally the same as that for the name, is dependent on two data properties, and therefore more of the class as a whole. It is not abstracted.

If one created classes for every combination of methods and the data properties they access within the base class, the class model would become even larger, possibly even unmanageably large. From a normalisation point of view, this abstraction into a "has a" super class should be done. From a design purity point of view, the author is writing heresy, but there is the inevitable design compromise.

With the facility of class composition one can now take logic to the third normal form. One of the authors developed the idea of the normalisation of logic being one of the basic features of object orientation, but could only show examples of this to second normal form (J. Hares, *op. cit.*, 1990, 1992). This book is able to expand on this idea and take it to third normal form, via the composition facility (Section 6.4.4.2).

The composition of the base classes and their abstracted data properties and related methods is defined with the use of the "has a" type semantic description. To recompose the base class of its constituent properties it is merely a case of following the "has a" relationships and rebuilding the base class through "inheritance" of the abstracted properties back to the base class.

2.2.2.3   Property inheritance

There are two types of property inheritance—class and aggregation.

Class/behaviour property inheritance   Class property inheritance is obtained where there is common behaviour between super and sub classes, that is they share common data and logic properties.

The inheritance relates to all the data properties. Thus in figure 2.2, Employee would inherit the data properties of Date of Birth by being a Person, No. of Legs by being a Man, and Warm Blooded by being a Mammal. The figure also shows that all the classes contain logic properties in the methods[1] Note that there is no data property of the Star Performer class. Here the bonus is calculated in the polymorphic method called Calculate Salary, the bonus being some $x\%$ of the basic salary, this being a data property inherited from Employee. The value of the basic salary is inherited from the Calculate Salary method in the Employee class, which issues a response to the message from Calculate Bonus.

A more complete example of data property inheritance with inheritance at the object instance level is illustrated in figure 2.5. Higher and Middle Management will inherit the pay property of Administrators and thus all three class objects will have a salary of £35,000. On the principle that the more particular/specialised information lower down the class model overrides the more general information higher up the class model, the Senior Executive Officers will override the Administrator's salary with their own salary of £15,000 and the Clerks with a salary of £8,000.

The most particular information of all is the instances of the class objects. Note that John Smith and John Jones are instances of the class Senior Executive Officers. All SEOs have a salary of £15,000 because the data property of Pay is instantiated with a value of that sum of money. But of

---

[1]   There has to be at least one method as the data properties cannot be accessed except via the methods.

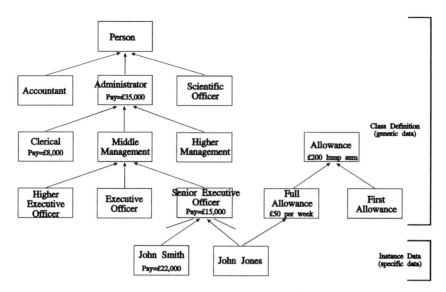

Figure 2.5 Data property inheritance

the two named instances John Smith has a pay value of £22,000. This is because he has negotiated a special deal. His special object instance level deal overrides the general class case. John Jones has no value for his salary and therefore inherits the general case salary for SEOs of £15,000. John Jones is a lucky person in that he can also inherit a Full Allowance of £50 per week and the ADP Allowance of a £200 lump sum. Jones has done well as regards allowances, Smith has done well as regards salary. The class structure shows that clerical persons get paid £8,000 but that higher management inherit a salary of £35,000.

The diagram shows that accountants and scientific officers will have no salary! The model is a variation of a model produced by a government consultancy body—perhaps there is a message here! If not there is a mistake in the model. If there is no mistake then accountants and scientific officers will have to live off charity.

There are two aspects to property inheritance—inheritance of the data properties, and inheritance of the logic properties. Both use different technology, although obtaining the same result.

Data inheritance is obtained from the concatenation of the class hierarchy as described in Section 1.8.1, this being a union of all the data properties higher in the class hierarchy than the class object being accessed. Logic inheritance is obtained from the object oriented software searching up the class hierarchy for the method named in the message to the method, starting the search from the class object defined in the object ID.

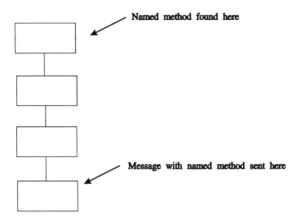

Figure 2.6   Logic inheritance (method may be at a distance from the message)

It needs to be understood that for logic inheritance the "location" of the method being invoked does not need to be known by the sender of the message. The message merely names the method, and the method is located within the Class Model by the object oriented software up the class hierarchy using the inheritance facility (figure 2.6). A message is sent to a class at the bottom of a class model and the method is a property of a class at the top of the class model.

There are two approaches that can be used to obtain property inheritance. The first is to send messages from the sub-class method to the super-class objects in the class hierarchy with the named method in the message. The process continues up the class hierarchy until the named method is found or until the Object object is reached (for Object object see Section 2.3.1.1). If no method is found an error message is issued. This is the approach used by object oriented languages that are not compiled before running, which do dynamic/late binding of the methods to the messages at run time. Such languages include SMALLTALK, which would issue the error message "doesnotunderstand" if no method is found. For this approach to work there has to be a message dictionary to list the methods of a class and the messages to which the methods can respond.

The alternative approach to dynamic explicit message searching up the class hierarchy is to compile the class hierarchy into the application program. This is the approach of strongly typed programming languages such as C++ and Object Pascal. The compiler can resolve the method message call to a simple subprogram call, and the compiled class hierarchy is searched. With such typed languages inheritance is not "do it yourself" at run time. It can be predefined.

G. Booch estimates that the dynamic approach for searching the methods takes about one and a half times as long as a simple subprogram call.

An example of searching for the method named in a message using the dynamic messaging approach is illustrated in figures 2.7–2.9. The business application is that of a chemicals company, which mixed standard chemicals in various standard and non-standard ways to produce generic and company-specific products.

In the first example from the event/business requirement "Conduct Test" the message is to the class Test to access the instance "123", invoke the method Formula "456" and pass to it the parameter of Concoction "789". The Test class is at the bottom of the class model. The test instance "123" is accessed and the named method is not found. The class of the instance is accessed and again the named method is not found. The class above Test is accessed and found to be Department. The method is not within the Department class object. The Company class above Department is accessed and again the Formula "456" method is not found.The Object class is finally accessed to find the named method. It so happens that Formula "456" is a standard universally true chemical formula and is therefore at the top of the class model. The method executes and returns a response to the event level class Conduct Test "123".

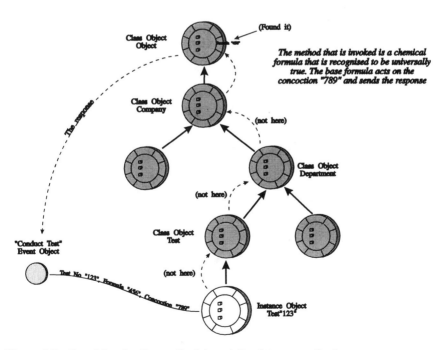

Figure 2.7 Searching for the method (specialised to general) - 1

The second example is the same as the first, except that there is a polymorphic modification to the formula made by the company. It is still the same named formula process but with a company variation, the variation being supported by adding a sub-class method in the Company class. The message to the instance of the Test class is therefore the same (here is an example of the benefits of information hiding and the change by addition capabilities of object orientation). Searching for the method up the class model is undertaken, and in this case stops at the Company class. The method in the Company class sends a message to the appropriate method in the Object class, with further searching up the class model hierarchy to obtain the response of the general case formula, and then adds the changes to the general case in the method invoked in the Company class. The method in the Company class sends the message response to the Conduct Test event class.

The third example extends the specialisation yet further. A Department within the Company has made a modification to the company's own modification of the general case formula. The message is sent as normal

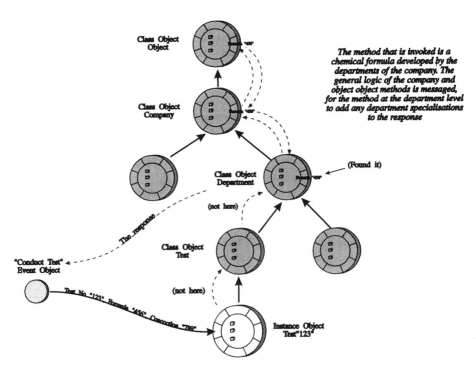

Figure 2.8   Searching for the method (specialised to general) - 2

and the searching stops at the Department class. This sends a message to obtain the response of the Company modifications, which sends a message to obtain the response of the general case formula—additional change on additional change on the base general case with repeated searching up the class model for the super-class model. The method in the Department class sends the message response to the Conduct Test event class.

Note that the inheritance of the sub-class methods of the super-class methods is explicit through the sending of messages one for each required method in the class model hierarchy. This is the SMALLTALK approach. With such object oriented programming languages inheritance is obtained by the application programmers needing to know that the method may or may not be anywhere within the class hierarchy and to send messages until it is found, with the messaging being handled explicitly and dynamically by the application programmer. With such technology, property inheritance is "do it yourself" in the DML of the programming language. Note also that the event level logic of the Conduct Test abstract class is totally isolated from the changes in the class hierarchy. It continues to receive the same message response.

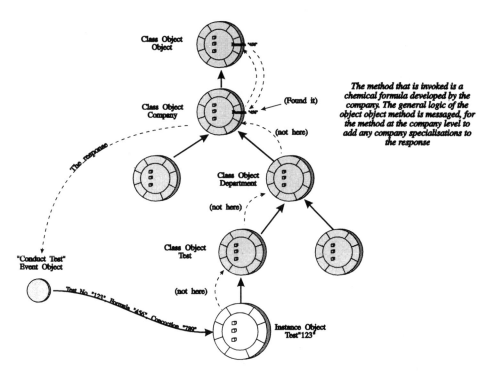

Figure 2.9   Searching for the method (specialised to general) - 3

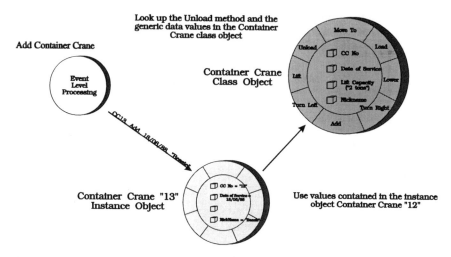

Figure 2.10 Accessing instance and class information

There is, unfortunately, no possibility of property inheritance being supported in the DDL of the database schema definition, even though the inheritance is following the fixed relationships of the sub class to the super class. It would be nice to have the DDL definition state that if there is a message to method XYZ then send a message to method ABC in such and such a super class. The problem is the inability to specify when the inheritance is required in the logic sequence in the method of the sub class (the messages could be sent any time between the begining and the end of the method logic), and to the fact that the argument(s) in the message from the sub class method to the super class method from which inheritance information is sought may well vary at runtime. It would be stupid to have the inheritance information "presented" to the sub class method at the end of processing if the requirement in the logic is for the information at the beginning of processing. The only way in which to have the inherited information presented at the correct time is for the inheritance messaging to be DML controlled in the sub class method.

Another more explicit example of property inheritance can be seen in figure 2.10. An instance of a container crane is being added into the objectbase. The Date of Service and the Nickname are passed as arguments but not lift capacity. This property is instantiated at the class level with a value of "2" tons, so that the value for the instance is inherited from the class. This example shows that the data property instantiation can be for concrete classes as well as abstract classes.

Class property inheritance can be to n levels in the class model. In the example in figure 2.5 there are four levels, and in the class model in figure 2.21 there are five levels.

Aggregation property inheritance   Aggregation inheritance is obtained when their data properties and their relevant/associated methods are abstracted as generalised super classes. The logic properties are in third normal form to a date property of the abstracted aggregation classes. An example of this is given in Section 2.2.2.2.

There can be n levels of aggregation hierarchy, just as there can be for class. There could be an aggregation hierarchy of an engine has cylinders has a piston has a rod has a... .

2.2.2.4   *Relationship semantics and semantic nets*

There are three kinds of semantic descriptions of the relationships between the classes in a class model (illustrated in figure 2.4). The semantic types are the "is a" semantic for class property inheritance, the "has" type for aggregation property inheritance, and the "free form" business semantics for the description of the business relationship between classes and no property inheritance. Each relationship between classes can be for one of these reasons, but only one. It would not be valid for a relationship between any two classes in the class model to have two semantic descriptions, for example a "is a" and a "free form" semantic description at the same time.

The class model at the top of figure 2.4 demonstrates the use of the "is a" semantic. It shows that the class Star Performer "is a" Employee, who in turn "is a" Person. The purpose of the "is a" semantic is to identify a class hierarchy/common behaviour between objects, from which class property inheritance is obtained. There is a class hierarchy of common behaviour between Star Employee, Employee and Person, with the sub classes inheriting the properties of the super classes.

The second type of relationship is the business relationship with free form semantics descriptions, describing the business purpose of the relationship between the classes. There are two types of business relationship, those that are optional and those that are mandatory at each end of the relationship. Where the relationship between two classes is mandatory there needs to be a grouping of the mandatorily related objects. Consideration has been given to making mandatorily related groups of object classes a further type of object class. Order has no value unless related to a Customer and Product. The problem with this is that the data properties for each of the three classes vary for each business requirement/event. This cannot be modelled in a class model. The optional relationship is between the Person and the House classes, the optionality indicated by the O symbol. Both classes can exist in their own right and do not, therefore, form a group of classes.

Note that with free form semantics there is a description at both ends of the relationship, from the master class to the detail class and from the detail class to the master class. This is because the business purpose of the relationship is different from the super class to sub class, and *vice versa*.

There is no super- and sub-classing of objects with business semantics, and there is no property inheritance. The free form type semantic description is not relevant to object orientation, and is not used by database file handlers.

There is a school of thought which says that this class- and business-based approach to data modelling is too crude and does not entirely model the full "richness" of the relationships between the individual data properties. The above "is a" and free form semantics are *inter-object relationship* modelling mechanisms only. They pay no attention to any relationships between the properties within an object. Yet there are such relationships, the third type.

The third type of semantic description is useful for composition modelling of the relationships at the data property level. What is being modelled here is *intra-object relationships*, that is the relationship of the data properties to the prime key of the class. The traditional data modelling approach has been to key based entities, where an entity is identified by a prime key data property and against which the other data properties are dependent. An entity could be a Customer with a prime key data attribute of Customer Number, and against the key would be an array of other data attributes that describe the customer, such as Customer Name and Customer Address. But the component of data modelling is the prime key of an entity and the dependent data properties.

The individual data properties can be pulled out as classes in their own right and related to the "home" class with the "has a" relationship, as in aggregation modelling. Thus Customer Name becomes a class in its own right and related to the prime key of the base class with the semantic description. It follows that Customer Number "has a" Customer Name. The relationship and semantic description is of the data properties to the prime key. It would be nonsense to relate the data properties to each other, such as Customer Name "has a" Customer Address, or the other way around. This data property abstraction should only be done when there is a method processing against the data property. If the data property was abstracted into an aggregation object class without an associated method it would not be an object oriented design, as the aggregation object class would not contain a method. Object orientation "says" that data properties can only be accessed via a method.

One can now create a full semantic net of a class model. A semantic net is an information structure that shows the three types of relationship

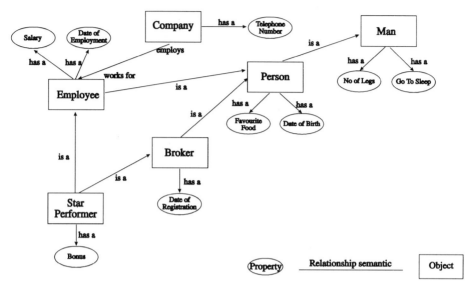

Figure 2.11 Semantic nets

between the business and abstracted class inter-object relationships and the abstracted aggregation intra-object relationships[1].

The significance of semantic nets to object orientation is that the semantic net happens to be a class model, and that object orientation makes use of the semantic descriptions to ascertain if the relationship between an object is a class and aggregation relationship (in which case property inheritance can be supported) and a business relationship (in which case property inheritance cannot be supported).

Semantic nets/class models model data at two levels, inter- and intra-object, between classes and between the data properties of the class. The inter-class support is with the "is a" and the free form semantic, while the intra-object relationship of the data properties within a class is with the "has a" relationship (figure 2.11). This figure is based on the class model of figure 2.2, with some extensions. The model shows the inter-object relationship between Star Performer and Employee and intra-object relationship with Employee having a Date of Employment and a Salary.

It should be appreciated that there are three modelling paradigms being used in parallel in the class model: the class and aggregation-based models superimposed on and

---

[1] Semantic nets are used mostly in expert systems as the description of the relationship between objects is in the form of facts—Customer has a name. Facts are in the form of what are known as triples—a subject (Customer), a relationship (has a) and a property (Name). When you join facts together one is able to represent knowledge and from this provide advice. This is the task of expert system products, not object orientation.

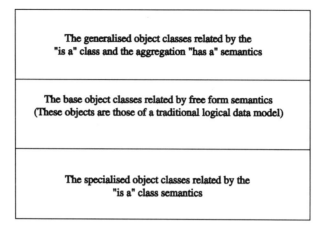

Figure 2.12 The information model semantic structure

surrounding the key-based model. The class model is an extension of the logical data model, the extension being the abstracted objects based on class and aggregation from the original entities, now also classes, based on keys. The relationship between the classes based on keys is still described by the traditional free form semantics of the logical data model, with the behavioural and composition semantics for the relationship between the abstracted class and aggregation objects.

2.2.3 Concrete and abstract objects

Objects can be at two levels—with and without instances. If a class object has no instances it is known as an abstract class. If it has instances then it is known as a concrete class. If it is abstract it is because it is a one-off object—here is only one occurrence (one instance) of the object in the world. As such it is often an object representing a concept or something intangible, such as Man or Mammal. If it is concrete, it is because there are n instances/occurrences of the object in the world. As such, concrete objects are tangible, typical examples being Customer and Order.

Objects are stored at the abstract and concrete levels, the abstract objects as definitions in the objectbase schema, and the concrete objects as "tables rows" in the objectbase. Figure 2.13 shows the class Container Crane defined and stored in the objectbase schema with four instances stored in the objectbase. The instances of the class are the individual containercranes in the container port. In a traditional database environment the classobject would be the record/table and the instance of the class would be the record occurrences/table row.

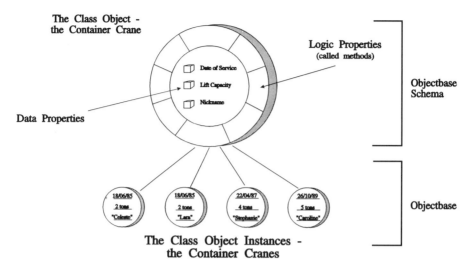

Figure 2.13 An object—its class and class instances

Some of the objects in a class model example may be abstract. Consider figure 1.7. The classes of Mammal and Man *have no instances: they are definitions of one-off objects*. These abstract classes contain information that is always instantiated with a value and only relevant/generic to the sub-class objects and their instances. For example, there is a data property Warm Blooded of the Man class with a value of "y", and all the sub class instances which can inherit from it are warm blooded.

Some of the abstract classes contain only a logic property(ies), that is a method(s). Examples of this are the class libraries and the event classes. The event classes contain the logic of the business requirements that are not normalisable to the business classes containing user data.

The class contains a template definition of all the information properties about an object that is generic to all the instances of the object. Thus, the class Container Crane for lifting and moving containers onto and off vessels in a container port would contain the data property definitions and the methods appropriate to all the container cranes. This is illustrated in figure 2.14, which shows the data and logic properties of the class definition of the container crane object.

There are three data properties and eight methods/logic properties. The data properties are obvious and are the same as for current database technology. The methods are blocks of logic unique to the class, with each method describing what the container crane can do, such as load a container onto a vessel and move left. The method Set Name updates the data property Nickname. The other methods are used for instructing the container crane to do something as detailed by the descriptive title to the

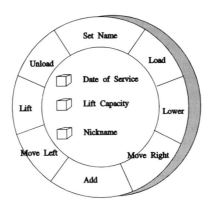

Figure 2.14   Container crane object

method (the application being a realtime system with embedded software), but would not update any of the data properties.

If the data or logic is at the class level it is generic information, relevant to all instances of the class. Thus, if all the container cranes had only one lift capacity, the data property lift capacity would have a value, be instantiated with a value, that would define the capacity. If the capacity were 2 tons a value of 2 would be defined as an instantiated data property at the class level, and all the container crane instances would be limited to 2 tons' lifting capacity. Of course, some of the container cranes could have a different lift capacity, but this is incidental to the fact that most of the container cranes will have the standard lift capacity. Any data property instantition is defined in the objectbase schema.

Some of the objects in figure 2.21 have bifurcated lines extending from the bottom of the class object. *This indicates that these are concrete objects.* Person, Employee, Broker and Star Performer objects are class objects, *and as such are defined in the objectbase schema,* and are also stored at the instance level—there are individual, real and live persons, employees, brokers and star performers, *and as such are stored in the objectbase.* These objects contain some properties that are not instantiated with a value at the class level. For example, the Date of Birth data property in the Person class is unique to each instance of Person. To instantiate at the class level would be meaningless, indeed it would be incorrect, as each instance of Person could have a different birthday.

The instance data properties values are not instantiated with data values in the dictionary. This is because the values to be stored in the instance data properties can vary with each instance of the class. Thus Person would have Date of Birth defined in the schema description of the class Person but stored with a potentially different value in the objectbase for each Person instance.

While the object instances are mostly used to contain unique values of the data properties for each instance of the class object, the object instances can also contain logic. This is new to information modelling and is not catered for in relational technology. Employee Mary could have a unique way in which her salary is calculated, and therefore requires a method to be stored at the instance level.

If the data or logic is at the instance level then it is only relevant to the single instance/occurrence of the object, and none other. It could be that container crane number 12 has a lift capacity of 3 tons.

There are those of the object oriented fraternity who believe that logic at the instance level is not appropriate, but why can't Mary have a unique method for the calculation of her salary? If Mary can have unique data values why not unique logic values? After all, object orientation normalises and stores logic in the same way as data. The two are no different. One of the authors has worked on a project producing an object oriented logical design (using the techniques described in Chapter 4), where some of the major parts of the business application methods were at the instance level. The application was for testing particular hardware/software configurations, each configuration being used for experiments on new types of telecommunications equipment. For example, tests of a particular nature were frequently being conducted, and for each test instance there were a variety of methods. Also, the logic of each test instance could vary.

This latter point illustrates another use of object instances—to overrule class information. Any class values can be overridden at the instance level of the class object—the instance information is more particular than the general class information and therefore overrides it. Consider the Employee class object. A method is defined to calculate the basic salary for all employees, *unless instantiated otherwise at the instance level.* Mary's method is more particular than the classes method, so Mary gets her salary and not that of the general employee. The same is true for data. At the class level Man is instantiated with a value of having two legs, yet poor Henry has his Number of Legs property instantiated with a value of "1". This is because Henry has had a leg amputated. None of the other Employee instances contain a value in the property Number of Legs, so they can inherit the generic value of "2" from the Man class object. By contrast, with the Date of Birth property there is no need for overruling as there is no instantiation of the property at the class level.

2.2.4 Property instantiation

With relational technology the values of the data attributes are stored only at the table row level, at the object instance level. This is true even if there is a value common to all the instances. For example, if the attribute was No. of Legs then all the table rows would have a value of 2 except for those poor persons who have had one or more legs removed. If there are 1000 persons there would 1000 values of "2" legs minus the number of amputees. This is clearly wasteful. A smart designer would create a separate table specifically for the generic value of "2" legs and use it as a table look-up for the general case. But the relational solution to the problem of generic data values is DIY.

Object orientation provides a built-in facility called property instantiation, the ability to define a generic value for a data property at the class level in the schema, and for the instances of the class to inherit the generic value.

The Mammal data property with an instantiated value of "Warm Blooded" is applicable to all mammalian species, and hence to all instances of the class sub-objects of Man, Person, Shareholder, Employee and Star Employee. The data property of Number of Legs with a class value of "2" is generally applicable to all instances of Man and to the sub classes of Person, Employee and Star Employee. All the sub classes within the class hierarchy inherit these generic values. However, the data property of Date of Birth as a property of Person is not instantiated with a value as it is not generally applicable to all instances of Person—each Person can have a different birthday.

The data properties of abstract classes must be instantiated with a value. It would be pointless to have any data properties that did not have a value, as there are no instance objects of the abstract class object to use the data properties with no value. The abstract class object would then serve no purpose, not even as a template description of an object. It can be seen in figure 1.8 that the Warm Blooded property of Mammal is instantiated with a value of "y" for yes and the "No. of Legs" data property for the Man class object has a value of "2". The most common abstract classes are those that contain methods only, the logic text being the instantiation of the logic property, the method.

2.2.5   Encapsulation

There are two parts to encapsulation—encapsulation of the data properties and encapsulation of the logic properties. As already described objects are composed of a data component in the form of attributes and a logic component in the form of methods, and the data component can only be accessed via the logic component. The data component is thus "encapsulated" by logic component. This is graphically illustrated in figures 2.14 and 2.15, with the methods surrounding the data. The great advantage of data encapsulation is that the user of the object, when sendinga message to trigger one of the methods, does not need to know and does not care about the format of the data properties.

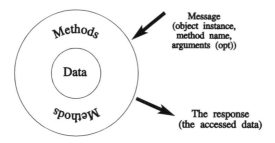

Data cannot be accessed other than via the methods, so its structure and contents hidden
Location and logic of the methods is not known, only the response to the message

Figure 2.15   Encapsulation

Abstract data type specifications describe class data structures not as a set of properties but as a list of services/methods available on the data structures. The only thing of interest to a user of the object is how the object appears in the interface—that is, the message and the associated response. The internal processing of the methods and the data properties they might access is irrelevant to the outside world, to the sender of the message and the receiver of the response. Therefore the methods are themselves in turn encapsulated by the interface.

2.2.6   Messages and responses

The message is the mechanism by which objects can "talk" to each other at application runtime. A message is sent from a method in one class or object instance to invoke a named method in another class object or instance. The invoked method executes, accesses the required data properties of the object instances to be accessed as specified in the message, and returns a response of the processed data to the source object that sent the message.

A message is therefore similar in role to a procedure call in current database technology. However, it is not a procedure call.

The format of a message (known as the signature) is shown in figure 2.16, and is different from the conventional program procedure call. There are three component parts to any message—the key/search criteria of the object instances to be accessed, the name of the method to be invoked, and any parameters the invoked method is to use.

The first two parts of the message are mandatory, but the parameter/argument list are optional. The first component of the

General Format

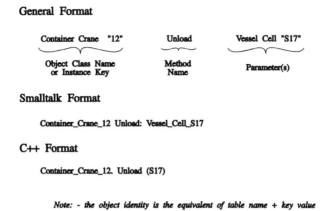

Smalltalk Format

Container_Crane_12 Unload: Vessel_Cell_S17

C++ Format

Container_Crane_12. Unload (S17)

Note: - the object identity is the equivalent of table name + key value

Figure 2.16   Format of a message

message makes the method similar in role to an SQL statement, but with the limitation that the access is record-at-a-time as in pre-relational database, and not the set access of relational database. The invoked method contains the access logic to the object instances specified in the first part of the message. The name method has to be a public method—messages are not able to invoke private methods. Messages can therefore only trigger logic of importance to the business rather than the system maintenance of the objectbase data.

The first component of the message distinguishes the message from a procedure call—the procedure call does not contain a specific component for the specification of the table rows to be accessed in the database. Procedure calls, of course, contain the name of the procedure to be invoked, and the argument list is the same in that it is optional.

Examples of messages to the Container Crane class are shown in figure 2.17. The first message invokes the method for unloading a container from Cell S17 of the vessel (cell number 17 on the starboard side of the vessel) the container crane is working on. The method accesses the Lift Capacity of thecontainer crane instance number 12 to ensure that the weight of thecontainer to be unloaded does not exceed the capacity. The second message invokes the method Add to insert a new instance of container crane number "12" with the data property values of a date of service of 15 May 1992, a lift capacity of 4 tons and a nickname of "Bessie".

Figure 2.18 shows a message sent to the Unload method, which accesses the Lift Capacity of the Container Crane to ascertain if it is greater than the containers to be lifted. An appropriate response is then sent back by the Unload method to the source of the message.

2.2.7 Methods

Methods contain the logic of the business application and of the system processes. The way in which they are incorporated into the computer system design is unique to object orientation. They can either be properties of the classes containing user data (a method for Calculate Salary as a property of the classes Employee) or as classes containing nothing but a method—the Date Edit routine, a common procedure or an event class.

There are two kinds of methods, private and public. They are discussed below.

2.2.7.1 *Private methods*

Private methods are system triggered when an object is accessed. They are private because they are not seen and cannot be used by the users. Their prime role is threefold—to edit the data properties in the objects as they are

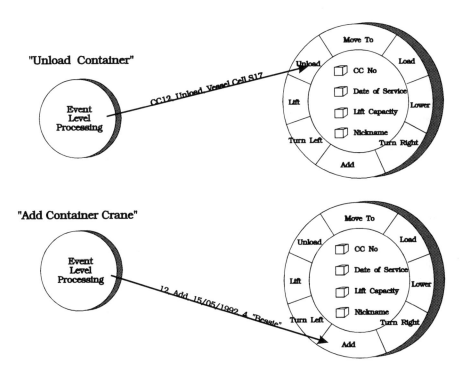

Figure 2.17 Messages to container crane (actually to the instances of the class)

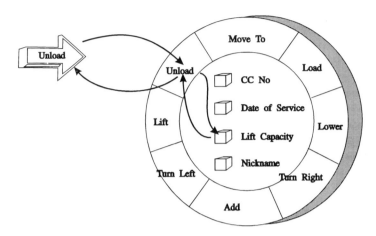

Figure 2.18   Method access to object data

inserted and updated into the objectbase, to prevent improper deleting from the objectbase (you cannot delete an employee if the Date Left Company property is blank), and to provide the usual objectbase referential integrity checking facilities. Private methods are therefore really concerned with data maintenance business requirements and objectbase integrity. For the first two roles many would recognise private methods as normal business processing, possibly developed as database procedures. In the latter role many would recognise private methods as database rules.

Both roles are now supported by most of the leading relational file handlers with stored procedures for public methods, triggers for private methods and rules for pre and post condition testing.

As database procedures the private methods can be defined for inserts, updates and deletes. For obvious reasons they can only be defined at the class level. For example, it could be that all employees' salaries are within specified value ranges for a given grade. The private method would be specified at the employee class level and automatically invoked whenever an employee is inserted into the objectbase, so as to ensure that the employee had a valid salary according to their grade.

However, a private method can also be defined at the instance level. This is only pertinent if the object is being updated or deleted, for the simple reason that the object instance must have been loaded beforehand and the private method specified subsequently for the instance. An object instance private method would be appropriate if it were necessary to edit in a unique, and not a general, way the data in an object instance that is being updated, or when an object instance is being deleted. For example, for an update private method it could be that the employee instance Mary's salary is the exception to the general rule, and that her salary is uniquely outside the general value range for her grade. A private method for editing Mary's salary would therefore be defined at the object instance level. Thus, if Mary's salary is being modified to reflect her special condition then the private method would be invoked whenever the salary update was being executed. As regards a delete it could be that at the class level employees cannot be marked as retired if their company pension information is not in order, but the employee instance of Henry has adopted a personal pension plan and opted out of the company's pension scheme. A private method for the Henry object instance would therefore be defined. Both Mary's and Henry's private methods, being instance particular, would override the class general method.

A private method can be triggered in three ways—by receiving a trigger from one of the public methods of the class to which the private method is private (Insert Object Instance public method triggers a private method to edit some of the data being input), or automatically whenever a business or database condition is obtained. This latter form of private processing is done particularly when the method is in the form of a rule. An example of a business condition could be that "WHEN stock level is below a certain level then create an order", the conclusion being the sending of a message to the method "Create Order" in the Order class. When the given condition is true, the stock level is below that specified, the conclusion can be drawn and an order is created. A database condition is typically a referential check of the type "When new order is created check customer exists".

2.2.7.2   Public methods

Public methods are unique to object oriented systems. They contain the application logic, the logic that supports a user business requirement, but logic that is normalisable to the classes containing user data. For example, the public method Calculate Salary for the calculation of an employer's salary is defined for and stored in the Employee class.

The public methods are those that are invoked by the receipt of a message from the event class of a business requirement, or from another class or object instance. The message contains the object instance value to be accessed, a method name, the name typically being a meaningful description of the function being called, such as Calculate Salary for calculating an annual salary, and relevant arguments. The method, of course, has been defined by name as a property of the class in the objectbase schema. The schema therefore points the message to the class specified in the method name, which then accesses the object instance(s) specified in the message. The public method will execute its logic, access the data properties as appropriate, process any arguments presented and return a result to the issuer of the message.

The initial message trigger for a set of public methods appropriate to a business requirement is from an application program event class. If the business requirement needs to access the data in multiple classes, then there need to be public methods appropriate to the business requirement in each class to be accessed. Each of these public methods has to be invoked by a message.

For example, when a business requirement has to access multiple objects, "For a specified customer display all orders for products greater than £10", then co-ordinated messages must be sent to the appropriate Customer, Order and Product classes to trigger the public methods. This can either be from the event object or from other objects previously accessed.

The data component in the objects can only be accessed by the public methods. It is the public methods that encapsulate the private data.

Public methods can contain what are called pre- and post-conditions. The prime purpose of this facility is to enable specified conditions to be true (usually in the form of data properties having a certain value that together indicate that the object instance being processed is in a given and correct state) before and after processing of the method. It could be that the method is for the painting of a Car class object. The pre-condition is an assertion that the state of the car instance being accessed is that the colour data property must be blank. The post-condition is an assertion that the colour of the car is non-blank.

Pre- and post-conditions are an excellent facility for ensuring that logic only executes under the correct conditions, and that the result of the execution is provably correct.

The EIFFEL object oriented programming language uses pre- and post-conditions for checking that the data being input and output is valid.

2.2.8 Polymorphism

Polymorphism relates to logic and therefore to the methods within objects. It is considered in this chapter with regard to its information modelling capabilities and how it affects the design of the objectbase.

Polymorphism is the ability of a function/process to have a common business purpose as defined by its name, but to have variations of its functionality/versions of its logic. Each version is defined as a method in a different class but with a common name. The version to be executed depends upon the class instance being messaged[1].

---

[1] Polymorphism therefore requires what is called dynamic binding (also known as late binding). Dynamic binding binds the methods to the message because the object instance to be accessed is not known until runtime. Static binding (also known as early binding) compiles the names of the classes and any variable to the logic of the application program.

There could be a method called Calculate Salary, but within this common name there could be a version for Employee and another version for Broker, or there could be versions for Salary Grade 1 and Salary Grade 2. Calculate Salary is polymorphic. Which version is executed depends upon the object instance being accessed. If the object instance being accessed is of the class Employee then the method version is for the Employee, and if the object instance being accessed is of the class object Broker then the method version is for the Broker. Polymorphism therefore allows the same message to a named method to refer to many classes, each of which can produce a different response depending upon the object instance being messaged. The sender of the message does not have to know that the named method is polymorphic. The message Calculate Salary for object instance "123" does not know whether the version of the method invoked is for an Employee or a Broker.

Polymorphism is a useful addition to the inheritance facility for aiding software reuse.

Consider figure 2.19. There are two examples of polymorphic methods. The business case is the container port authority. In the upper of the examples there are three classes—Container Crane (for loading and unloading of containers onto and off vessels), Van Carriers (for picking up containers from the ground and moving them at slow speed to another location) and service trailers (for the higher speed movement of containers over longer distances). Each of the classes have a method for checking the status of the container mover—is it free for allocating to the movement of a container? The business purpose of the three methods, one for each of the classes, is essentially the same, that is to access the status data property and ascertain the status of the container mover and if the status is free to allocate the free container mover to a container waiting to be moved. The variation of the functionality is that the instructions that go with the movement of a container differ depending on the type of container mover and how this information is to be presented to the user.

The methods can be made polymorphic, and being common they can be generalised as for normal information abstraction. A super class of Port Vehicle is created, and a polymorphic method with a suitably generalised name of Check Status is defined in the Port Vehicle class. The three original base methods are referenced by the common name of Check Status with a common signature/message format. Each base method is still stored on disk as part of the definition of the base class as illustrated, but as a "submethod" of the polymorphic method Check Status.

A message is sent to invoke the method Check Status, that is the method in the Port Vehicle class. The object oriented software recognises that the name is a polymorphic signature, or interface, reference to the three subclasses Check Status methods. If the container mover key reference in the

74

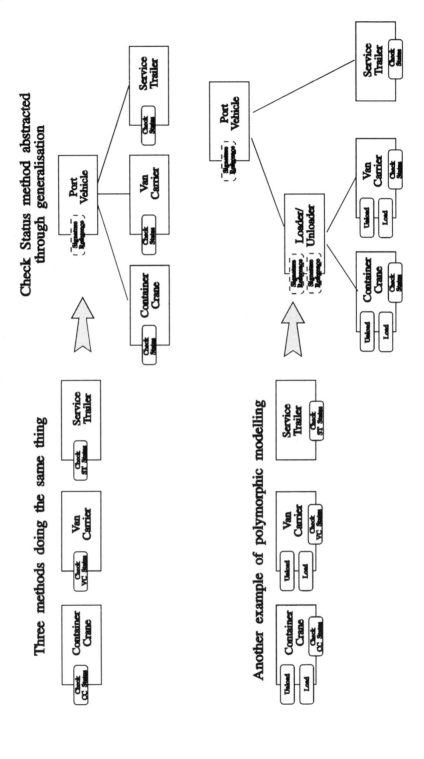

message is a van carrier, then the base Check Status method in the Van Carrier class object is "invisibly" invoked. This is not seen by the sender of the message, who merely has to say "move container 12345 with van carrier 54321" with the Check Status method.

This generalisation of the Check Status method to a super-class object can be seen in the top right of figure 2.19.

The second example takes the polymorphic modelling of methods a stage further. The Check Status method of the first example is still present, but there is again another common method of Unload in the Container Crane and the Van Carrier class objects, but not the Service Trailer class object. Both container cranes and van carriers have the ability to load and unload/pick up and drop containers, but if this is being done by a container crane then it is in relation to a cell in the vessel being loaded or unloaded. There is no relationship to a vessel as far as the van carrier is concerned. The Unload method can be made polymorphic, but because it does not relate to all the container movers it cannot be generalised to the Port Vehicle. A new class that is a super class to the Container Crane and Service Trailer and a sub class of Port Vehicle needs to be created. This is illustrated in the bottom right of figure 2.19.

It has been argued that polymorphism will eliminate much of the use of the condition IF/CASE statement when used for a given entity/class in application programming.

```
if Container Crane
    then do;
if Van Carrier
    then do;
if Service Trailer
    then do;
type code would disappear
```

It is also a more powerful modelling facility for conditional logic. There could be some logic for the Employee class object which states that if the length of service is less than 10 years then do this, if more than 10 years then do that, and if more than 20 years then do the other. There are several problems with this long practised approach—the conditionality is hard coded and potentially laborious. With polymorphism there could be three separate methods for each of the above two sets of conditions, each condition given a suitable polymorphic name and treated as a polymorphic method with a signature reference in a super class. Problem solved—and one could add new methods to new conditions without affecting the existing methods.

Figure 2.19   Polymorphic information modelling

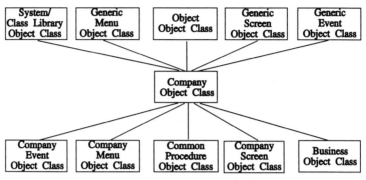

System classes include libraries, windows and menu and dialogue screens
Business classes include entities in the logical data model and their abstractions
Event classes are the business requirements
The Object Object class contains universal truths

Figure 2.20   Basic structure of an object oriented information model

2.3   THE CLASS MODEL

The class model is to object orientation what the logical data model/entity model is to relational technology.

The basic structure of an object class model and the different types of classes are illustrated in figure 2.20.

There are two basic groups of classes—the business objects that support the application being designed and developed and the system objects that support the computer system on which the application will run.

2.3.1   The business object classes

The origins of many of the business class objects in a class model are as entities in a traditional logical data model. The Employee entity becomes the class Employee. The business classes are thus based on the entities, and are therefore classes containing user data. But there may well be other derived business classes abstracted as super classes through generalisation or as sub classes through specialisation of the base entities according to object oriented abstraction rules. These business classes of the base entities and their class and aggregation abstractions contain both user data and methods.

The other business classes contain a method property of the event level logic of the business requirement. Each business requirement is a "Do something" event, such as "Calculate Salary" and "Make Payment". As

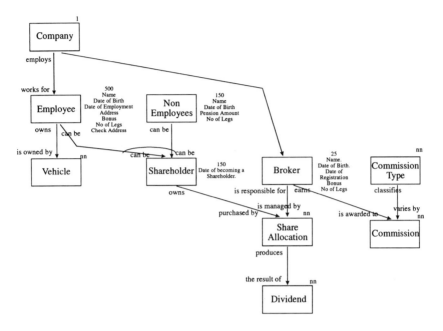

Figure 2.21 The logical data model

already explained, some 80% of the logic of the event can be normalised to the classes containing user data. Part of the logic of Calculate Salary relates to Employee, and is therefore defined as a method for the Employee class. The residue of the logic is not normalisable to the classes containing user data and remains at the event level. This logic becomes a method only event abstract class.

Given that the base entities of a logical data model continue to be preserved in a class model but can be abstracted into further super and sub classes, plus the addition of the event and system classes, it follows that a class model is larger, usually much larger, than the equivalent logical data model.

The base entities of a logical data model are shown in figure 2.21 and the resultant class model is shown in figure 2.22. Each rectangle in the logical data model represents an entity, a "thing of interest", to the application system about which data can be recorded, and the line between the entities with an arrow at one end represents a relationship between two objects, the arrow indicating the direction of detail entity to the master entity. Commission is a detail of Broker. Each rectangle in the class model represents a class, and the line between the objects with an arrow at one end represents a one-to-many relationship between two classes, the arrow indicating the direction of property inheritance and pointing to the super

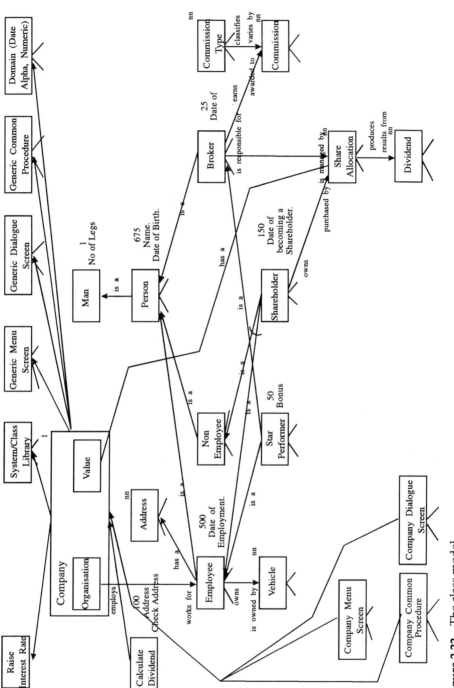

Figure 2.22 The class model

class, with the arrow's base pointing from the sub class. Employee is a sub class of Person. When the arrowhead points downwards the relationship is between the business classes remaining from the source logical data model entities from which the class model has been abstracted. This can be seen with the Broker and Share Allocation classes. Where the relationship arrowhead points upwards this is because of class or aggregation generalisation abstraction of super classes or a class specialisation abstraction of sub classes.

The generalisation from the base entities in the class object model are Man and Person and the specialisations are Star Performer and Star Bonus. There has also been sub-typing in that the Company entity has been split into two sub-types. Some of the data properties are relevant only to the Employees of the company and others to the Valuation of the company. The data about the internal organisation of the company is relevant only to the Employees, and the data about the financial value is only relevant to the Share Allocations of the Company. The Company class object has therefore been split into Company/Address and Company/Valuation.

There are six additional business classes in the class model than entities in the logical data model—two super classes, two sub classes and two sub-type classes.

2.3.1.1   The Object class[1]

Object orientation is able to model information to its appropriate level of abstraction. As described in Chapter 1, this is not possible with logical data modelling. The result is that objects "higher up" the class model are more general than objects "lower down" the class model. The more one goes up the class model the more general the information, and the more one goes down the class model the more specialised the information. It therefore follows that information which is universally true must be at the top of the class model.

The Object object is the class that contains information which is recognised to be universally true (such as the world is round, and that if you are in location A you cannot be in location B) and of relevance to the business application. One of the authors worked on a project concerned with chemical formulas. The company worked within the universally accepted laws of chemistry but mixed the various chemicals in such as way as to produce company or departmentally specific products. The raw chemical formulae were defined as method properties of the Object object and the results of the mixing were defined as specified methods in classes

---

[1]   This is sometimes called the base class. In SMALLTALK this class object is called Object, and in Object Pascal TObject. For C++ the top class object is anonymous.

lower in the class model, such as the Company and Department classes. This example was used in figures 2.7–2.9 to show the inheritance of methods.

2.3.1.2   The Company class

This class contains information that is more specific, more specialised than universal truths, but which is information that is applied corporate-wide. Typical company information could be a business rule stating that overtime for all employees is standard pay × 1.25. This would be stored as a method within the company class as the method logic is applicable to all employees within the company. This is an important class in the class model. All the classes above the Company class are effectively bought-in classes, such as system routines, application packages and window classes. All classes below the Company class are developed in-house.

2.3.1.3   The Business class

The most common classes in the class model are the business objects, all based on the entities in a logical data model. A typical business class would be Employee, which contains the data and logic that is pertinent/normalisable to employees. Examples of this could include the Telephone Number of the employee for the data component and the Calculate Annual Salary of the employee for the logic component.

Users of relational databases would recognise the business class as a standard entity/table of data. The business class almost always contains user data, as in a conventional logical data model. The only business classes with no user data are those where the data has been abstracted.

All the entities in figure 2.21 logical data model are in the OO class model with class and aggregation abstraction creating additional object classes. Examples of generalisation from the logical data model are the classes of Person and Man, and of specialisation are the classes Star Performer and Star Bonus.

Large parts of the logical data model remain unchanged, such as the Broker, Share Allocation and Commission and Shareholding entities. These objects are classes in their own right, in that they all have an objectbase schema template definition, but none of them belong to a class or aggregation hierarchy because there is no abstraction of factored out common or composition information.

It need not be assumed that information abstraction is appropriate to all parts of a logical data model. Much can remain unchanged.

Not all object oriented facilities are universally applicable all of the time.

2.3.1.4 The Event class

The event classes contain the logic that is relevant to the event/business requirements of the application and not to the classes containing the user data. Typically, they contain the 20% of logic that is not normalisable to the user data classes. They become classes in their own right, but containing a method only.

But being specific to a business requirement, event classes are the only portion of a class model that is not application independent.

The Event classes generally contain the logic for the beginning and the end of the application program. The beginning logic would typically be for the receipt of the input screen information, the initialisation of the variables and the sending of the messages to one or more classes, mostly business classes, in the class model. The end logic would typically be any final processing of the response information and the presentation of the output screen. The logic in between would be for the sending of messages to the classes containing the user data the business requirement needs to access and the synchronisation of the responses before final processing.

Since each event is unique and distinct in its own right, it cannot be part of a class hierarchy.

The placement of the Event class in the class model has been a matter of some debate. Perhaps the best place to put it from the point of view of information abstraction is as a sub-class of the company object, as the events are obviously relevant to the company. Such a company event could "Receive Customer Order". These events are triggered by the company's internal operations, but there are events that are of interest to the company that are not company specific in that they are not triggered by the company—they are events which are external and also affect other companies, but nevertheless the company is interested in such events as it needs to react to them. Such events can be classified as generic as opposed to company-specific. A generic event could be a government's decision to raise interest rates. Another example. The company could be a chemicals manufacturer and the events regarding the manufacture of generally available chemicals are not specific to the one company, but to any company manufacturing chemicals.

From an object oriented information modelling point of view there thus needs to be a distinction between generic and company events. Being generic to n companies, generic events need to be modelled as super-class event classes to the Company class. Company events are specific to the company and need to be modelled as sub-class event classes to the Company class. This can be seen in figure 2.22 where some of the events are identified as being above and some being below the Company class .

Event classes have most important roles to play within object orientation, specifically:

- being the main procedure to an object oriented application program and acting as a controller of the "central policeman" messaging strategy (see section 6.4.7.5);
- acting as the "glue" between the business and the system classes. This is discussed further in Chapter 7.

2.3.1.5   *The Menu Screen class*

Menu classes can be used at both the company business and bought-in levels. Those for the business of the company are designed for the user to select business requirements. Usually there is a main menu for each user role for the appropriate user to select a high level business function from an array of functions relevant to the user role. There is then a cascade of subordinate screens for the progressively more detailed selection of individual business requirements. These business menu screens are sub classes to the Company class. The bought-in system level menu screens would typically be windows classes.

2.3.1.6   *The Dialogue Screen class*

The dialogue screens support the selected business requirement from the business level menu screens. If the format of the screens is unique to the company, then this class is a sub class to the Company class. If the screen is not unique to the company, typically because it has been bought in with application package software and therefore not only relevant to the company but also to other companies, then it is a super class to the Company class.

2.3.1.7   *The repeating value object*

This type of class is illustrated as the Address class in figure 2.22.

Relational data analysis works on the principle that the data is dependent on the prime key, and that there is only one value for the data item for a given value of the prime key. Thus there could be n customers, each with an address and all living at the same address. The address value would be repeated for each of the customers without breaking any of the rules of data normalisation. Relational data analysis would not spot the wastage of disk space, which could be considerable (number of the repeated addresses × address length). An example of this is illustrated in figure 2.23. Of the five employees in table, three live at the same address of 12 Chase Side. This is a 60% duplication of this representative table. The class model shows that this address has been generalised and made a super class to all the classes with addresses, and supported by composition inheritance.

Object orientation is able to cater for this situation in that the address data property can be abstracted as a super class to those business classes with an address data property. In the OO information model this has been done with the address class.

A relational solution to this design problem is to create a separate table of the addresses and use the table as a "table look-up". The separate table would fulfil the role of the abstracted super class.

2.3.2   The system classes

The system classes are new to information modelling. These non-business classes are unfamiliar to those from a traditional data processing background, and are not found in a logical data model. They are unique to object orientation. They are classes that contain information for the running of the application on the hardware/software configuration. The system classes contain the logic supporting system functions, such as general data edit routines, print routines and technical processes such as windowing and file handling. Many of these system classes can be purchased from specialist vendors of classes.

All system classes, being of generic functions, are above the Company class in the class model. They are almost all abstract, containing a method of the functional purpose of the system process.

Employee Table					
Employee No	Name	Address	Date Of Employment	Salary	Retirement Date
12,345	Henry Smith	12 Chase Side Slough Berksire	15/01/86	17,000	31/12/1999
12,346	Mary Bloggs	12 Chase Side Slough Berksire	17/06/82	42,000	12/11/1995
12,347	John Brookes	The Form Field House Close Ascot Berkshire	25/11/80	17,500	12/07/2005
12,348	Susan Parker	17 High Street Edinburgh Scotland	12/12/78	25,750	15/09/2001
12,349	Andrew Eagle	12 Chase Side Slough Berksire	15/02/77	35,000	13/02/2010

Relational data analysis fails to spot an address values repeats, so wasted data

Figure 2.23

2.3.2.1   The Domain class

The concept of the domain is the same for object orientation as it is for a relational file handler. There is no difference. Domains, therefore, also contain information that is universally generic such as date, or generic to a company such as the salary range being between £10,000 and £20,000. All the classes that contain the Date and Salary domain will inherit all data and logic pertinent to valid values of date and salary. Date would be a super class to Company and Salary would be a sub class.

2.3.2.2   The common procedure object

The common procedure is a class that contains only a logic component, the logic being a common procedure that is application generic and relevant to the event classes as well as the methods in the application classes.

The methods in the Common Procedure class or object instances are therefore similar to the classical common procedure of conventional application programming, but limited to the commonality of the functionality in the event classes. In the class model the Common Procedure class is a sub class of the Company class as it is relevant to all the business classes in the class model.

2.3.2.3   The Class Library class

The instances of this class are usually supplied as what are called class libraries. Typical class libraries are classes for system software support, such as bit string handling, array handling, inserting an object, deleting an object, character editing, numeric editing and printing an object. There are a number of vendors of class libraries, both independent third party such as Glockenspiel, and suppliers of object oriented programming languages such as AT&T for C++, Interactive Software Environment Inc. for EIFELL, and Xerox Parc for SMALLTALK.

These class library objects are of a very generic nature, to the extent that they are universal type functions for system processing, and could therefore be stored as super-class methods to the Company class, as shown in figure 2.22.

2.4   SUMMARY

This chapter shows that:

- a class contains both data and logic properties. The data properties are optional;

- there are two kinds of abstracted classes—class and aggregation. The aggregation classes are those which contain a method that relates to a data property that is not the prime key of a class;

- the data properties are encapsulated by the methods, and the methods by the messages. There is complete information hiding of the data and logic in a class;

- the only interface with classes is via the messages, these containing the key of the object instance(s) to be accessed, the method to be invoked and any input data to be processed as arguments. The response to the messages is the processed output data;

- super classes contain more general information than sub classes;

- if the relationship between classes is a behavioural "is a" or an aggregation "has a", then there is property inheritance, with the sub-class property inheriting the properties of the super class;

- polymorphism is where processes of the same name can have different logic depending on the object instance being accessed.

3

OBJECTBASE FILE HANDLER TECHNOLOGY

This chapter first describes the technology of current database file handlers, in particular the data storage, pointing and data access mechanisms, and then the added facilities required for object oriented file handlers, with particular emphasis on the object ID collection facilities and their uses. The weaknesses of current file handlers are also assessed.

Given that object orientation provides additional information modelling facilities to those supported by conventional and database file handler technology, do object oriented file handlers have to be different from the current technology? Are object oriented file handlers like:

- a conventional flat file handler of pre-database days, with the record defined as a set of data properties of a known format and size and the relationships between the records based on symbolic pointers and under program control, and with one record per file?[1];

- a pointer-based objectbase as above, but with the relationships between the object instances maintained through a director indirect address pointing mechanism of some kind? Access to the object instances would be under programmer control with record-at-a-time access, and there can be *n* records per file;

---

[1]   A file is a named area on disk that contains the tables rows defined for the file.

- a relational type objectbase where the relationships between the objects are supported by symbolic pointers, with access optimised through indexes and query optimisers under file handler control, with a database access sub-language supporting set access?[1] There is one record per file;

- a new information storage and access mechanism?

The consideration of object oriented file handler technology is based on the pointing and information storage and access mechanisms they must use to support the additional information modelling facilities object orientation provides.

Although information access and storage are considered separately, they are in fact very much interlinked, as each uses the other to work.

The descriptions below are basic, with generic file handler facilities only described in terms of what they are and not how they do it, and even this is only to a level of detail necessary to understand how object oriented file handlers work and the degree to which they are different from current technology[2].

Before this can be done there needs to be an explanation of terms, some of them new to object orientation. The reason for this will become clear. The terms are:

Primary and Secondary Keys   Keys are user allocated data properties to identify, for commercial reasons, one or more concrete object instances. Assume the object classes are Customer, Order and Product. A primary key is required to identify an instance of Customer from an instance of Order and an instance of Product, and to identify one instance of a Customer from another instance of a Customer. A prime key is a named data property that has a unique value for each instance of the object. Customer Number would be an excellent prime key for the Customer object, Order Number for the Order and Product Code for the Product. A user can now access an object instance of the three classes by specifying the appropriate prime key value. Prime keys are required for persistent objects and cannot be modified while the object instance is in the objectbase. They remain unchanged for the

---

[1]   A set is *n* object instances as specified in the query and can be from *n* classes where access to multiple classes is required. One compound access command detailing the search access criteria is issued and all the object instances are retrieved as one set of records for the programmer to subsequently process a record (object instance)-at-a-time.

[2]   A detailed description of the internal workings of file handlers, such as the different mechanisms for calculating optimum access paths around the database, the different index optimisation techniques and the different approaches for reorganising large volatile direct address pointer-based databases with n relationships between the records and the whys and wherefores for the facilities and how they should best be used, would require a book on database design technology and techniques, of which there are many. As that is not the purpose of this book they are not described.

duration of the life of the persistent object. An object oriented term for primary keys is "identifier" keys.

Secondary keys are different. They are also data properties of the object but do not have to have a unique value for each instance of the object class. They are a facility enabling the user to access one or more concrete object instances on a search criteria other than the prime key. For example, a user may wish to access Customers on the secondary key of Customer Name. "List all Customers with a Name of 'Smith' ". There can be *n* instances of Smith in the objectbase. Secondary keys can be modified. After all, a female Smith can be married and change her name from the née of Smith to the married name.

These keys are user decided, their values user allocated, and they are used by users for the operational running of the business. They are also used by the file handler for direct access on the prime key, searching on the secondary key and as symbolic pointers for the relationship between the tables/class objects.

Keys therefore have a dual role, for the user to use to access data and for the system software to use as a means of accessing the data *and* of relating classes together.

Persistent and Transient Objects   These are object oriented terms for the different ways in which objects can be stored. Like all new technologies object orientation has generated its own set of terms, most of which, quite frankly, represent facilities that have long been used by current file handlers for many years. Many of the object oriented terms could be discarded as there are perfectly good terms in widespread use today[1].

Persistent objects have a life that lasts longer than the duration of a transaction that processes them (from a BEGIN statement to a COMMIT statement), and therefore need to be stored on a storage medium of some kind, usually a disk. Those familiar with current database technology would recognise persistent objects as being nothing more than standard database records.

Transient objects have a life limited to the duration of the transaction, and are held only in processor main memory and then discarded. These objects are typically used in realtime systems, and could include radar signatures of an object that lasts for the duration of a few turns of the radar aerial. The

---

[1] The generators of these new terms for old technology are no more "sinful" than their predecessors. The relational vendors did the same when advocating the advantages of relational file handlers over the Codasyl and hierarchical database file handlers. The need to market new products encourages the need for new terms. It gives the impression that there are new facilities in a new product. The real situation is that the "new product" is often merely an extension of the old product and uses much of the old technology. As we shall see, this is the case with object orientation. The object oriented term object instance is the relational equivalent of table row, is the Codasyl equivalent of a record, is the hierarchical equivalent of a segment. This is but one example

icons used in window graphics is another example. Special object oriented facilities are provided for the management of transient objects, such as garbage collection. These facilities are discussed in Chapter 5.

This section on object oriented file handler technology is only concerned with persistent class objects.

Business object 1–N relationships.   Database technology and the design techniques have long used the term master–detail relationships between tables/objects. Those of the Codasyl fraternity use the term owner–member. All relationships between tables/objects are on the basis that one of the records/tables is the master and the other the detail. Which is the master and which is the detail is based on the one-to-many facility, one master to many details. Thus Customer would be the master and the Order would be the detail, as a customer can have many orders and an order can only be for one customer. With concrete objects for which there has been no abstraction the master–detail relationship is one-to-many—one master Customer to n detail Orders.

Master–detail record relationships are key-based technology, with the Order containing a symbolic user-defined pointer to the Customer. The Order would contain the Customer Number as a foreign key/symbolic pointer to the Customer to which it relates.

Class 1–1 relationships for concrete objects   Where there has been class abstraction from the source objects because of common data properties then the relationship between the super and the sub classes with the source object class is always one-to-one. This is illustrated in figure 2.4, where the source classes of Employee and Broker with common data properties created the generalisation into Person and specialisation into Star Performer. For each of the 120 instances of Employee and Broker there is an instance of Person and for each instance of Employee and Broker with star features there is an instance of Star Performer.

Since Employee and Broker are concrete objects any abstractions are usually also concrete objects[1]. Person and Star Employee are also concrete objects. The relationships between abstracted concrete objects is also based on user defined prime keys, the keys being the keys of the source class objects. Thus, in the example in figure 2.4 both Person and Star Performer have the keys of Employee ID and Broker, this reflecting the source objects from which they have been derived. *There is thus the situation in object orientation that an abstracted concrete object will have n prime keys, one for each source object class from which it has been derived.*

The class relationship between concrete objects is supported by the traditional user defined key. This can be supplemented in physical design

---

[1]   The abstraction into generalisation does not have to be a concrete object. The Employee and Broker concrete objects abstract into the Man and Mammal abstract classes.

by the pointing mechanisms discussed in Section 3.1.1.

Class hierarchy 1–1 relationships   With object orientation, abstract classes are related to the other abstract and concrete object classes—they both are part of the same class model. Mammal to Man is an abstract class relationship and Man to Person an abstract to class concrete object class relationship. Since all abstract classes are one-offs the relationship between abstract classes has to be 1–1 and the relationship between an abstract class and a concrete object class has to be 1–N.

The mechanism to support class relationships is discussed in section 3.3.3.

Aggregation hierarchy 1–N relationships   This is illustrated in figure 2.4 with the example of the Address object class. Address is an aggregation class as it has been abstracted because there is some processing against the Address data property. With this situation there will be more object instances of the source object than for the abstracted aggregation class. In the example there could be *n* Employees residing at the same Address.

The mechanism to support aggregation class relationships is discussed in section 3.3.3.

There therefore needs to be support for abstract, class and aggregation class relationship modelling on top of the key based modelling of the traditional data model. Keys are still within the class model, to be used for maintaining the relationship between concrete classes. Another facility is required to support the relationships between abstract, class, aggregation and transient objects —this facility being what is called the object ID.

What this means is that for the physical implementation of an objectbase there needs to be three sets of key/pointer mechanisms:

— the user defined prime and secondary keys for user access to the concrete objects;
— the set of traditional database pointers for access along the user defined symbolic/foreign key relationships of the source objects from the logical data model and their object oriented abstractions;
— a set of system pointers/object IDs for the modelling of the relationships between abstracted and transient objects. These object IDs cannot be used as a user defined key for direct access to object class instances. Object IDs are system created and, as such, not understandable or usable by the user.

User keys, system keys and system pointers   User keys are data properties of an entity/object that are defined by users for the identification of an instance of the entity/object. They are therefore prime and secondary keys as defined above. They are required to enable users to access the appropriate data in the objectbase.

Database and object oriented file handlers can use the user keys not only as a means of access to the data but also as a means, through symbolic pointers, for relating tables/class objects together.

System keys are system allocated surrogate keys and have the benefit of overcoming the theoretical disadvantages of user-based prime keys that they cannot be altered[1]. System keys are used by the system software for direct access to an object instance, and not for relating objects together.

A system pointer is the means by which file handlers relate classes and their instances together to build an information structure as modelled in a class model. They are direct address pointers of the location of the object instance being pointed to on disk. The pointer can be in an index (much used by relational file handlers), placed as a prefix to the object (the approach used by the first two generations of database file handlers) or held as an array (the ADABAS approach).

3.1   POINTING, STORAGE AND DATA ACCESS MECHANISMS

3.1.1   Pointing mechanisms

There are a variety of pointing mechanisms to maintain the relationships between the persistent object instances, the relationships being defined in the class template definitions in the objectbase schema. There are two groups of pointers, those that directly point and those that indirectly point to the location of an object instance.

3.1.2   Indirect pointers

Symbolic pointers, with indexes   This facility is used mainly by relational database managers. Symbolic pointers are also known as foreign keys. This is the facility where the key of the master object class is defined and stored in the detail object. The Order class contains the Customer Number class key as a data property, so that an Order instance points to the Customer instance to which it relates. The pointer is symbolic in that the disk address of the customer instance is not given, merely a key value. This means that a file handler searching access mechanism is required in support of the symbolic key. The relational approach is a serial/physical sequential scan of the "file" containing the table rows/object instances or a direct access via an index,

---

[1]   The disadvantage is theoretical in that there is no practical need ever to want to change the value of the prime key. No user user would ever want to change the value of an invoice number.

using the key value to be accessed on. The index provides fast access to the object instances, but it has to be maintained by the file handler software.

The index contains a direct address pointer for each instance of the class object pointed to. In a sense, the index facility is like the direct address pointers but with one crucial difference; the pointers are not stored with the object instances and hence spread like "grass seed" around the objectbase but clustered separately in the index. This means that when there is a reorganisation of the objectbase it is possible to reorganise individual classes and their instances and any associated indexes. Reorganisation can thus be a class at a time—it does not have to be for the entire objectbase.

Indexes provide the means for relating classes together. There could be an index on the Order class for the key/identity of Customer Number. This is a much faster access to an object instance than the serial scan, so indexes are also used as a relationship access optimisation facility. The same facility supports direct access *and* master–detail relationships. The indexes need to be used in conjunction with symbolic pointing.

It will be seen later that this use of symbolic pointers as foreign keys is one of the main criticisms levelled against relational database file handlers by the devotees of object orientation.

The use of symbolic pointers has been of immense benefit in the development of query languages, a feature of relational file handlers. Symbolic pointers are user allocated keys to the classes with the appropriate values allocated to the object instances. Customer Number is the allocated prime key for the class object Customer and a value of Customer Number "12345" is allocated to the object instance Customer "12345".

Since they know the value of the customer instances they wish to access, and as the relational file handlers have database access technology that can use the symbolic pointers automatically, users can now pose queries on the relational database dynamically without programmers having in advance to write tailor-made query programs, as in pre-relational database days. The use of direct address pointers has meant that the database file handler cannot use the user's search criteria to access the database, there being no symbolic relationship between the table rows, only direct address relationships. Although the users could pose queries against the database, it still needed an application program to convert the user's query into an explicit database access path by following the pointer's paths on the basis of the search criteria specified in the user's queries. It all needed careful design and programming against predefined queries. *Ad hoc* querying cannot be supported by direct address pointers.

In discussions with a vendor of an object oriented product the salesmen kept on saying "But we can do that! All we have to do is write a program to access the objectbase .....". Game, set and match to relational technology and symbolic pointers. Symbolic pointing is a much underrated facility. Object oriented file handlers would do well to use them.

And this is what some of the object oriented products are now supporting —the use of direct address pointers *and* symbolic pointers, the former to be used by the production application programs and the latter by the *ad hoc* query languages. This is the case with the Objectstore product.

Inverted list   This is similar to an index, with a list of all the key values to access, a count of all the object instances which have that value as a key (the key may not be unique if it is not the prime key), and an associator that relates that value to a disk address. The end result is the same as an index. This is the approach used by the ADABAS database manager.

Serial/physical sequential/entry sequenced   This is the only mechanism that can be used on a tape storage medium. Table rows/object instances are related in that they are physically juxtaposed together, one after another. There can, of course, be only one relationship between object instances, class A and its instances, or a fixed hierarchy, a class A instance, the instances of class B that are details of class A, and so on.

Object instances need another form of pointer while under program processing in processor main memory. This is supported by memory references as to the location of the object instance. This is discussed in Chapter 5.

3.1.3   Direct pointers

Direct address pointers.   These are stored with the object instances on disk and point to the disk address of the target object instances. The pointers are usually of 4 bytes in length and stored as prefixes to the object instances. For each relationship as defined in the class model, there could be a pointer to the super-class master objects, the sub-class detail objects and forward and backward pointers to "daisy chain" each master object instance and its related detail object instances together in a predefined sequence. The sequence could be, for example, in prime key sequence of each object instance. The Customer object instances could be chained in an ascending sequence of Customer Number and the detail Order object instances in the sequence of Order Received Date within Customer Number.

The format of the pointers is a two part structure—the page/block the object instance is stored in and an offset position of the object instance in the page, usually in the form of n bytes from the beginning of the page. This is the classic structure of direct address pointers.

The advantage of this mechanism is fast access from one object instance to another. Direct address pointers cannot be beaten for retrieval access performance from one object instance to another. The disadvantage is the insertion and deletion of object instances and database reorganisation. If there are many relationships, especially where there are broad network data structures of n master objects to one detail object, there is heavy disk I/O when accessing the master objects to maintain database referential integrity.

Since the relationships are a direct reference to a disk location when reorganisation of the data is required due to insertions and deletions making the database "untidy" (the place where the object instance should go based on the design criteria specified for the objectbase is full because of n insertions or excessively empty because of n deletions), the entire database has to be reorganised, including those objects which are stable and are not "untidy". If one detail object instance is moved as part of the reorganisation, then all the pointers pointing to the moved object instance also need to be altered, even though the other objects may not have been moved. The pointers in the other object instances that point to the object instance just reorganised must be updated to reflect the new address of the reorganised object instance. Volatile and large databases/objectbases with many relationships are bad news for direct address pointers.

The direct address pointer facility has been used by the first two generations of database managers, the hierarchical type, such as IBM's IMS, and the Codasyl type, such as IDMS from a variety of vendors.

The other disadvantage of direct address pointers, as already discussed, is their inability to support *ad hoc* query languages.

The disadvantages of this type of pointer led to their demise for the third generation database managers, the relational file handlers.

Randomising   This is an alternative to indexing. The prime key of the object is converted into a disk address by the randomising algorithm. A typical randomiser is the division/remainder technique, the divisor value being the page/block for the object instance and the remainder being the placement of the instance within the page, the value of the remainder being the *n*th record position in the page/block. From a disk storage point of view, the technique only works efficiently if the sequence of the prime keys is ascending/descending without too many breaks in the key values. The breaks result in empty spaces on disk.

Relative record[1]   Relative record is where the "slots" on disk are of fixed length and the record occurrence/object instance is allocated to the slot on the basis of its key value. Object instance with a prime key value of Customer Number 123 would be allocated to slot 123. The records/objects have to be a fixed length to match the disk format and for the location of slot 123 to be calculated (record length × 123). This provides extremely fast access to the object instances, there being no need to go via a search algorithm, pointers

---

[1]   There are variations of the Relative mechanism, such as Relative Track. They are not described as they are not widely used.

or indexes for direct access. But the relative record approach is very wasteful of disk space. There could be 500 slots but only customers 123, 321, 456 and 654 currently in the application, this being a 99.99% wastage of disk space. The randomiser and relative record mechanisms are of use only for direct access to a specific instance of a class. They cannot be used to support relationships between classes.

3.1.4 Storage mechanisms

The storage of data is in the form of flat records as described above for all types of file handlers, the only thing that is different being the means of maintaining the relationships between the table rows/object instances through the pointing mechanisms, and from this the building of data structures either as hierarchies, networks or relations.

The records can be stored on disk in a variety of ways, the main ones being:

- serial/physical sequential (explained above);

- key sequential. The object instances are stored in the sequence of a specified key, either ascending or descending. If the chosen key is Customer Number ascending then the Customer instances would be stored in the sequence of Customer Number 1, Customer Number 2, and so on;

- clustering—the placement of a detail object instance in the same page or page range as the master object instance to which there is the most frequent access, thus reducing disk I/O. The object oriented file handler Gemstone supports this facility, the cluster being within a "bucket" page range.

If a data property contains no value, is empty, then most file handlers support the null facility. The empty property is defined as a length of n in the class definition but is marked on disk as a null value for the object instance with a blank or zero value, possibly of a byte or less in length.

The object instances are stored in pages/blocks within the file to which they are allocated. Their placement in the file and pages is dependent on the storage mechanism used. The file is located on disk x, starting on cylinder y and track z, and has n pages of such and such a size. The space allocation on disk could be physically split over n page ranges on n disks, but it is nonetheless one logical file page range. The calculation of the page in which the object instance should be stored is a simple matter of the storage and access mechanism used.

3.1.5   Access mechanisms

The main access mechanisms are scanning in either serial/physical sequential scanning, keyed sequential, following the pointers or direct access through a randomiser, a relative record position or an index. Given the previous sections, they are not explained further here.

If accurate statistics of the cardinalities of the relationships between the class object instances are maintained, it is possible to produce what are called QuEPs—Query Execution Plans. This is the ability of the file handler to calculate the best access path around the database when needing to access multiple classes and n instances of the classes. A Customer could have, on average, 100 Orders and a Product, on average, 50 Orders. If the query was "For a specified Customer and Product get all Orders" then the cardinality statistics would show that it is much more efficient to access via Product than via Customer. The QuEPs are used by the query optimisers of relational file handlers, and they vary considerably in sophistication. The pointer facilities are then used to provide the fastest access along the QuEP calculated path[1].

All the pointing, storage and access mechanisms described above are available for object oriented file handlers to use.

3.2   FILE HANDLER FUNCTIONS

There are many functions that a file handler needs to do beyond the storage and access of data. This book is not about the details of file handler technology, so the functions are merely listed and then put in the context of what an object oriented file handler does. There are numerous database books that describe these file handler functions. The functions include:

- Concurrency Control. This is the locking of the object instances so as to ensure concurrent access to a table row, or to less granular locking such as to the table, when multiple users need simultaneous access. There are different kinds of locks appropriate to the type of access required, the main ones being the "S" type lock for read access, and the "X" type lock for update.

- Transaction Control, this being achieved through the BEGIN and COMMIT commands. The appropriate lock is established between these two commands

- Recovery, with the use of the before image log for the rollback of failed

---

[1]   QuEPs are not used by the database file handlers using the direct address pointers for the simple reason that the access paths are under programmer control, but there is no intrinsic reason as to why they cannot be so used.

transactions and the after image log for the recovery of failed hardware—this facility being used in conjunction with the transaction control facility.

- Reorganisation of the database to place records in the correct location in the database from their displacements due to the addition of new records in full pages and to recoup empty spaces due to record deletions.

- Security, this being through the subschema for application program data access restriction (this by pre-relational database file handlers) and the view and GRANT/REVOKE facilities for user access restriction (this by the relational file handlers).

All these functions are required of and are supported by object oriented file handlers. The fundamentals of file handler technology have not been altered because object orientation is being adopted. The underlying technology is the same.

3.3 THE DIFFERENCES REQUIRED OF AND SUPPORTED BY OBJECT ORIENTED FILE HANDLERS

There is no reason as to why the pointing, storage and access mechanisms for the data properties of object classes and the file handler functions detailed above need be any different from current database managers. However, object orientation does require additional facilities because of the more powerful forms of information modelling provided. These facilities are discussed below.

3.3.1 Class concatenation (objects within objects)

The data properties of the object instances are a concatenation of those defined in the class and aggregation hierarchies the object is in. This can be seen in figure 3.1, where the base table in the relational model is Employee, with 500 table rows. The abstractions in the object oriented class model is that there are 500 instances of the super class Person with the data property of Date of Birth, 500 instances of Employee with the data property of Date of Employment, and 50 instances of Star Performer with the data property of Bonus. 50 of the 500 Employees are Star Performers—in object oriented terms they are not Employees but Star Performers who inherit the properties of the Employees they have been derived from. The stored model on disk is divided into the "pure" object oriented approach of the new object oriented products and the approach that will almost certainly be adopted by the relational vendors.

Figure 3.1 Different information models

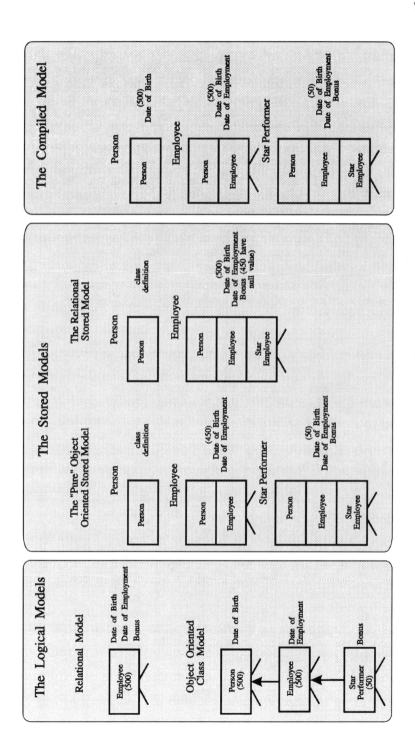

With the "pure" object oriented approach there will be 450 instances of Employees inheriting the Date of Birth property and storing it with Date of Employment—Employee within Person—and 50 instances of Star Performer with all three data properties—Star Performer within Employee within Person. There is a 1–1 relationship of the abstracted concrete class of Person from the source class of Employee. This is stored as a single flat file rather than two files and thus disk space and disk I/O is saved.

What figure 3.1 shows is that if there is concrete object generalisation of the data then with the pure object oriented approach the data is stored in the source class. But if there is specialisation of the data properties then the specialised data properties are abstracted not only as a new class in the objectbase schema definition, but also as a new file on disk. There will thus be 450 Employees and 50 Star Performers on disk in two files.

Basically, what is happening is that the class definitions are defined as high as possible in the class model and the instances and their values are stored as low as possible in the class model with the pure object oriented approach, and at the level of the original source class from which any abstractions have been made for the extended relational products.

The relational approach will be to store the data values exactly as in the table rows of a relational file handler that is the 500 Employee object instances, of which 450 will have the bonus data property with a null value. The object oriented storage of data will not change with the extended relational model. To make a relational database object oriented all that will be required to redefine the database schema object oriented data abstraction will be limited to writing SQL DDL, not rearranging disk storage.

The object oriented "database" benefit gained is that there is no repetition of the Bonus property for the 450 Employees who are not Star Performers. With the extended relational file handlers the property would be declared as null and stored as an indicator of one byte or less for those 450 instances of Employee.

One could extend the object oriented disk storage model to reflect exactly the logical class model, such that there would be 500 instances of Person with Date of Birth, 500 instances of Employee with Date of Employment, and 50 instances of Star Employee with Bonus. This approach would not save disk storage but would increase disk I/O, with three files instead of two.

The compiled model of the same base structure is different from the stored model. If the application program accesses the Person, then the "view" of the class is that it is composed of the data property of Date of Birth. If the application program accesses the Employee then the "view" of the class is that it is composed of the data properties of Date of Birth and Date of Employment. If the application program accesses the Star Performer then

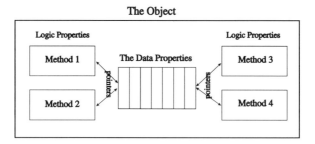

Figure 3.2   Common storage structure of a class

the "view" of the class is that it is composed of the data properties of Date of Birth, Date of Employment and Bonus. This concatenated view of the class and aggregation hierarchies is, of course, property inheritance.

3.3.2   Class definition (and disk space)

Object orientation stores logic properties as well as data properties in the classes, these logic properties being the methods that act on the data properties. Indeed, they must store the logic properties to ensure encapsulation of the data in the classes

There are two approaches for the storage of the methods,[1] to store them with the class definitions as variable length properties or to store them as separate variable length records, one for each method, and with pointers between the "home" class and the methods. The authors are not aware of any object oriented file handler that uses any approach but the second. This means that the basic storage structure of a class is as in figure 3.2. If each of the four methods are 1K in length and the name description, format and length definitions of the data properties is 50 bytes each, so that for the seven data properties the data definition needs some 350 bytes, the total disk space requirement of the class definition is 4350 bytes.

Assuming that the storage lengths of each data property is 10, 20, 30, 30, 30, 20, 10 bytes, and assuming that there are two data properties inherited from super classes each of 30 bytes, then each instance of the class is 150 bytes of data in size, to which is added 60 bytes of inherited data from the super class at runtime.

---

[1]   There can also be methods at the object instance level. A case of this would be where Mary, an employee, has negotiated a special bonus for herself, this bonus being based on a complex formula. This formula would be a method stored at the object instance level, that is Mary.

One of the authors has recently worked on a project producing an object oriented model of the application. Some 20% of all the methods were at the instance level.

The amount of additional disk space for the pointers of each concrete object depends on the pointing mechanism used and the number of relationships to maintain. This can easily be calculated. If direct address pointers are used, the pointers are 4 bytes each and there are pointers from and to the master and detail classes, with forward and backward pointers then, for each relationship in the class model the overhead would be 12 bytes or 9 bytes if the class had no super or sub class to point to. The pointer overhead can be substantial.

3.3.3   Object identifiers

Much reference in articles and books on object orientation is made to the facility of object identifiers, often referred to as object IDs. What are they and what role do they play?

There seems to be some confusion about object IDs. They have been defined as the key to identify an object instance (Customer Number 12345). In this context object IDs are the same as user defined keys/symbolic pointers as used in current file handler technology (Khoshasfian and Abnous, 1990, p. 152). Somewhat confusingly, Rumbaugh et al. (1991, p. 24) argue that the object ID is not required when modelling the class model. This view is decidedly out of line with traditional entity modelling, where the prime user allocated key of the entity is always identified. Object IDs have also been described as relating the object instance to a memory or disk address and relating object instances together based on their relationships as modelled in the class object model. In this context they have a system purpose—addressing—and hence are system allocated direct address pointers (Taylor, 1992, pp. 46; Khoshasfian and Abnous, 1990, p. 164).

The problem is that identifiers cannot be both a user identification key and a system addressing pointer at the same time. A user allocated key is not an address, which is why there are the various types of direct address pointers (described earlier) to support rapid searching for object instances in the objectbase, the direct address pointer addressing the user defined key reference values.

It is further argued by some (Khoshafian and Abnous, 1990, p. 143) that the database pointer mechanisms described earlier compromise identity, in that the reference of one object instance to another object instance is an external mechanism and is environment dependent—a certain database type uses a certain type of pointer which may be within or external to the object instance record. And symbolic/user named keys need costly joins when accessing from one object to another. The current database pointing mechanisms are felt to be deficient. "An address based (direct address pointers) or a descriptive based (symbolic pointers—authors' brackets) identity mechanism compromises identity and corrupts the computational model of the language. Identity is a machine or implementation independent notion associated with objects." An alterantive objectbase pointing mechanism is required.

According to these authors, in an object oriented system each object instance is permanently allocated a system generated object ID. The ID is internal to the object and is allocated when the object instance is created. The object ID uniquely identifies the object instance, and the object instance remains associated with the object ID throughout its lifetime. In a sense, the object IDs are what has long been called surrogate keys, not user allocated keys, such as Invoice Number and Customer Number, but surrogate keys allocated by the system software for the system software to use. But object IDs are more than a surrogate key, as they contain a reference to the location of the object instance in the object oriented system, be that location main memory, disk or a device. Object IDs are therefore not merely system generated surrogate keys, but also location references.

There is a dichotomy here, even a contradiction and error, which many books (Khoshafian and Abnous, 1990; Taylor, 1992, to mention but two) on object orientation have not answered. An object ID is an "arbitrarily assigned value ...assigned and maintained by the system .... *and* (authors' and) that point to an actual address or to a location within a table that gives the address of the referenced object" (Taylor, 1992, p. 46) and "each object will be given an identity that will be permanently associated with the object. Its purpose is to represent the individuality of an object *or* where it resides" (Khoshafian and Abnous, 1990, p. 144).

These two statements are exactly the same, with one exception. The Taylor description states the object ID is a system key *and* a location referencing mechanism, whereas the Khoshafian and Abnous description states that the object ID is a user defined key *or* a location referencing mechanism.

The difference is important—which is correct? The Taylor statement is partly contradictory. The object ID cannot be a permanently allocated key value and a location reference pointing mechanism to an actual address at the same time, for the simple reason that object instances are moved around the disk locations, not only when the objectbase is periodically reorganised but often when object instances are being inserted. If the file design is key sequenced and the block/page the object instances need to be inserted into to maintain the sequence is full, then a number of file handlers (VSAM being one) split the block/page and move half the object instances to a new empty block/page. And if, as suggested, the key value is arbitrarily allocated and is a location reference, it does not say much for the objectbase design on disk.

If the object ID points to a table that gives the address of the referenced object, so that the object IDs refer to objects by some indirect pointing mechanism, then the object ID can be an identifier *and* a referencing mechanism.

But this is no different from current technology. The user allocated key is pointed to by an index which also points to a disk address.

And the Khoshafian and Abnous statement is equally puzzling. How does the system software decide whether the object ID is a user defined key value or location address pointer reference?

So what are objects IDs—are they user defined keys to identify object instances for user access to the objectbase, disk address pointers for system access to the objectbase, or surrogate keys for transient object instances? An object oriented file handler will need to use:

- user defined keys to support user access to the concrete objects. These will be the same as the current user defined keys, being either the prime or secondary keys;

- direct address pointers (either via indexes, pointer chains or inverted lists) to model the master–detail key based relationships between concrete objects on disk (Order 12345 relates to Customer 54321). These will be the same as current file handler pointers. Object IDs could be used for this—see figure 3.3, but if this is their use what is different about object IDs from current pointer types?;

- the new object oriented facility of the object ID to model the composition relationships. The current database pointers are not used for this because class and aggregation abstraction are new facilities unique to object orientation. There is a problem here. In the example in figure 3.4 there is the aggregation class of Address. Address is a concrete object in that there are *n* addresses to process. But there is no user defined key for the address other than the address itself. Textual keys of this kind are prone to keying errors. No user could use the full address as a key for accessing a specific address. And to put a foreign key of the full address in the Employee class would negate the very purpose of aggregation objects.

  The solution is to create an object ID and to use that as the foreign key to relate the aggregation object class with the source object class, to relate Address to the Employee.

- the object ID facility to model relationships between concrete objects and abstract objects. Abstract objects do not have a user defined key as they are definitions of one-off objects in the objectbase schema and are usually about objects that are intangible, the examples used in Chapter 1 being Man and Mammal. Not having a user defined key they need a system allocated key—the object ID. The ID could, of course, be the name of the class. The other objects related to the abstract objects can now use the object ID as a foreign key in the standard manner. This is shown in figure 3.4.

Figure 3.3 Object ID pointing

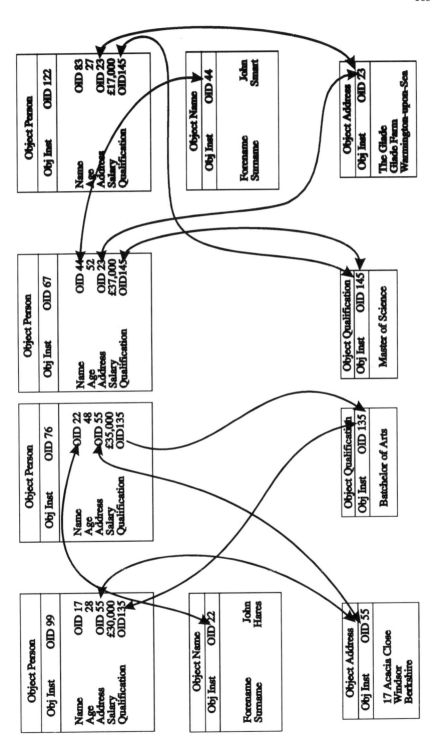

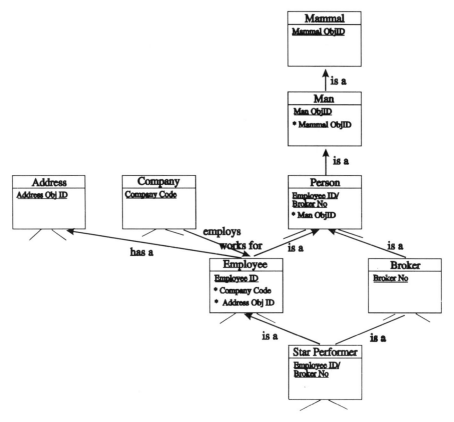

Figure 3.4   Class and aggregation abstraction sit on top of keys

Surrogate keys for transient objects   On a project one of the authors is working on, system created object ID surrogate keys are being used for simulation testing of an advanced weapons system. None of the object instances have any user defined keys, with the memory resident transient object instances having a life of anything from a few seconds to several tens of minutes.

The author does not consider that object IDs are designed to enable persistent concrete object instances to relate to each other—if that were the case there would be no difference with the pointers of current database technology for the objects created through object oriented abstraction. Their purpose is to relate aggregation classes to their source class for which they have been abstracted, abstract classes to the relevant concrete object classes in a class hierarchy and to identify transient object instances.

Object ID can also be used for system management purposes, that is to relate the transient objects together. In this context pointers are virtual memory addresses. Languages such as Pascal and C use a heap facility to allocate dynamically memory for data types reference via the pointers, the heap being linear address spaces allocated at run time (and hence dynamically) to the object instances.

As system allocated key values, for whatever role, object IDs are of no use to the users of an application system, for the simple reason that the user does not know what the system allocated object ID is for invoice 12345 and customer 54321. User keys have a known and possibly meaningful value to the user and are user decided and allocated. All computer systems use user keys, they have to, otherwise the users could not use a computer system in support of a business. System generated and allocated keys such as object IDs do not have a known or meaningful value to the user. Object oriented systems will therefore still have to use user allocated keys to the object instances just as in relational and pre-relational database technology. *User allocated keys will need to function for business purposes alongside object IDs for object oriented information modelling and system purposes.*

This means that for the location of persistent object instances on disk the address reference will require the two classic features of a disk address, given current disk technology, of the page/block the object instance is located in and the offset position of the object instance within the page/block. Given that the persistent objects are stored on disk they have to have these two features. This can be seen in figure 3.3, where the pointing is exactly the same as with the Codasyl database managers, but with the absence of the pointers between the instances of the same class object. The chain is from the master to the detail and detail to the master but not detail to detail, so it can support class models but not the chain relationship between instances of a class object. And they are stored with the object instance just like direct address pointers of the Codasyl type of database file handler managers.

But objects do not have to be persistent—they may have a life for the duration of a transaction, for the running of the application program. This is where object IDs are more powerful than merely disk address pointers. They can also be used for the address of the transient object instance in main memory, or on some device in a networked system.

3.3.4   Object ID mechanisms

Various mechanisms have been proposed for object IDs. The mechanisms reflect the confusion in the industry, as they include both user allocated and system keys. They include:

User Defines Primary and Secondary keys.   This is the approach used by database file handlers. All object instances have to have at least a user allocated prime key, but do not have to have a secondary key. The alleged problem here is that the prime keys cannot be modified.

It is argued by Khoshafian and Abnous (1990, p. 153) that using such "identifier" user keys for object ID "confuses identity and data values (object state as defined in the value of the data properties—authors' brackets)" and has a number of problems:

— One cannot modify the keys. While true this concern of the devotees of object orientation is more one of "noise" than practical reality. There is no business sense in having any need to modify a prime key. The key of an Customer, Order and Product never changes during its life. If it did then there would be operational chaos in the running of a business—there would be no common point of reference for the users of the business. If the prime key was subject to change then it is a bad key as it provides no permanent point of reference for the system users . An example of this is if the prime key is Surname and therefore subject to change when the person is married. All one has to do is choose a prime key that is stable during the life of an object instance. That has never been a practical problem—that is the way users run their business, computer system or no computer system, object oriented or not object oriented.

   And secondary keys are not used specifically to identify an individual instance of an object because the key may not be unique. They can equally be used to identify sets of object instances—all the instances with the name of "Smith" being an example. And secondary keys can be modified.

— There is non-uniformity. The same key in different objects may have a different format.
   The designer of the system should be fired.

— Different prime keys This often happens when companies merge, where one company identifies employee instances by Employee Number and the other company used Social Security Number. What's the problem? Make one of the two candidate keys a primary key and the other a secondary key which also happens to contain a unique value for each object instance and is therefore also suitable as a candidate key, and provide a direct access mechanism to both keys. The most used direct access mechanism is the index facility.

— Unnatural joins when accessing multiple objects. The example given is of the need to join the Department and Employee tables "Where

Employee.DeptName = Department.Name. This is claimed to be unnatural in that what the user "really wants instead of DeptName is the actual department tuple/row". Why the user requirements were not included in the relational design is not explained. Assuming that the database design is able to support the user requirements, the WHERE clause now becomes "Where Employee.DeptNo = Department.DeptNo". There is no problem.

The book then goes on to say that relational tables are in first normal form (p. 154) (the repeating groups have been taken out). No, they are not—they are in third normal form, so that the data properties are dependent on the prime key and have only one value for a given value of the prime key. If they weren't in third normal form, not only is there the problem described at the end of Section 3.4, but the data properties could well be stored in the wrong tables, such that the user poses a sensible query and could obtain a nonsensical response. There could be a Stock table in first normal form composed of the data properties of Product Code, Depot Code, Product Description, Depot Name and Stock Quantity. Product Code and Depot Code are the prime keys of the table. And there is no Product Description in the Product table or Deport Name in the Depot table. A pretty awful design, but nevertheless in first normal form. The user poses a query requesting a Product Description from the Product table, a reasonable request, and is presented with no description, it being in the wrong table.

- Surrogate keys, this being the allocation of system generated globally unique keys. But of themselves surrogate keys are not enough—for the running of business two other types of keys are needed to operate alongside them. Since the user will have no knowledge of the surrogate keys, user allocated prime keys of the object instances will still be required, as will direct address pointers to point to the address/location of the target object instance.

- Structured identifiers. This is very much the mechanism used by the file handlers supporting operating systems. This can only support hierarchical data structures. An example of this is the MS DOS directory mechanism.

- Direct address pointers, both for the virtual main memory address space if the object instance is transient and the page/offset position on disk if the object instance is persistent.

This is the approach currently being most widely used by the new emerging object oriented file handlers, such as Objectstore from Object Design, by some of the conventional programming languages, such as

Pascal, and the object oriented programming languages such as C++ and EIFFEL. They function in the same way as the pointer chain technology of the Codasyl database file handlers. Given that object IDs point to the location of the target object instance, they can also be used as direct address pointers. This is the approach illustrated in figure 3.3.

Indeed, it is noticeable that object oriented file handlers are reverting back to pre-relational file handler technology for persistent objects. Come back Codasyl, all is forgiven! Long live IMS—as a hierarchical file handler it is almost perfect for the modelling of class and single property inheritance. Direct address pointers are an excellent mechanism for object IDs. The only problem is that if the object ID is the physical placement of the object instance then it cannot be a randomly assigned key, as claimed by the vendors of object oriented products. Random allocation of object IDs that are placement-based would produce a random objectbase design. For reasons of access and storage performance, the placement needs to be carefully designed.

All in all, direct address pointers come out on top as the best of the object ID facilities.

3.3.5 Collections

Collections are classes that encapsulate the management of sets of other classes and selected object instances *for a business requirement.* These classes have methods for performing such functions as creating the collection, accessing an object instance of a collection, deleting an object instance of a collection, inserting an object instance of a collection and iterating access over the object instances of a collection. A collection therefore does not have the generalised functionality of a file handler, rather tailored functions for storing and accessing object instances appropriate to a business requirement.

There could be a business requirement to list all customers with red hair and the associated orders placed within the last six months, this being a requirement that is constantly triggered. It would be extremely efficient to create a class with all the appropriate instances, the set of customers with red hair and associated orders. All subsequent triggers of the business requirement would have an optimised access path to the collection class and its instances, with no wasted accesses to any table rows.

These classes are called collections, each containing the methods for storing, accessing and manipulating the instances of a class object the collection class supports. The methods in the collection class undertake the functions of storing object instances, sorting them, accessing and deleting them as appropriate. As orders for customers with red hair and their orders

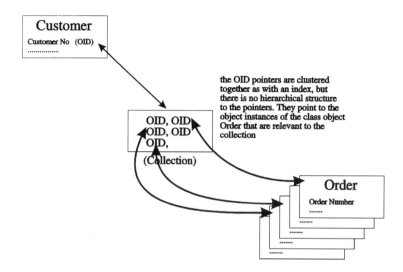

Figure 3.5 The collection facility

placed within the last six months come and go so the appropriate methods insert and delete object instances from the appropriate collection. To build a collection, a file of object instances, all that needs to be done is to create new instances of an existing collection class.

A collection is a subset of all the instances of a class. There is fortunately not a duplication of data event though there are actually two sets of object instances—the objectbase instances of the class and all its instances and the collection instances appropriate to the business requirement. Rather, the collection is a selected set of the objectbase class object(s) and its instances pointed to by the collection facility.

This can be seen in figure 3.5.[1] Since the collection of pointers is created under program control the sequence could be serial, in the order the object instances are created, or in the sequence of a user key in the object instances, in Order Number order for example, or Order Number within Customer Number order. There is thus the benefit of an indexing-like capability under programmer and not system control. And this means that a "daisy chain" of the set instances of a detail class to the appropriate instance of the

---

[1] This is an approach to the use of direct address pointers in a way not used by the first and second generation pointer chain database file handlers. With these file handlers the pointers were stored with the object instances and hence were "grass seed" dispersed around the database. With the relational approach the direct address pointers were grouped as pointer arrays at the bottom of the hierarchically structured B-tree indexes. With the approach adopted in figure 3.5 the object ID pointers linking the Customer class to "its" instances of the Order class (or another array of collection pointers for a business requirement for the customer orders for product XYZ) are grouped as an serial array, as in the inverted list facility.

master class can be created in any order the programmer wishes. There can thus be a "daisy chain" of pointers linking the Customer to its Orders. The pointers can be made to link in a forwards, a backwards, an upwards and a downwards direction as desired by the programmer. The programmer has complete control.

3.3.6   Multi-source class library compatible repositories

As indicated in Chapter 1, object orientation offers the ability to build application systems "mechano" style with the event classes "cherry picking" from the methods in the business object classes containing the user data, and from class libraries of common procedures and system routines, and then linking them together to form an application program.

There are several sources for these class libraries of application independent class object methods. Many generic functions are attached as class libraries to the object oriented programming language (C++ usually has over 100 depending on the vendor), there are specialist vendors of class libraries supporting business functions (the days of buying entire business application packages may be coming to an end) and one can develop home-built class libraries.

One is therefore moving to a situation where the sources for the application independent component of application systems can be various. Some of the method only classes could therefore be from several programming languages, from several specialist vendors and from home development.

Support for this varied source situation is required in the repositories of the object oriented file handlers. This is not the situation with the database repositories of the database file handlers where the common procedures are all from a common source—programmer written code.

3.4   CRITICISMS LEVELLED AGAINST CURRENT FILE HANDLER TECHNOLOGY

Much is being made by devotees of object orientation about the deficiencies of current database file handlers and the solution offered by object orientation. These criticisms need to be considered and put into context. The criticisms include that:

- if a data property is not filled in with a value, disk space is wasted. Assume the Customer Address field in an object instance is blank, the 150 bytes defined for it in the database schema definition are wasted.

  Not so. The field needs to be declared as a null field so that if the field is blank then all that is stored for the object instance is a null value indicator, of some one byte in size;

- if the same data property has the same value for n instances of the class, disk space is wasted. Assume that 20 Customers all live at the same address, then the address is repeated 20 times and some 2850 bytes of disk space (19 × 150) are wasted.

  If this is a problem then create a separate table of addresses as in the example of the abstracted repeating value class objects in Section 2.3.1.7. The design solution for conventional and database file handlers is the same as for object orientation.

- there is no ability to alter the value of the prime key of an object instance. If the prime key of the Customer class object is Surname, then this key cannot be altered in the objectbase even though there is a business need to change the surname due to marriage.

  The problem is more apparent than real. Choose a key that does not require alteration, like Customer Number—and there has never been a practical problem in finding prime keys for a class object definition which fulfils this requirement.

- the real problem with current pointer mechanisms is the foreign key/symbolic pointer. There may be a situation where the detail entity/table/object is exclusively related to two master objects. A person is either at home or at work and there is a foreign key in the Person record that needs to indicate by its value that the object instance is at work or at home. The foreign keys need to be changed to reflect the change in the state of the object instance. Object orientation does not like the situation where the state of the object instance requires a change in the object reference, the object ID. This is a valid criticism, so use the alternative approach of direct address pointers—but this then leads to the problem of objectbase reorganisation.

  With the relational approach, with the use of symbolic pointers between tables (the indexes are access optimisation facilities) one can reorganise the database one table at a time and an objectbase one class object at a time. With direct address pointers one is required to reorganise the entire objectbase—if one moves an object instance through the reorganisation then the pointers in the other object instances that point to it have to reflect the new address. The pointers in these other referenced objects therefore also need reorganisation. One cannot, therefore, reorganise the objectbase a class at a time, it has to be the objectbase as a whole. Yet large parts of the objectbase may be very stable and may not need reorganisation, the object instances still being "tidily" organised on disk. All very wasteful—direct address pointers are not good for objectbase housekeeping if the objectbase is large, volatile and has many relationships. If the object ID is used as a direct reference to the location of another object instance, then there has to be a change to the object ID during objectbase reorganisation—one cannot avoid it. If the object ID refers to objects by some indirect look-up mechanism, to a look-up table that contains the address, then the problem of direct address pointing is avoided.

But reverting to the dislike of object orientation of the situation where the state of the object instance requires a change in the object reference, the object ID. The point is valid, but is it significant? The book by Khoshafian and Abnous (*Object Orientation: Concepts, Languages, Database, User Interfaces*, Wiley, 1990) gives an example of the alleged weakness of the foreign key pointer mechanism (p. 156). "In some cases the state of the object which is the value of an object instance (i.e. the state of the prime key—authors' brackets) is modified. For instance, assume Jim Brown, like John Smith, works in the same Hardware department. Then if we change the budget of John's department, we had better make sure all copies of the budget of the hardware department instance occurring everywhere are updated consistently. With object identity this is unnecessary. There is only one copy of the hardware department instance in the whole system."

If a relational design is properly conducted with the tables in third normal form then there will be a separate table for the department budgets and one table row for each department budget value. There is no

FNF Relation - Project/Person						
Project Code	Person	Name	Grade	Salary Scale	Date Joined	Alloc Time
ABC001	2,146	Jones	A1	3	1/11/86	36
ABC001	3,145	Smith	A2	3	2/10/7	36
ABC001	6,126	Black	B1	9	3/10/87	17
ABC001	1,214	Brown	A2	3	4/10/87	17
ABC001	8,191	Green	A1	3	1/11/87	12
XYZ002	6,142	Jacks	A2	3	1/11/87	5
XYZ002	3,169	White	B2	10	2/11/87	5
XYZ002	6,145	Dean	B3	10	14/11/87	3

Figure 3.6

duplication of data. So why the need to go checking that "all copies .... ". It is only if the relational design is poor and not in third normal form that this kind of problem could occur, and that is the fault of the designer, not the foreign key.

The holding of redundant data in a table to which it doesn't rightly belong (for example, the budget information not being in the Department table) creates "storage anomalies". Figure 3.6 illustrates a number of such anomalies.

Here a table is in first normal form. Strictly speaking, there should be three third normal form tables—project, person and a link table showing the time that a person has spent on a project.

By producing a physical design from a table in first rather than third normal form the following inefficiencies occur:

— One cannot insert a person until that person has been allocated to a project.

— Deleting a project also wipes out all associated person data.

— If grade A1 is switched to salary scale 4 it would be necessary to read the entire table and make multiple amendments where only one should be necessary (this is the situation in Khoshafian and Abnous).

The solution to the above problems does not require object orientation and object IDs—it requires a good designer to put the tables in third normal form. The criticisms of foreign keys is rejected.

3.5 OBJECT ORIENTED PERFORMANCE

Claims are made both ways as regarding object oriented performance—that it is typically 100 times faster with complex data structures (Taylor, 1992) to "Object oriented database have developed the reputation of being 'rich in functionality but poor in performance' " (Khoshafian and Abnous, 1990). Given the above descriptions of the technology used and that it is essentially the same as current database technology, there is no intrinsic reason why object oriented file handlers should perform faster or slower than current database file handlers.

It needs to be realised that file handlers are like human beings, they have a character. Depending on the facilities they are provided with (direct *versus* indirect pointing, for example), they perform differently under different conditions. Direct address pointing is excellent for fast retrieval but poor for objectbase housekeeping, randomisers are superb for fast direct access but poor on data storage efficiency if the prime key sequence being randomised is frequently broken with large breaks (as they usually are); and so on.

All that has to be done to get a set of good performance figures is to match the file handlers' facilities to the data and access requirements of the application system, and to run on a suitably sized hardware configuration.

The claims made that object oriented objectbases are n times faster than relational databases need to be treated with the same degree of caution as the claims made about the productivity gains of the 4GL programming languages over the 3GL programming languages. Orders of magnitude in

The Current Database Approach

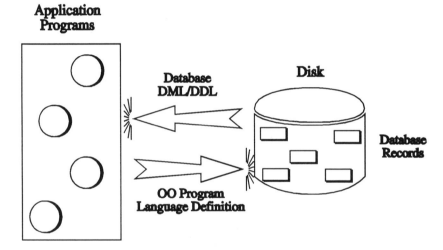

The Object Oriented Approach

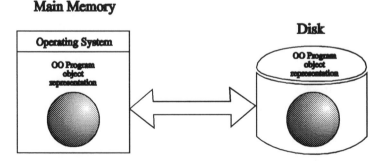

Figure 3.7   Impedance mismatch

improvement were promised. Unfortunately, the claims did not take into account that, no matter what product one uses, one still has to write code, line by line down to the last dot and comma. And so it is with file handlers. One still has to store the object instances, to access them from disk pages/blocks, pull them into a buffer pool and from there into the application program's main memory, and one still has to link the related object instances together with a pointing mechanism of some kind. And there still have to be user recognisable keys for the user to operate the application system. If the file handler decides to use system keys such as randomisers, direct address pointers and indexes, then there are two sets of keys, user keys for commercial operation of the application, and system keys for computer system operation of the application system. *There are still the same user and system requirements for the storage and access of data—object orientation does not alter these fundamentals.*

There are, nevertheless, some facilities which object oriented file handlers do provide that do offer optimised performance compared with current database file handlers:

- *No impedance mismatch*   There is one facility offered by pure object oriented file handlers that is not provided by current database technology— the fact that the physical representation of the object instance in main memory is exactly the same as that stored on disk. There is no translation required to go from the database form to the application program form. The benefit is that there is no overhead in the formatting and reformatting of the data when there is transmission from memory (program form) to disk (database form) and disk to memory. The schema definition of the objectbase can be obtained directly from the application program source code rather than from a separate file handler schema definition. With the separation in current database technology of the data definition language (DDL, exclusively SQL) from the data manipulation language (DML) there is a translation required between the application program language (DML) and the database language (DDL) with *every access to and from the database*. Given the different application and file handler languages, all classes need to be defined twice, once in each form. The DDL language is declarative in form, the DML procedural and the SQL data types may be different from those of the programming language. This mismatch is called the "impedance mismatch" (illustrated in figure 3.7). The overheads saved on this are claimed to be substantial, although no figures have been released by the vendors of pure object oriented file handlers.

- *The elimination of the buffer pool*   The current approach is to retrieve data from disk, pull it into a buffer pool and from there into an application program storage working storage area. There is therefore logical I/O from the buffer pool to the working storage. From figures obtained from a number of relational vendors, the average machine instruction overhead (for a typical IBM MVS operating environment) for a physical disk I/O from disk to the buffer pool is some 5000 instructions, and from the buffer pool to the working storage the logical I/O overhead is some 1500 instructions, this being the logic overhead for data management of the buffer pool. This means that there is some 30% extra processor overhead for the movement of data from the buffer pool to working storage. Object Design with their product Objectstore have eliminated the buffer pool facility, and move data from disk directly to the working storage area. There is therefore an automatic saving of 30% of processing overhead on the processor for the movement of data between the processor and the objectbase. Given that the disk I/O overhead has proved to be somewhere between 30% and 60% of the total program overhead, the total application saving can be as high as 20%. This is a significant saving for a single facility.

The proportion of program overhead to the total overhead varies according to the speed of the processor. If the processor is fast then the proportion declines, if it is slower it is larger.

3.6   OBJECT ORIENTED FILE HANDLER EVOLUTION

The driving force for object oriented file handlers was to:

- overcome the information modelling deficiencies of current database technology. The requirements of object orientation are more demanding than current database technology can support—there is now the need to model logic with the data, to model class and aggregation hierarchies, to enforce encapsulation and to support property inheritance etc. The approach that has been adopted is the usual one of adding these facilities to the existing technologies of current file handlers, choosing those facilities that are best suited (record at-a-time access and direct address pointers) to the requirements of object orientation. The result is that object oriented file handlers are able to combine the best of all the previous information storage and access technologies with their own facilities. An elegant solution that preserves existing technology and skills.

- centralise the definition of the structure of an objectbase base and take it out of the hands of the application programmer. Schema definition is a corporate task and should not be pitched at the event level in the application programs. The need for this is potentially in conflict with the next point.

- resolve the impedance mismatch overheads incurred when moving information from/to memory and disk from the mismatch of the database DDL language and the application programming DML language. This need spawned new products where the file handler was an extension of the programming language, products such as ONTOS from Ontologic and Object Design with ObjectStore. From an objectbase administration point of view, putting the definition of the structure of the objectbase in the hands of programmers to prevent the impedance mismatch overhead is a dangerous policy.

There is, in fact, not much to worry about. Programmers do not need to define the objectbase structure. Schema definers can define the object classes and organise the data properties and relationships appropriately. They just need to know the DML language facilities to use. The devotees of object orientation argue that one can just as easily define an objectbase schema in DML as the devotees of database technology argue that the schema should be defined in the DDL. Once the definition is made, the application programmers then merely need to know about the methods, the messages to pass to them and the responses to receive from them.

The evolution of the object oriented file handlers will be in two stages, of which the first is coming to an end and the second is announced and emerging.

The first stage has seen the emergence of new file handlers specifically designed for object oriented support. They have mostly been developed by new companies that have seen the benefits of object orientation and the market opportunity that go with the emergence of a "new" technology. There has therefore been a plethora of new startup object oriented companies and associated products. Some of the main ones are Ontos Inc. with Ontos, Object Design with Objectstore, Objectivity Inc. with Objectivity/DB, Servio Corporation with Gemstone, and Versant with Versant OODBMS.

The second stage is the response from the relational vendors. Two things are certain—the relational vendors are not going to abandon the database market to the new specialist object oriented vendors and their products, and they are not going to abandon relational technology (nor should they and nor do they have to).

Several of the relational vendors have made announcements that they will produce object oriented versions of their products. The vendors of the Oracle, Ingres, Informix and Sybase databases have all announced object oriented developments. Oracle Inc. have announced that the next release of the Oracle product will be object oriented, Informix have entered into an agreement with Hewlett Packard regarding their OpenODB, and Sybase have purchased Gain Technology in the United States, a supplier of object based software. And Ingres and Sybase already has many object oriented facilities built into their product, as discussed below.

The enhancements being made to relational file handlers to support the information modelling requirements of object orientation has become known as the extended relational model, the original model being based on Dr. Codd's 12 rules. This term nicely encapsulates the fact that the relational vendors will not abandon relational technology, but will extend it by adding object oriented facilities to it. There is much in the relational model that suits the process of addition—a table can be the basis of a class and a table row is the equivalent of an object instance. And the latest enhancements to the products already enables them to define public and private methods, such as stored procedures and triggers, with rules for pre and post condition testing. *There is nothing in the relational model that is anti the object oriented model.*

Indeed, on a recent assignment using Oracle 7 (and this would be true of any relational product with stored procedures, triggers and rules) it was proved that 13 of the 14 object oriented information modelling facilities could be supported, either directly or without much difficulty. Only polymorphism cannot be supported. This capability is impressive. It shows you do not have to buy an object oriented product to adopt object orientation.

3.7 SUMMARY

The chapter shows that:

- object oriented file handlers continue to use the same pointing mechanisms to relate object instances together as current relational and earlier database file handlers;

- the class and aggregation facilities sit on top of the user defined keys for identification of all the instances of the classes;

- the object ID facility is the pointing mechanism for relating abstract and aggregation classes together;

- relational vendors will continue to store class data without change when adopting object oriented technology. It is the database schema definition that reflects any class and aggregation abstractions and their relationships with each other;

- a collection is a program created class object file of class object instances that have to support a specific business requirement's access needs. For example, there could be a collection of all customers with red hair;

- some of the new object oriented file handlers have considerable performance advantages over the relational file handlers. There is no

overhead for impedance mismatch—translation of the database definition of the structure of the database data into a form recognised by the
application program. Neither is there any overhead for the buffer pool,
which has been eliminated;

- the latest versions of relational file handlers can be used in a very object
oriented manner. Seven of the facilities for modelling information in an
object oriented way can be supported. The stored procedures become
public methods and the rules the private methods, abstract class objects
supported with pseudo/surrogate keys, and property inheritance is "do
it yourself messaging".

4

OBJECT LOGIC TECHNOLOGY

This chapter describes the concepts, associated with the expression of program logic, of:

- Encapsulation,
- Abstract Data Types,
- Function and Operator Overloading,
- Classes,
- Inheritance,
- Polymorphism,
- Genericity;

by taking an example of a simple piece of logic which is evolved to exploit each of the above concepts. The purpose, benefits and consequences of each concept are discussed to show how the concepts complement each other, and why they are all essential features of any Object Oriented Programming Language (OOPL).

4.1 THE FEATURES OF OBJECT ORIENTED LOGIC

The previous chapters have indicated that the major advance offered by object orientation is the association of logic with the data objects to which it relates; the logic is normalised in the same way that data is normalised. This gives the logic, like the data, an intrinsic value of being dependent on an object and independent of a business application. It therefore enables the logic to model the behaviour of the objects it supports in a way that allows the same logic to be reused in several different business applications.

Associating logic with data objects is a different way of organising and packaging logic from that used in traditional programming languages. In a traditional approach, particularly where functional decomposition is used for the modelling of the logic, the requirements of a business event are translated into a bespoke sequence of logic that implements that specific event by accessing and manipulating whatever data objects it needs. While the logic may contain many common sequences of code, they cannot be reused because they depend upon the logic that surrounds them to establish the correct context for their successful execution. The logic associated with a business event only has value as part of that business event.

The object oriented approach to the organisation of logic enables a number of additional programming techniques and mechanisms to be incorporated into the program description of the logic components. It is the combination of all of these features which provide a much more expressive and powerful way to structure and organise the logic. These new features can significantly increase the intrinsic value of a piece of logic by making it more reusable, more resilient to change and suitable as building blocks for dealing with more complex objects and business requirements.

The features that are increasingly recognised as being part of the object oriented logic portfolio are:

- encapsulation, as the means of hiding information,

- abstraction, where data types are defined by the operations they support,

- classes, as user defined data types,

- objects, as instances of a class,

- methods, as operations on an object,

- inheritance, whereby subclasses can be derived from superclasses,

- message passing, as the means of invoking methods,

- function name and operator overloading

- polymorphism and runtime binding,

- genericity.

In Chapter 3 the benefits of these facilities were described in relation to modelling information in an object oriented way. In this chapter we shall look at each of these features of object orientation to show how they complement each other to give the benefits that are possible with an object oriented approach to the construction of logic, where the logic is an integral part of the data objects it helps to define.

4.2   AN EVOLVING EXAMPLE—MANIPULATING DATES

The above features of object oriented logic will be looked at by considering a straightforward example of programming logic using a familiar data type. The logic will initially be expressed using the features of traditional programming languages. The features listed above will then be introduced, one by one, and the example progressively modified to incorporate their use and the benefits that result will be discussed.

Dates are reasonably familiar data objects that look like abstract data types[1] in most software development environments. They can be read into a program and written out into reports in a variety of formats, such European or American ordering. Within a program they are ordered so that one can distinguish dates in the past from dates in the future. We would not expect to have to handle Dates in any other way.

To demonstrate the value of encapsulation and of abstract data types, let us consider an environment where Dates are not already supported and we have a programming language which only has built in support for the primitive data types of Integer and String. Consider, as a simple example, a program to read in two dates, subtract one from the other and print the result as the numbers of days that separate the two dates.

We shall use a pseudo language whose syntax is based on the Ada Programming Language because of the clarity it provides. However, some of the examples are used to explain concepts and mechanisms that are not supported by the Ada language and these therefore cannot be legal Ada code but are simply expressed in an Ada-like style.

In this environment Dates could be represented by a String, but this would make any arithmetic operations on Dates very complex and inefficient. A more effective representation for supporting arithmetic operations would be the use of three Integers; one for the year, one for the month of the year and one for the day in the month. So the variables needed to hold a Date would then be declared thus:

Year, Month, Day: Integer;   – – the three variables that represent a Date

---

[1] The term Abstract Data Type, in the field of formal specification languages, is used to describe a data type which is characterised solely by the set of operations that can be applied to values of the type and for which the actual representation is irrelevant. This is the meaning being used in this chapter and its application in a programming language context will be described in Section 4.5.

The term should not be confused with an Abstract Class, which is applied to classes for which no object instances can be created.

For these three integers to represent a valid date they have to satisfy the rules of the Gregorian calendar. For simplicity, we will assume these rules are applied when a Date is converted from a String representation, on input into the program.

The arithmetic operations on Dates can be written in terms of years, months and days in a messy way. A fairly simple operation is subtraction, to produce the number of days between two dates. We will assume that such an operation is available in a Program Library together with operations to convert Dates to and from a printable String representation. In a traditional programming language the operations in a Program Library all have to have unique names, so we will name these operations:

Date_from_String;

Days_between_Dates;

String_from_Days;

The first problem we encounter when Dates are represented as three separate Integers is how to define the interfaces, or signatures, for these operations. Assuming that a String is a built in data type supported by our programming language and that Days is represented by an Integer data type then the operations, *Days_between_Dates* and *String_from_Days* can both be defined as functions returning values of built in data types. These functions could have an interface specification like this:

function Days_between_Dates (Year1, Month1, Day1, Year2, Month2, Day2: Integer)
return Integer;

function String_from_Days (Days: Integer) **return** String;

The operation *Date_from_String* cannot be a function returning a Date, since a Date consists of three Integer values and a function can only return a single value. The operation has to be implemented as a procedure that takes three output parameters of type Integer; the interface specification for this procedure would be:

procedure Date_from_String (Text: **in** String; Year, Month, Day: **out** Integer);

Given these three operations and the operations *Get* and *Put* to read in a string and to print out a string respectively, our example could be coded as a procedure *Date_Example_1*, as shown in figure 4.1. This procedure declares local variables to hold two Dates, a Day and a String. The logic simply reads in a string and uses the operation *Date_from_String* to convert it

```
procedure Date_Example_1
        Y1, M1, D1:  Integer;
        Y2, M2, D2:  Integer;
        Days: Integer;
        S: String;
begin
        Get (S);
        Date_from_String (S, Y1, M1, D1);
        Get (S);
        Date_from_String (S, Y2, M2, D2);
        Days := Days_between_Dates (Y1, M1, D1, Y2, M2, D2);
        S := String_from_Days (Days);
        Put (S);
end Date_Example_1;
```

Figure 4.1 Date as three integer variables

into the three Integer Values *Y1, M1* and *D1*. This is repeated for the second Date. Then the function *Days_between_Dates* is used to compute a value for Days which is converted into a String and printed.

Despite having encapsulated the logic for three complex operations inside a procedure and two functions, we cannot be sure that the interfaces that these operations provide are correctly used, even if our programming language applies type checking. This is because the interfaces only require that values of the built in types, Integer and String, are supplied. The language can check that a use of an interface is given a value of type String where a String has been specified and a value of type Integer where an Integer has been specified. But the language cannot check that the right sort of Integer has been supplied. One could supply the Date variables in the wrong order when invoking the procedure *Date_from_String*, thus:

Date_from_String (S, D1, M1, Y1);

and the program would still compile and execute, but the results would be wrong! The procedure *Date_from_String* has no way of knowing that its parameters have been given the wrong meaning by the user of the interface. Thus, representing application data in terms of primitive data types, like Integer and String, cannot ensure that the application data is correctly manipulated since the real meaning of the data has been lost.

4.3 USER DEFINED TYPES

The problem, of associating different meanings to objects of the same type in the programming language, can be overcome by defining a different data type for each different meaning, such as Years, Months and Days. This means that the language has to allow its users to define their own data types, and that the language provides mechanisms with which instances of such user defined types can be specified and controlled.

Given the facility to define our own data types we can now define a Date to be represented by a value of type *Years*, a value of type *Months* and a value of type *Day_in_Month*. To complete our example we also need to define the type *Days* to represent a period between two Dates. *Days* should be a different type from *Day_in_Month* because they have a different meaning; instances of the latter type can only legitimately have values in the range 1 to 31, whilst instances of the type, *Days*, may have negative as well as positive values with a range determined by the range of Dates supported by the logic encapsulated inside *Date_from_String*.

With these user defined data types we are able to specify a more specific, and safe, interface for the three operations we are using, thus:

function Days_between_Dates (Year1 : Years; Month1 : Months; Day1

        Day_in_Month;

        Year2 : Years; Month2 : Months; Day2 : Day_in_Month) **return** Days;

function String_from_Days (The_Days : Days) **return** String;

procedure Date_from_String (Text : String; Year : **out** Years; Month : **out** Months;

        Day : **out** Day_in_Month);

Now our language can check that the right type of values are supplied to all uses of these interfaces. The language may even allow us to specify, when defining a new data type, the range of values it is expected to contain so that the program can ensure that the specified range is never exceeded and that invalid values will not be accepted by the program. The Ada language supports the specification of range constraints on numerical data types so that, for example, the data type Day_in_Month could be defined in Ada as:

type Day_in_Month **is range** 1 .. 31;

The coding for our example now looks like the procedure *Date_Example_2* in figure 4.2. The only difference from *Date_Example_1* in figure 4.1 is the way that the local data variables are declared as instances of the three user defined types; these differences are highlighted in italics. Whilst declaring these local variables as two instances of the user defined types Years, *Months* and *Day_in_Month* ensures that the correct data type is given to the operations that need them, it does not ensure that the three variables that actually represent a Date are always correctly used together. One could supply, to an operation, a set of variables of the right types which were not the member variables of a single Date, thus:

```
procedure Date_Example_2
      Y1, Y2: Years;
      M1, M2:  Months;
      D1, D2: Day_in_Month;
      Time: Days;
      S: String;
begin
      Get (S);
      Date_from_String (S, Y1, M1, D1);
      Get (S);
      Date_from_String (S, Y2, M2, D2);
      Time := Days_between_Dates (Y1, M1, D1, Y2, M2, D2);
      S := String_from_Days (Time);
      Put (S);
end Date_Example_2;
```

Figure 4.2   Date as three user defined types

Date_from_String (S, Y1, M1, D2);

and the program would still compile and execute. But the results would not be as expected unless the wrongly supplied variable happened to have the same value as the one that should have been supplied. The problem is that the component parts of a Date have not be grouped together, that is, encapsulated, into a single entity.

4.4   ENCAPSULATION OF DATA

To ensure that a set of related data values are always used together they need to be encapsulated into a further user defined type. This can be defined as a record, or an object, containing the necessary set of data values, thus:

type Date **is record**
      Year :   Years;
      Month :   Months;
      Day :   Day_in_Month;
end record;

Now the three values that represent a *Date* are encapsulated into a single object that can be referred to and passed around a program as a single entity. This also overcomes the inconsistency we had by defining the interface to the operation *Date_from_String* as a procedure when a Date was represented by three separate variables. The operation can now be defined, like the other two operations, as a function since a *Date* is regarded by the programming language as a single object, thus:

function Days_between_Dates (Date1 : Date; Date2 : Date) **return** Days;

function String_from_Days (The_Days : Days) **return** String;

function Date_from_String (Text : String) **return** Date;

Encapsulating all the data values that make up a particular type of object—in this case a *Date*, into a user defined type ensures that the set of data values are always kept together and treated as a single entity by the programming language. Being able to treat objects, which are represented by several related values, as a single entity helps to simplify the expression of the logic. The logic of our example, when *Date* is defined as one, multi-valued, user defined type, shows this simplification, which is highlighted by italics, in the procedure *Date_Example_3* given in figure 4.3.

Encapsulating the components of a user defined data type into a single entity does not usually, in a traditional programming language, prevent the user of objects of that type from accessing or manipulating the components individually. For instance, the procedure Date_Example_3 could include the logic to increment the *Day* component of a *Date* entity, thus:

Date1 .Day := Date1.Day +1;

if addition is an operation that can be applied to entities of type *Day_in_Month*. Even if the addition operation for Day_in_Month ensured

```
type Date is record
        Year  : Years;
        Month: Months;
        Day   : Day_in_Month;
end record;
procedure Date_Example_3
        Date1: Date;
        Date2: Date;
        Time: Days;
        S: String;
begin
        Get (S);
        Date1 := Date_from_String (S);
        Get (S);
        Date2 := Date_from_String (S);
        Time := Days_between_Dates (Date1, Date2);
        Put ( String_from_Days (Time) );
end Date_Example_3;
```

Figure 4.3   Date as a single user defined type

that the result could never exceed 31 (the maximum number of days in a month), it could produce an invalid Date such as 30th February or 31st June. The ability of the user to manipulate the components of a user defined data type means that the supplier of the logic that resides inside the function, *Days_between_Dates*, who is expecting to subtract one Date from another cannot be sure that the values he receives represent valid dates.

To be sure that the algorithm being used to subtract the dates always works correctly the supplier must include logic to verify that the component values given do represent valid Gregorian dates. This additional logic will have to be applied every time the interface is used, just in case the user of the interface has made the values of the encapsulated components inconsistent. This additional logic would be an object oriented private method.

The supplier of the encapsulated logic could avoid having to include such checks if it could be guaranteed that the values supplied as the components of a *Date* could not have become inconsistent since the entity was created.

4.5   ABSTRACT DATA TYPES

To ensure that the component values of an entity of a user defined type are always consistent, one has to stop the user of that type from being able to access and manipulate the components individually. The user of a user defined type must be forced to treat it as a "black box" for which the internal structure is not accessible; the structure and representation of a user defined type must be hidden from the user. The user can only manipulate a user defined data type defined in this way by the operations (methods in object oriented parlance) specifically provided for that user defined type. On the other hand, the supplier of operations for such a user defined type must be able to access and manipulate its components. This approach uses the concept of information hiding to ensure that objects of such types cannot have their component parts manipulated by users of the type, and defines what is known as an Abstract Data Type.

An Abstract Data Type defines a data type in terms of the operations it supports rather than by its representation. For the *Date* example there are two operations defined so far: *Date_from_String* and *Days_between_Dates*. The definition of this type as an Abstract Data Type is shown in figure 4.4. Note that the first definition of the type *Date* simply defines it to be **private**. This indicates that the representation of *Date* is not accessible to users of the type. Associated with the **private** type declaration are the specifications of the two operations that support the Abstract Data Type; the name of the type and the signatures of its publicly accessible operations constitute its public specification. The keyword **private** indicates that what follows is not

```
package Calendar is
        -- the public interface for the type
        type Date is private;

        function Date_from_String (Text: String)        return Date;
        function Days_between_Dates(Left, Right: Date) return Days;

private   -- the following information is not publicly available:-
        -- Implementation details for the type
        type Date is record
                Year  : Years;
                Month: Months;
                Day   : Day_in_Month;
        end record;
                -- this may include private operations
end Calendar;
```

Figure 4.4   Date as an abstract data type

publicly accessible; the information only needs to be known by the supplier of the Abstract Data Type and, possibly, by the language compiler.

The private part may include a definition of the structure of the implementation of the Abstract Data Type, as in figure 4.4, which will be used by the implementation of the public operations. The private part could also include additional operations which can only be used by the implementation of the public operations; these operations are known as private operations or private methods.

There are two approaches to allocating space in memory for instances of data types. A language may need the compiler to allocate space in the program's storage memory for objects of the type when compiling a program that contains objects of the type. In this case, the language compiler will need to know the implementation details of an Abstract Data Type so that it can compute the storage space required and allocate the space at compile time. Alternatively, the allocation of memory space for objects can be performed during the execution of a program. In this case, the size of an instance of an Abstract Data Type only needs to be known a runtime, and does not need to be known by the language compiler at the time that the Abstract Data Type's public interface is defined.

Each approach has its advocates. If the language compiler is able to allocate storage for Abstract Data Type objects then it does not have to be done when the program is executing, and the program will run faster. In addition to simply allocating storage for objects, the compiler is also able to manage this storage and can arrange to recover the space and reuse it for another purpose when the original object is no longer being used. However, if the representation of the Abstract Data Type is changed then all parts of a program that declare objects of that type will have to be recompiled so that the size of the objects can be recomputed. The program parts will not have to be changed since it is known that they could not make use of the implementation details of the Abstract Data Types they were using. They simply have to be recompiled so that the language compiler can allocate the right amount of storage for the Abstract Data Type objects that the program parts use.

On the other hand, if objects are to be created at runtime, it is possible to change the representation, and therefore the size of an Abstract Data Type object, without having to recompile all uses of that data type; only the definition of the implementation details of the Abstract Data Type has to be recompiled. However, because objects now have to have their storage allocated while the program is executing, the program will take longer to run. There is also the question of how the memory space that has been allocated to an object at runtime is recovered and reused when the object is no longer needed. If the memory space is not recovered then there will be a danger that the program will eventually run out of memory space, particularly if it runs for a long time. The mechanisms that languages provide to deal with the management of memory space during the execution of a program are described in Section 4.11.

When objects are allocated storage at runtime they have to be represented within the program by an object, often called a "handle", which contains the address of the storage that has been allocated to them. This means that objects allocated memory storage at runtime also use more storage than those allocated storage by the compiler because there is the storage needed to hold the address of the object in addition to the storage needed to hold the implementation details of the type.

If this policy is applied to all user defined types then the additional storage can become significant. For example, a *Date* can be represented by three objects, as in figure 4.4. If these objects also require an address pointer to each of them, then a *Date* object will use four address pointer values in addition to the storage needed to store values of the types *Year*, *Month* and *Day_in_Month*. In some cases, an address pointer may occupy more space than the value to which it refers. Remember that a *Month* only needs to hold the values 1 to 12 and a *Day_in_Month* only needs to hold the values 1 to 31; these could each be stored in a byte. An address pointer typically occupies four bytes. The storage for the values of a *Date* could be a low as four bytes whereas the storage for the address pointers will be at least 16 bytes; that represents a fourfold overhead.

Using address pointers, or memory references, to represent user defined types can also lead to discontinuity in the meaning of assignment in a language where built in data types use copy semantics. For instance, if X and Y

are variables of the built in type *Integer* then the assignment:

X := Y;

will mean that the value of Y is copied into X. This is known as copy semantics. If Date1 and Date2 are objects of the user defined type Date, which are represented by address pointers, then the assignment:

Date2 := Date1;

will mean that the address that refers to the value of *Date1* will be copied into the object that contains the address of *Date2*. Now *Date2* refers to (that is, points at) the same value as *Date1*. This is known as pointer semantics. The difference is shown diagrammatically in figure 4.5. The significant semantic difference is that if the value represented by *Date1* is subsequently changed, this also changes the value represented by *Date2* which will not be the case for values of the built in types. This is not wrong, it is just a different way of implementing an assignment operation. The problem occurs when both copy semantics and pointer semantics are used implicitly within one language; the user has to be aware when each form is used. If a language uses copy semantics for built in data types then it is more consistent, and easier to use, if it also uses copy semantics for user defined types. To achieve copy semantics for objects of user defined types that are created at runtime (and therefore need an object that contains an address pointer) the value pointed to has to be copied. This is known as a "deep" copy because

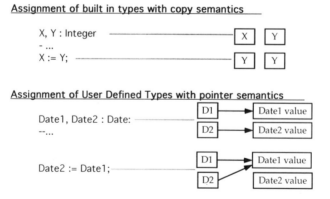

Figure 4.5   Copy vs. pointer semantics

```
procedure Date_Example_4
        Date1: Date;
        Date2: Date;
        Time: Days;
        S: String;
begin
        Get (S);
        Date1 := Date_from_String (S);
        Get (S);
        Date2 := Date_from_String (S);
        Time := Days_between_Dates (Date1, Date2);
        Put ( String_from_Days (Time) );
end Date_Example_4;
```

Figure 4.6   Using the date abstract data type

it has to be applied recursively to any user defined type that contains any instances of other user defined types.

4.5.1   The benefits of abstract data types

An advantage of Abstract Data Types is that the logic of a program does not depend upon how a user defined type is represented. To return to our example, the procedure to read in two *Dates*, subtract them and print the number of *Days* between them can be written as shown in figure 4.6 when *Date* and *Days* are implemented as Abstract Data Types. This is identical to figure 4.3, except that the representation of a *Date* is not included. This is because the logic does not need to know how a *Date* is represented if it is an

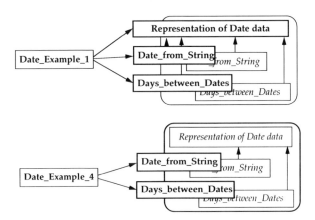

Figure 4.7   Date examples: compiling diagrams

Abstract Data Type; it only needs to know the interfaces, or signatures, of the operations that can be used on objects of the type *Date* (and *Days*).

Abstract Data Types decouple the users of the type from the way the type is implemented. The implementation of an Abstract Data Type can be changed without affecting, in any way, the logic in the programs that use that type as long as the signatures (the specifications of the interfaces) of the public operations for that type do not change. This reduction in coupling is shown in figure 4.7.

The upper diagram in figure 4.7 shows the dependency of the first implementation of the example logic in the procedure *Date_Example_1*. It depends upon the data representation chosen for objects of type *Date* as well as the signatures of the two Date operations that it uses.

The lower diagram in figure 4.7 shows that the procedure *Date_Example_4* only relies upon the signatures of the Date operations that it uses. The only logic that depends upon the way that a *Date* is represented is that which is encapsulated within the operations *Date_from_String* and *Days_between_Dates*. This total encapsulation means that the effect of changing the way that an Abstract Data Type is represented is contained and predictable; only the operations that have been implemented as part of the definition of the Abstract Data Type can possibly be affected. The worst that can happen to the logic that uses the public operations of the Abstract Data Type is that it will need to be recompiled.

With the data representation for an Abstract Data Type only accessible to the operations for that type, it becomes possible to choose a representation that is the most appropriate for the set of operations to be supported. For example, the operation to subtract two *Dates* would be much easier to implement if a *Date* was held as a single value representing the number of *Days* since a specific *Date*, such as 1 January 1900. With this representation the subtraction of two *Dates* becomes a simple subtraction between two Integers; all the complications associated with maintaining the Gregorian Calendar can now be encapsulated in the operations to convert a *Date* object to and from a printable text string. For an Abstract Data Type it becomes more important to design an appropriate set of operations and their signatures rather than the details of the type's data representation; the latter can be chosen once the needs of all the operations has been established.

Furthermore, the supplier of the logic that is encapsulated in an operation (like the function *Days_between_Dates*, which will subtract one *Date* from another) can rely on the fact that the values he receives cannot have been tampered with since the last operation was performed on the Abstract Data Type. The values of an Abstract Data Type cannot be tampered with because a user of the type is unable to manipulate the components of an Abstract Data Type. The supplier of the operations on an Abstract Data Type is therefore able to control the state of the objects of the type, even to the extent of ensuring that the operations are applied in a particular order.

4.5.2 Initialisation of Abstract Data Types

To ensure that the values encapsulated within an object of an Abstract Data Type are always self-consistent it must not be possible to create such an object in an undefined state. This means that whenever an object is created it must be initialised. Since the user of an Abstract Data Type cannot know how to initialise it the supplier of the Abstract Data Type must provide one or more operations to initialise all instances. For example, the function *Date_from_String* creates a *Date* object from a *String* object and provides one way to initialise a Date object. Another way could be to provide a function that converts objects of type Year, Months and Day_in_Month into a date Object, thus:

function Date (Year : Years; Month : Months; Day : Day_in_Month) **return** Date;

It can be seen that the operations which initialise an object are essentially operations that convert one or more objects of other types into an object of the desired type; they perform type conversions.

It can be seen in figure 4.6 that the local objects *Date1*, *Date2*, *Time* and *S* in the procedure *Date_Example_4* do not appear to be initialised when they are declared and therefore created. Whether they have actually been initialised or not depends upon the way in which the objects have been implemented by the language.

If objects are implemented as pointers to storage that is allocated at runtime, then the compiler can initialise these pointers to be invalid or illegal addresses; these are usually known as null pointers. Now if a user of the object tries to access its value before the actual object is created and initialised, the program can trap the error at runtime, and report that it does not yet exist. But now the programming language must be told when the object is to be created at runtime. This is achieved by providing a special operation that is part of the language; this operation is called an allocator and is usually denoted by the word **new**. This implementation model for objects would require the example procedure to be written as shown in figure 4.8, where it is called *Date_Example_5*.

If an object can be allocated storage by the compiler then the object must be initialised when it is declared, otherwise the value of the object is undefined until a value is assigned to it. If an object is not initialised at the point of declaration, then it is possible for the object to be used in an operation before a value has been assigned to it. To avoid this problem it becomes necessary to be able to delay the declaration of objects until the logic of the program can sensibly provide values for them. In our example, the value for a Date cannot be provided until a String has been read, so the Date object should not be declared until after the Get (S) statement has been executed.

```
procedure Date_Example_5
      Date1: Date;
      Date2: Date;
      Time: Days;
      S: String;
begin
      Get (S);
      Date1 := new Date (Date_from_String (S));
      Get (S);
      Date2 := new Date (Date_from_String (S));
      Time := new Days (Days_between_Dates (Date1, Date2));
      Put ( String_from_Days (Time) );
end Date_Example_5;
```

Figure 4.8   Runtime allocation of objects

This means that the language must allow objects to be declared in amongst the executable statements rather than requiring them all to be declared before any executable statements are written. This requirement is only supported by the traditional block structured languages by introducing additional levels of block structure into the program, as shown in figure 4.9, which can become very cumbersome. It is notationally much more convenient to be able to write declarations in amongst the statements as in C++. With such a facility in the language the example procedure can be written as shown in figure 4.10[1], where it is named *Date_Example_6*.

It should be noted that because the procedure *Date_Example_5* is written using the language facilities shown in figure 4.8, the language compiler can only implement it by allocating objects at runtime. If the logic is written with the language facilities used in figure 4.10, then it may be implemented, as described above, with the storage for objects being allocated by the compiler. It could also be implemented with the objects being allocated at runtime. The facilities used to express the logic in the procedure Date_Example_6, shown in figure 4.10, do not dictate which implementation model for the allocation of storage for objects should be used and the logic can therefore be written without the need to know which implementation model will be used. The logic thereby gains in intrinsic value because it uses a higher level of abstraction. A language with such facilities may even allow the implementor of an Abstract Data Type to choose which storage allocation model to use for the objects of individual types. *A language is only able to provide such a degree of freedom to the implementor of an Abstract Data Type because of the lack of coupling which is achieved by hiding implementation details behind an interface that is clearly defined and supported by the language itself.*

---

[1]   The code in this example is not legal Ada. It is given in Ada-like syntax to emphasise the notational convenience and clarity over the legal Ada syntax given in figure 4.9.

```
procedure Date_Example_6
    S: String;
begin
  Get (S);
  declare
    Date1 :  Date:= Date_from_String (S);
  begin
    Get (S);
    declare
      Date2 : Date :=  Date_from_String (S);
      Time  : Days :=  Days_between_Dates (Date1, Date2);
    begin
      Put ( String_from_Days (Time) );
    end;
  end;
end Date_Example_6;
```

Figure 4.9   Compile time initialisation of objects

4.6   FUNCTION NAME AND OPERATOR OVERLOADING

4.6.1   Function name overloading

The term "Function Name Overloading" is used to describe the features of a programming language that allow more than one operation with a particular name to be visible and callable at the same point in a program. Traditionally, programming languages have required that, at any point in a program, all the visible procedures and functions defined by the user of the language are uniquely named. This constraint simplifies the job of the compiler writer and often allows the same names to be also used during the program linking phase when separately compiled parts of a program are bound together to produce an executable program. The constraint imposes a discipline on the user of such languages to ensure that the names of functions and procedures never clash. This discipline is not too onerous on

```
procedure Date_Example_6
    S: String;
begin
    Get (S);
    Date1 :  Date:= Date_from_String (S);
    Get (S);
    Date2 : Date :=  Date_from_String (S);
    Time  : Days :=  Days_between_Dates (Date1, Date2);
    Put ( String_from_Days (Time) );
end Date_Example_6;
```

Figure 4.10   Declaring initialised objects

a small project and can be managed on a large project with the use of data dictionaries and configuration management tools.

However, problems can arise when externally supplied libraries of functions are used if attention has not be given to the use of naming conventions. The problem with naming conventions is that they often add little or no additional meaning to the names and make the names longer and more difficult to remember. An object oriented approach will generate many more operations than a traditional approach, so choosing a unique name for every operation would become very onerous and the possibility of encountering name clashes with operations in program libraries would be that much greater. Since object orientation greatly increases the opportunities for reusing code it would be unfortunate if the reuse of code was inhibited by the occurrence of name clashes with program libraries. This becomes highly relevant to object oriented development as one is able to obtain class libraries from a variety of sources.

Allowing function names to be overloaded solves the problem of name clashes within the language rather than relying on the user avoiding the problem; it allows the user to concentrate on choosing names with the most appropriate meaning without worrying about where else the same name might be used.

Obviously, if there is more than one function with a particular name accessible to a program, there has to be a way for the programming language system to decide which one was intended to be called. This is known as overload resolution and relies upon the functions having signatures which are sufficiently different to be distinguishable by the language system.

A distinguishing feature of a function's signature is the number of parameters it takes. For example, the following function was introduced in Section 4.5.2:

function Date (Year : Years; Month : Months; Day : Day_in_Month) **return** Date;

to initialise a *Date* object to the values given by a *Year*, *Month* and *Day_in_Month* objects. There is also the function *Date_from_String* which initialises a *Date* object to the date represented as a printable text String. Using function name overloading this function could also be named Date, thus:

function Date (Text : String) **return** Date;

The language system would be able to decide which of these two functions to use simply because the first one takes three parameters and the second one takes only one parameter. Since not all functions are going to have different numbers of parameters another means of distinguishing between several uses of the same function name also has to be used.

The other method for recognising the signature of a function relies on the language system being able to distinguish between the data types of the parameters that are being passed into the function. For example, if another function named *Date* was defined with the signature:

function Date (Day : Day_in_Month; Month : Months; Year : Years) **return** Date;

then it has the same number of parameters as the first one above, but the parameters are specified to be in a different order. However, the first and third parameter of each function is of a different type, and this fact can be used by the language system to identify which one is intended when a functions call is written. The way such overloaded functions can be used is shown in figure 4.11. Note that each of the uses of the function *Date* which take objects of type *Year*, *Month* and *Day_in_Month* as parameters has had the parameter values qualified by the name of the type the parameter is intended to have. These qualifiers are, in fact, functions that initialise objects of that type name to the Integer values given. It would not be possible to simply write a use of one of these functions with numeric literals as the parameters, *viz:*

New_Year :=Date (1, 1, 1992);

since the numeric literal values are Integers and there is not a function with the signature:

function Date (Day : Integer; Month : Integer; Year : Integer) **return** Date;

```
package Calendar is
      type Date is private;
      function Date (Text: String) return Date;
      function Date ( Year  : Years;
                      Month: Months;
                      Day   : Day_in_Month) return Date;
      function Date ( Day    : Day_in_Month;
                      Month: Months;
                      Year  : Years) return Date;
private
-- The representation of type Date
end Calendar;
-- Now use these overloaded functions:
First_Date   : Date:= Date ("1/1/1992");
Second_Date : Date:= Date (Year(1991), Month(1), Day_in_Month(1));
Third_Date   : Date:= Date (Day_in_Month(1), Month(1), Year(1991) );
```

Figure 4.11   Date with overload functions

The ability of a language system to be able to distinguish overloaded function names by the types of their parameters relies on all objects, including numbers, being of a known type, as described in Section 4.5. The type of an object may be determinable during compilation of a language or during the execution of the language. In the former case the language is said to be **statically** type checked, whereas in the latter case the language is said to be **dynamically** type checked. In either case, the language is strongly typed and this is a prerequisite for the support of function name overloading in a language. Strong typing is also needed to support other features of object oriented languages such as polymorphism.

The benefit of a language being statically type checked is that the language compiler is responsible for determining whether a piece of logic is type safe. Errors in the use of the language's type system are reported during compilation rather than when the program is executed. This can reduce the number of abortive test runs of a program at the expense of having to go through a "compile, link and execute" cycle for each test run. There is no type checking to be done at runtime so program execution can be efficient.

On the other hand, a dynamically type checked language will allow programs to be translated into an executable form very quickly because little, or no, validation needs too be carried out during its translation. This is at the expense of carrying out type checking during program execution which can cause the program to execute more slowly.

4.6.2   Operator overloading

Operator overloading is the term applied to an extension of function name overloading where the programming language allows the operators, which are used with the language's built in data types, to be used for operations on user defined types. Such operators usually include:

- the arithmetical operators: +, -, * and /

- the relational operators: =, /=, <, <=, > and >=

- the logical operators: **and, or, xor** and **not**

and may include:

- the assignment operator: :=

- an array indexing operator: []

- a function call operator: ()

The main advantage of being able to overload the language's operators is the ability it provides for manipulating user defined types in the same way as the built in types. This provides a notational convenience which can improve the clarity of of the code. For example, if a language allows one to write:

W := X + Y + Z;

when *W*, *X*, *Y* and *Z* are objects of the the built in type Integer then if the language supports operator overloading one is also allowed to write:

C := D + E + F;

when *C*, *D*, *E* and *F* are objects of a user defined type, such as *Days*. The intent of such a statement is both clearer and shorter than:

C := Add (D, Add (E, F));

In the case of the Abstract Data Type, *Date*, the operation *Days_between_Dates* could be expressed as an overloading of the subtract operator thus:

function "-" (Left : Date; Right : Date) **return** Days;

and additional operator overloadings could be specified which allow a Date to have an object of type Days added to it or subtracted from it:

function "+" (Left : Date; Right : Days) **return** Date;
function "–" (Left : Date; Right : Days) **return** Date;

By using a language's facilities to overload functions and operators the definition of the Abstract Data Type, *Date*, can be expressed as shown in figure 4.12 and used by the example procedure, *Date_Example_7*, as shown in figure 4.13.

Note that in figure 4.12, all the relational operators have been overloaded. In practice it becomes necessary, with Abstract Data Types, to overload most of the operators that can be applied to the built in types because the language system is unable to create the operators for an Abstract Data Type itself. This is a consequence of hiding the data representation and the fact that an Abstract Data Type may have many data properties encapsulated inside it. If *Date* actually holds the data properties shown in figure 4.4 then obviously the language is unable to create an operator "<" for it, since it cannot know how to compute such a relationship.

```
package Calendar is
      type Date is private;
      function Date (Text: String) return Date;
      function Date (Year  : Years;
                     Month: Months;
                     Day   : Day_in_Month) return Date;
      function "-"   (Left: Date; Right: Days) return Date;
      function "+"   (Left: Date; Right: Days) return Date;
      function "-"   (Left, Right: Date) return Days;
      function "="   (Left, Right: Date) return Boolean;
      function "<="  (Left, Right: Date) return Boolean;
      function ">="  (Left, Right: Date) return Boolean;
      function "<"   (Left, Right: Date) return Boolean;
      function ">"   (Left, Right: Date) return Boolean;
      function String (a_Date  : Date) return String;
private
      type Date is record
      Year  : Years;
      Month: Months;
      Day   : Day_in_Month;
      end record;
end Calendar;
```

Figure 4.12   Date with overloaded operations

It becomes the responsibility of the supplier of the Abstract Data Type to decide which operators can be given a sensible meaning for the type and to provide those operators as as part of the type's interface definition. An operator should only be overloaded if it can be given a **sensible** meaning, otherwise the reader of the logic will be misled and confused.

The arithmetical operators should only be overloaded if it is sensible to do arithmetic on the objects. For instance, it is not sensible to add two *Date*s together but it is sensible to subtract two *Date*s; therefore "+" should not be overloaded but "−" could be overloaded for Dates. It would be very confusing, for instance, if "+" was overloaded to have the same meaning as the overloaded "−".

The relational operators should only be overloaded if there is some well defined ordering of the objects. There is an obvious ordering to *Date*s. Objects of a type *Name* that held the names of persons could be defined to be ordered alphabetically so it is sensible and helpful to users of these objects to define the relational operators for these types. On the other hand, there is no

```
procedure Date_Example_7
      S1, S2: String;
begin
      Get (S1);
      Get (S2);
      Put (String_from_Days (Date (S1) - Date (S2) ) );
end Date_Example_7;
```

Figure 4.13   Using the date overloaded operators

obvious order to objects of type *Address*, say, so the relational operators should not be defined for that type.

Operators defined for Abstract Data Types often have to be used with care. For instance, if the operation *Days_between_Dates* uses an overloaded "–" operator then an expression which subtracts three *Date*s, thus:

Time := Date1 – Date2 – Date3;

is incorrect since it will be interpreted as:

Time := (Date1 – Date2) – Date3;

This produces an expression which expects to subtract Date3 from an object of type *Days* (which is the result of computing (Date1 – Date2)). Unless there is an overloaded "–" operator which subtracts a *Date* from a *Days*, this expression will be rejected by the language system. To ensure that expressions involving the use of overloaded operators are interpreted as intended, parentheses should be used, thus:

Time := Date1 – (Date2 – Date3);

The only operations that can be applied to an Abstract Data Type are those defined as an integral part of the type definition. This means, in principle, that one is not able even to make a copy of an instance nor compare two instances for equality unless these operations have been defined for the type.

For example, given the type definition for a *Date*, shown in figure 4.12, where the assignment operator ":=" has not been defined, it should not be possible to assign one Date object to another:

Date1 := Date2;

Similarly, without defining the equality operator "=" it should also not be possible to compare two *Date* objects, thus:

if Date1 = Date2 then ...

However, it would be very tedious for the supplier of each Abstract Data Type definition to always have to provide definitions for operations to copy and compare objects of the type. In practice, a language that supports operator overloading will provide default versions of the copy and the compare operation for each Abstract Data Type defined. These default versions allow

```
procedure Date_Example_8
        Date1, Date2 : Date;
        S1, S2: String;
begin
        Get (S1);
        Get (S2);
        Date1 := Date (S1);
        Date2 := Date (S2);
        if Date1 = Date2 then
                Put ( "The Dates are the same!")
        else
                Put (String_from_Days (Date1 - Date2) );
        end if;
end Date_Example_8;
```

Figure 4.14 Comparing two dates

the assignment operator ":=" and the equality operator "=" to be used on objects of any user defined type. These automatically supplied operations will provide a "standard" way of copying and comparing objects[1].

The "standard" way to copy objects will depend on the way objects are implemented by the language system. If objects are implemented as pointers to storage then pointer semantics will be used for the assignment operator. If objects can be allocated storage by the compiler then copy semantics will be used. This was discussed in Section 4.5.1.

If the language uses pointer semantics then one would expect the equality operator to compare the values of the pointers to the objects. This, however, would only indicate that two objects were "equal" if they were, in fact, the same object. That is, the objects would only be "equal" if they had the same pointer values. Suppose, as in figure 4.14, our example procedure, now called *Date_Example_8*, wanted to compare the two textual Dates that had been read in to establish whether they represented the same Date. With pointer semantics the comparison statement:

if Date1 = Date2 **then**

would never achieve this because the objects Date1 and Date2 are different objects, that is they are represented by different pointer values; they have different identities and are two distinct objects. To establish whether two distinct objects contain the same values then it is necessary to compare the

---

[1] The Ada language always provides default assignment and equality operators for each **private** data type as "bitwise" copy and "bitwise" compare but it does not allow them to be redefined by the user. Default versions of the ":=" and "=" operators are not provided for **limited private** Ada data types and only the "=" can be defined by the user.

values of each property in both objects. This is, in fact, the semantics that is applied to the equality operator "=" even in languages that implement pointer semantics so that object comparison has the normal meaning. Of course, if an object contains instances of other objects then the equality operator for these other objects will have to be called to establish whether they have the same values.

4.7 CLASSES

In an object oriented context an Abstract Data Type is usually known as a Class. A class has all the properties of an Abstract Data Type that have been described above. A class encapsulates together all the data properties and all the logic properties that are characteristic of all object instances of that class. It is a template for objects with the same properties.

An object in the context of software development is analogous to an object in the real world. An object has state and behaviour, i.e., an object has a set of data properties with values which together contain its state at a point in time, and a set of methods that defines its behaviours—that is, how it responds to external stimuli. Packaging together this state and behaviour is the process of designing a software object, also referred to as encapsulation. The encapsulation defines an Abstract Data Type or a Class.

Any system, real world or otherwise, has many objects that are of the same type while not necessarily of the same state (for example, there are many Ford Sierras of the same type but of different state). In computer systems, these objects can be grouped into a class which defines their attributes and behaviour, while each object in the class is able to have different state.

For example, a computer model of a vehicle fleet might define a class Family Saloon Car, having data properties of Maximum Passengers and Current Passengers. Each instance of class Family Saloon Car would have its own values of these properties, and would thus be in a different state from the others.

Any software system will consist of many different objects, just as in the real world. Some of these objects will share similarities while other are clearly different. Design and development are greatly simplified by grouping similar objects together into classes. To take an example, consider the average family saloon car. Such cars typically have four doors, four wheels, an engine, and so on. They also have a number of common behaviours, such as being able to accelerate, to cruise, to brake and stop. These behaviours are some of the operations (methods) which one expects a saloon car to provide. The visible interface to these operations are the accelerator and brake pedals in a car. There are a number of generic

• Template for objects with similar properties:
- set of operations (methods)
   - set of properties (attributes)
     - state variables

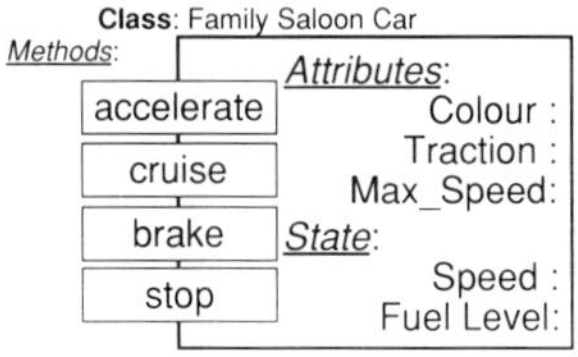

Class: Family Saloon Car

Methods:
accelerate
cruise
brake
stop

Attributes:
Colour :
Traction :
Max_Speed:

State:
Speed :
Fuel Level:

Figure 4.15   Classes

properties, shared by all saloons, that serve to categorise them; examples of such generic properties are that they all have four doors and four wheels and are driven by the front or rear wheels. A specific saloon car also has a number of other properties. It might be painted red, have a sunroof, have a dent in one of the door panels, etc. A specific car is, in object oriented parlance, an "instance" of the class of family saloon cars. It has a state which relates to both its class (four doors, etc.) and itself (it is red, etc.). All the instances will have the same behaviour, in that they will all respond to the same set of operations such as accelerate, cruise, brake and stop because they all have an accelerator and a brake pedal (the same visible interface). Providing the same interface for the operations does not necessarily mean that the behaviour of all cars is the same. If the internal state of a specific car indicates that the engine is broken, then pushing the accelerator pedal will not make the car accelerate; the effect of invoking an operation on a specific object may, and often will, depend upon the internal state of that object.

The characteristics of a class that could represent a number of different Family Saloon Cars are shown diagrammatically in figure 4.15. The diagram uses a common notation of encapsulating all of the data properties in a box, to indicate that they are not accessible from outside the box. The public methods (operations) are shown protruding from the data box to indicate that they constitute the publicly accessible interface to the box and that they themselves do have access to what is inside the box. The data properties have been separated into Attributes and State variables to emphasise that the State variables are expected to change their values over the lifetime of a specific instance of the class. For example, the Speed and Fuel Level of a Car instance will change while it is being driven around, and their values may determine how the Car responds to the operation *accelerate*. If it has no fuel it will not accelerate! Attributes, on the other hand, do not usually change their value during the lifetime of a specific instance. For

- Instances of classes
  - same set of methods
    - own set of attribute values
      - own state

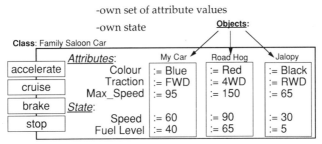

Figure 4.16   Objects

instance once a Car has been painted red, or fitted with four wheel drive, during its manufacture it is unlikely to change—unless it has been stolen! Even so, the values of an Attribute may affect how that particular car instance will behave. For instance, a car's maximum speed will determine when it will stop accelerating. Figure 4.16 shows some instances of the class Family Saloon Car, showing that each instance has its own value for each data property but that all the instances share the same logic properties, that is they all respond to the same set of messages by providing the same interface to the outside world.

It is the message interface that defines what objects will do and what can be done to them, and it is the class definition which defines the complete set of message formats (or signatures) that all objects of that class will respond to. The maxim for an object oriented approach to designing a class is given in figure 4.17. By considering what objects of the class should be able to do the messages, or methods, that it needs to provide will become apparent. This will enable the class definition to be specified by the set of operations.

The behaviour of the operations will determine the set of data properties that need to be encapsulated within each object instance of the class.[1] For instance, the *accelerate* operation of the class *Family Saloon Car* needs to know a car's maximum speed to know when to stop accelerating; therefore, the maximum speed needs to be a data property for the class. On the other hand, if the only operations provided by a *Family Saloon Car* are those given in figure 4.15 then the data property *Colour* will serve no purpose as it probably does not contribute to the behaviour of any of these operations. If none of the operations use a data property it has no use, since it cannot be utilised by the outside world.

---

[1] The author is here arguing in favour of the process driven approach to information modelling. This, and other approaches, are discussed in Chapter 6.

> When designing a Class ask:
> **"What will it do?"**
> *rather than:*
> **"How will it do it?"**

Figure 4.17   Object oriented maxim

In general, software objects follow the same pattern. They can have state variables and methods that relate to both the class and to the specific instance. Classes are defined in the text of the program. The example of *Date*, expressed as a Class definition in the pseudo language used so far, is shown in Figure 4.18. *Note that the Class definition only specifies the logic properties.* This ensures that objects of the class can only be manipulated by use of the public operations; the class is a true Abstract Data Type.[1]

The other significant characteristic of Class definitions in an object oriented language is that the signature of an operation, or method, does not have a parameter signifying the object to which it applies, as is the case in figure 4.18. It is unnecessary because the operations are specified as part of the class definition to reflect the fact that they apply only to instances of the class; the language system "knows" that these operations must be given an object instance upon which to operate. It is therefore redundant, and would be a potential source of error, to include, in an operation's signature, a parameter specifying the object type to which it applies. It also emphasises that invoking a method on an object instance of a class is not the same as making a procedure call. Invoking a procedure causes a set of parameters to be sent to a piece of free-standing logic; that is, the data is sent to the code. Invoking a method involves sending a "message" to an object to apply a method to itself. The message may contain parameters which are, in effect, other objects. Invoking a method involves sending objects to another object with "instructions" (the method) of what the object is to do. For example, the message "–" with a *Date* as a parameter instructs a *Date* object to subtract the parameter from itself to provide a response which is the number of *Days* between itself and the supplied *Date* object. To service a message the logic inside a method will need to be able to refer to the object instance upon which it is to operate. An object oriented language allows this to be done by giving the object instance, upon which a method is to operate, a special name; usually "self" or "this".

All instances of a class, that is objects of a class, have the same methods

---

[1] A Class definition that does not define the data properties of the Class can only be used in a programming language that does not need to allocate storage for objects at compile time (as described in Section 4.5).

```
class Date is
    function Date (Text: String) return Date;
    function Date ( Year  : Years;
                    Month: Months;
                    Day  : Day_in_Month) return Date;
        function "-"  (Right: Days) return Date;
        function "+"  (Right: Days) return Date;
        function "-"  (Right: Date) return Days;
        function "="  (Right: Date) return Boolean;
        function "<=" (Right: Date) return Boolean;
        function ">=" (Right: Date) return Boolean;
        function "<"  (Right: Date) return Boolean;
        function ">"  (Right: Date) return Boolean;
        function String return String;
end Date;
```

Figure 4.18   Date as a class

and attributes—each instance has (potentially) different values of the attributes which may change during the lifetime of an object. However, the state of classes, as opposed to their definition, can change at runtime—for example, it may be useful to monitor at the class level how many objects of that class have been created. While it would be possible to have different methods for individual objects, such as the calculation of Mary's salary, this is rarely useful and not often supported by object-oriented systems.

4.8   INHERITANCE

The encapsulation of all the methods (the logic properties) and all the attributes (the data properties) of a set of objects into a class ensures that all these objects have the same set of properties which can only be manipulated by the methods defined for that class of objects. The data properties are only accessible to the logic within the methods and cannot be accessed directly by the users of those objects. This provides all the benefits that were described for Abstract Data Types in Section 4.5.1.

The encapsulation provided by classes requires that each new class defines all the data and logic properties for objects of that new class. If there was no way to share properties between classes the construction of a new class would be very tedious and repetitive.

To continue the car example, consider defining a class for Racing cars. They, like Family Saloon Cars, have four wheels, an engine and so on. They also respond to the messages, that is they have methods, to accelerate, cruise, brake and stop. With just the class mechanism all these properties, that Racing cars have in common with Family Saloon Cars, would have to be defined again in the Racing Car class. Replicating all these properties would be:

- prone to error,

- difficult to ensure that any changes were applied to all replications,

- wasteful of resources, both human and machine.

The replication would waste human resources replicating lots of identical information from one class to another; replicating the logic will also waste machine resources by creating many copies of the same code in a program. Humans are not very good at carrying out repetitive tasks accurately, so it would be much better if the computer could do it instead.

Inheritance is the mechanism that allows the properties common to two or more classes to be shared rather than replicated. Inheritance is a mechanism that is widely used in human endeavours to assist with the classification of things in the real world. Many things in the real world have common properties and these common properties are used to develop classification schemes so that we can manage the seemingly infinite complexity of the world. For instance we classify living creatures into mammals, insects, birds, fish, etc. These main classifications are then divided into subclassifications according to their common properties, and these subclassifications are subdivided again and again until the set of things that fit into a classification all have a set of properties that is unique to that set. Such classification schemes are hierarchical, so that each subclassification is more specialised than the one from which it is derived. Each subclass is the same as its superclass, but some properties have become more specialised or additional properties have been added. A class hierarchy supports the "is a" semantic form of relationship.

To return to the car example, although Racing cars are significantly different from Family Saloon cars they are also recognisable cars; that is why they are both called cars! Both racing cars and saloon cars are sub-classes of the class car. The class car encapsulates all the properties that Racing cars and Family Saloon cars have in common. Cars are, in their turn, a sub-class of the class motor vehicle, which in turn is a sub-class of the class transport system. Aircraft and ships are other sub-classes of the class transport system, whilst trucks and buses are other sub-classes of the class motor vehicle. This hierarchy of property inheritance in shown in figure 4.19.

Similarly, classification schemes can be applied to software classes by the use of an inheritance mechanism which allows one class to inherit all the properties (logic as well as data) of another class. The new class is then said to be derived from a base class. It can also be said to be a subclass of the class from which it inherits; in which case the base class is called its super-class.

There are two important characteristics of inheritance of software classes.

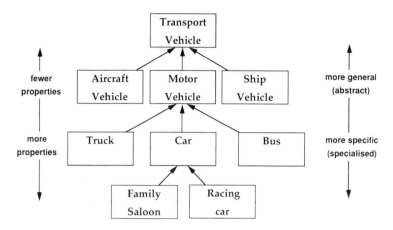

Figure 4.19   A property inheritance hierarchy

First, the derived class has all the data properties of its base class. This avoids the definition of these data properties having to be replicated in the definition of the derived class. The data properties of the base class automatically become the data properties of the derived class. The derived class may add new data properties but it cannot remove any of the data properties of its base class.

But even more important, the logic properties—the methods, defined and implemented for the base class, are **shared** with the derived class. That is, the derived class reuses the same pieces of logic that were created for the base class; the code is not replicated. *This reuse of existing code can generate a massive increase in software productivity (as shown in Chapter 7), without a corresponding increase in the amount of new code that must be maintained in the future.* It can also significantly reduce the overall size of a software system compared with a development environment that cannot exploit such commonality of the logic. The derived class may add new methods but it cannot change the interface to any inherited method. However, a derived class may provide a different implementation for an inherited method as long as it maintains the inherited signature of the method. If it changes the signature it becomes a new method by virtue of the rules of function name overloading.

It is the ability of object oriented programming languages to support inheritance in this way that differentiates them from convention languages. The inheritance hierarchy provides a **structure** *within which code can be placed at the right level of generality. It is inheritance alone that provides the environment for increased reusability of code; encapsulation is valuable in providing more maintainable software, but it does not in itself help reusability.*

As a simple example of inheritance applied to a software class, consider

```
Class American_Date inherits Date is
public
        function American_Date (Text: String) return American_Date;
        function String (a_Date: American_Date) return String;
end American_Date;
```

Figure 4.20   American date as a derived class

the Date class defined in Figure 4.18. Let us assume that the original Date class handled the textual representation of dates in a European format where a date is written as Day_in_Month/Month/Year, e.g. 31/12/91. Now suppose we also wanted to handle dates that are written in American format; that is, as Month/Day_in_Month/Year, e.g. 12/31/91. These additions do not require that the way that a date is represented by the class to change in anyway, because an American Date "is a" Date. We just need two new methods; one to read a textual Date in American format and one to convert a Date into an American formatted textual string. All the existing methods of the Date class will still be applicable. A class to handle American Dates can therefore be derived from the Date class using inheritance, and the two new operations can be added to it.

The new class for *American Dates* is shown in figure 4.20 as a class that inherits from *Date* and which defines the two new operations that it supports. The function *American_Date* reads in a textual string that is in American date format whilst the new overloaded function *String* converts a *Date* back into its American date format. These new operations could be implemented in terms of the operations supported by the *Date* class by manipulating strings into the format used and produced by Date's operations. Alternatively, they could be implemented in a similar way to the corresponding Date operations if they were able to access the data properties of the Date class. This would, of course, violate the encapsulation principle of a class and should not be allowed, but, as will be seen in Chapter 5, some object oriented languages do allow controlled access to a base class's data properties by methods of a class which has been derived from it.

4.8.1   Multiple inheritance

Real world objects can inherit properties from more than one super-class. Consider a toy car, for example. This has attributes common to both the class of toys and the class of cars; it displays the characteristic of multiple inheritance.

Multiple inheritance changes the inheritance picture from a hierarchy to a network, more closely modelling the way we think about real world objects.

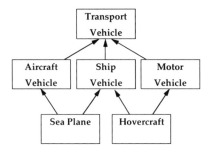

Figure 4.21   A property inheritance network

Consider the inheritance hierarchy for Transport Vehicles in figure 4.19, and where Hovercraft and Sea Planes would be placed in such a hierarchy. Hovercraft obviously have properties in common with Ships and Motor Vehicles; when they are at sea they behave like Ships, whilst on the land they behave like Motor Vehicles.   Similarly, Sea Planes have properties in common with Ships and Aircraft. The multiple inheritance network, shown in figure 4.21, is the natural way to model these relationships.

Some object oriented language systems support multiple inheritance while others do not. For example, C++ supports multiple inheritance but Smalltalk does not.   Many systems with single inheritance force the programmer to chose which of two (or more) superclasses a new class will be derived from; this is usually done by specifying a superclass name along with every property name that has been inherited from more than one class.

Support for multiple inheritance further increases the opportunities to reuse code in an object oriented system, and allows such a system to model the real world more accurately.   An important aspect of multiple inheritance as compared to single inheritance is that classes within the inheritance network (which is a directed acyclic graph) produced by multiple inheritance can share information without forcing that information towards the single root of an inheritance tree. With multiple inheritance it is possible for sibling classes, like Aircraft and Ships, to share information in a common base class, like Transport Vehicle in figure 4.21, without affecting other classes in an inheritance lattice. This can overcome a problem with single inheritance systems, whereby information that needs to be shared tends to drift towards the common root of the tree which acts as a global container of lots of unrelated properties. For example, a property of Ships is that they are registered whereas a property of Motor Vehicles is that they have a Road License. If a Hovercraft has to be registered, like a Ship, and has to have a Road Licence, like an Motor Vehicle, then these properties need to be inherited. With multiple inheritance these properties need only to be properties of Ships and Motor Vehicles for them both to become properties of a Hovercraft. With a single inheritance system these two properties would need to become properties of Transport Vehicles so that whichever class (Ships or Motor Vehicles) was used as the parent class for Hovercraft it would inherit both properties. But now all Transport Vehicles have both of these properties just so that Hovercraft can share these properties with Ships and Motor Vehicles. With multiple inheritance properties can be more effectively abstracted to the level of their role and generality; *there are no restrictions on correct information modelling*.

As another example of the use of multiple inheritance consider the *Date* class. This handles time in units of a Day. Suppose there is another class, *Time of Day* which deals with the time of day in seconds. This would no doubt have a method, like *String* in *Date*, which translates the time of day into a textual string format like that of a digital watch, e.g. 17:22:45. A new class, *Clock*, could be derived from these two classes with multiple inheritance which would exhibit all the properties of both *Time of Day* and *Date*.. For example, adding a *Days* object to *Clock* would automatically add it to the *Date* component of the *Clock* object, whereas adding an *Hours* object to a *Clock* would automatically add it to the *Time of Day* component of the *Clock*. To get the *Date* component of a *Clock* incremented when its *Time of Day* exceeds 24 hours it is necessary for a *Clock* to have a private method, or daemon, that deals with the occurrence of this situation. For a *Clock* to deal with this it needs to know when a *Time_of_Day* object overflows twenty-four hours, which should be part of the response of the *Time_of_Day* 's method to add Hours. To ensure that the user of a Clock does get the expected effect when Hours are added to a Clock the *Clock* class must overload the name of *Time_of_Day* 's method to add Hours to make it become *Clock* 's method to add Hours. The need to do this reflects the fact that the "Add Hours" method for Clocks has a different behaviour from the "Add Hours" method for Time of Day.

4.9   POLYMORPHISM

Polymorphism is the feature of object oriented language systems that enables an application to be easily extended by adding new derived classes which do not cause an existing application to be changed or even recompiled.

Polymorphism means "of many forms" and is applied to a software mechanism which allows operations with different meanings (they have many forms) to be expressed in exactly the same way. In a sense, the overloading of function names and operators is also a form of polymorphism. For example, a programming language statement of the form:

W := X + Y + Z;

can have different meanings which depend upon the types of the objects W, X, Y and Z. They could be *Dates*, *Time of Day* or any other object for which a "+" operator had been defined. In an object oriented language the above statement is performed by:

Sending a message "+"(Y) to object X; to "add" object Y to X and return an object T1,

Sending a message "+"(Z) to object T1; to "add" object Z to T1, and return an object T2,

Sending a message ":="(T2) to object W, to "copy" object T2 into object W.

These messages will only succeed if there is a method with the right signature in the class of each object, or in any of the classes from which the class has been derived. The binding of the message to a method is achieved by searching, from the class of which the object is an instance, back through its base classes towards the root of the hierarchy until a method with the right signature is found. This search can either be carried out during the translation of the logic (in a statically typed OO language) or during the execution of the program containing the logic (in a dynamically typed OO language).

In a statically typed language the search has to start with the class that is identified by the static type of the object being referenced; the language translator cannot know whether the object could be of a different type when the logic is executed. The result is that the message will always be bound to one specific method because the program code has been statically bound. This static interpretation of overloaded functions is not polymorphic because each use of any of the overloaded functions has a single interpretation; it is monomorphic!

In a dynamically typed language the class of the object to which a message is sent may be different each time the program is executed. This will cause the search for the method to start at a different place in the class hierarchy and this may result in a different method with the right signature being found and executed. The result is that the message has been dynamically bound to a method. The same message may invoke a different method each time the program is executed. Obviously, if the class of an object is too different from that which was anticipated when the logic was written the message may not find a method and the program will fail.

It is the ability to dynamically bind messages to methods that differentiates polymorphism from function name overloading (which can be achieved statically).

To show the power and benefit of polymorphism, where the same message (or request to invoke a method) may take on many forms dynamically

```
procedure Date_Example_9
       S1, S2: String;
       Days_Later : Days;
       a_Date : Date;
begin
       Get (S1); a_Date := Date (S1);
       Get (S2); Days_Later := Days (S2);
       Put(String (Days_ Later));
       Put (" days after ");
       Put (String (a_Date));
       Put (" is ");
       Put (String (a_Date + Days_Later ) );
end Date_Example_9;
```

Figure 4.22   Date example 9

consider, once again, the *Date* example that has been developed throughout this chapter. In figure 4.14 the procedure *Date_Example_8* constructed two *Date* objects by reading them in as *Strings* before it subtracted them to produce a *Days* object which was converted back into a *String*. A similar procedure could be developed that created a *Date* and a *Days* object from a *String* and added them to produce a new *Date* object which was converted back to a *String*. Such a procedure is shown as *Date_Example_9* in figure 4.22.

This procedure would become more useful if it did not create the *Date* and *Days* objects from *Strings* but allowed its caller to supply them as parameters. This procedure, called *Date_Example_10*, is shown in Figure 4.23. This procedure can be used by a piece of logic that can supply it with a Date and a Days object as parameters; this logic could itself create these objects from Strings, as in Figure 4.24. If this logic read in the Date "31/12/91" and the Days "365" then the call of Date_Example_10 would produce the output:

365 days after 31/12/91 is 30/12/92

Now consider the need to be able to do the same thing with *American_Dates* which are a class derived from *Dates*, as in figure 4.20. Obviously, the logic to create the objects must change because an object of class *American_Date* has to be created to represent an American date. This logic is shown in figure 4.25. The important feature to note is that this new logic also calls the procedure *Date_Example_10* but in this case the output will be:

365 days after 12/31/91 is 12/30/92

The behaviour of procedure *Date_Example_10* has changed because it has been applied to different objects. In the first case *Date_Example_10* was given an object of class *Date* and in the second case it was given an object of

```
procedure Date_Example_10 (a_Date: Date; Days_Later : Days)
is begin
        Put(String (Days_ Later));
        Put (" days after ");
        Put (String (a_Date));
        Put (" is ");
        Put ( String (a_Date + Days_ Later));
end Date_Example_10;
```

Figure 4.23   A useful operation on date object

class *American_Date*. The procedure *Date_Example_10* was able to accept an object of class *American_Date* because this class is derived from *Date* which implies an *American_Date* object "is a" *Date* and therefore an *American_Date* can be used wherever a *Date* is expected.

But how does *Date_Example_10* "know" that it has been given an *American_Date* instead of a *Date*? The answer is it does not have to "know" if the language system dynamically binds messages to an object's methods, that is, the language supports polymorphism. The procedure *Date_Example_10* specifies , in the expression:

a_Date + Days_Later

that the message *"Add a Days object"* be sent to the object *A_Date*. When the object *A_Date* is given at runtime turns out to be of the base class *Date* then the message will be bound to *Date*'s "+ Days" method. If the object that *Date_Example_10* is given at runtime turns out to be an object of a class that is derived from *Date* , like *American_Date*, then the message will be bound to the derived class's "+ Days" method. The logic is dependent on the object instance it is given. Each of these methods create a new object instance of their own class; this new object is sent the message String, that is "convert

```
declare
        S1, S2: String;
begin
        Get (S1); Get (S2);
        Date_Example_10 ( Date (S1), Days (S2) );
end;
```

Given the date: **31/12/91** *and* **365** *Days*
the above logic will generate the String:

365 days after 31/12/91 is 30/12/92

Figure 4.24   Using this operation on date objects

```
declare
      S1, S2: String;
begin
      Get (S1); Get (S2);
      Date_Example_10 ( American_Date (S1), Days (S2) );
end;
```

Given the date: **12/31/91** *and* **365** *Days*
the above logic will generate the String:

365 days after 12/31/91 is **12/30/92**

Figure 4.25   Using the operation on American date

yourself into a textual String". An *American_Date* object does this differently from a *Date* class object; hence the different behaviour of the procedure *Date_Example_10*.

The ability to reuse the procedure *Date_Example_10* on new derived classes becomes even more apparent when additional classes are derived from the *Date* class. Figure 4.26 shows a class *Clock* which has been derived from *American_Date* and from the class *Time_of_Day* by using multiple inheritance. If this new class implements the method String to produce a textual string containing both the date and the time of day then that is what will be produced when the existing procedure, *Date_Example_10*, is given an object of class *Clock*, as shown in figure 4.27.

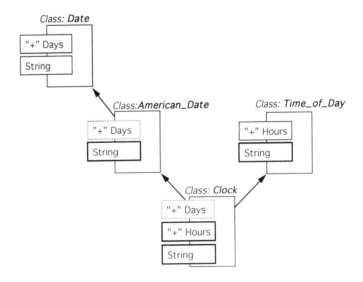

Figure 4.26   The clock class network

```
declare
      S1, S2: String;
begin
      Get (S1); Get (S2);
      Date_Example_10 ( Clock (S1), Days (S2) );
end;
```


Given the date & time: 12/31/91, 17:30:00 *and* 365 *Days*
the above logic will generate the String:

365 days after 12/31/91, 17:30:00 is 12/30/92, 17:30:00

Figure 4.27   Using the operation on clocks

This dynamic binding of messages to methods has a very significant benefit. The procedure, *Date_Example_10*, is able to exhibit this different behaviour without being modified, in any way, when a new class is derived from the *Date* class; it does not even need to be recompiled or retranslated into its executable form when a new class is derived from *Date*.

This means that logic that has been developed and tested before new classes are derived from the classes it uses will continue to work correctly even when it is given an instance of such a new derived class. Not only will it still work with the classes that it specifies it uses but it will work with any instance of a class that has been derived from the class specified, even if this class provides a new implementation of a method, such as String, that was defined in the base class. This ability of polymorphism to accommodate new derived classes within existing systems allows a systems to be easily and gracefully extended. *It is a powerful facility for handling change.*

This allows existing logic to continue to be used, untouched, even when the business requirements change so long as the changed requirements can be expressed by deriving new classes from those already used by the business application logic.

It has been estimated that some 70% of a business's software effort is expended in understanding, maintaining and upgrading existing systems. Object orientation's support for polymorphism can provide the opportunity to significantly reduce this effort in the future, and to provide software systems that have much more intrinsic value by virtue of their increased stability, reusability and extensibility.

4.10   GENERICITY

The final feature of importance to object oriented language systems is generics, or templates. This supports the facility for defining a class in terms of parameters; such a definition becomes a "template" from which several actual classes can be instantiated by specifying the values of the parameters. This facility is very useful for defining classes which can manipulate collections of other objects.

For example, it could be useful to maintain a list, or collection, of Dates which are, say, Dates of Employment of the employees of a Company so that Service Awards can be calculated. This list would become a class in the object base which grouped together, by the mechanisms provided by its methods, the instances of Dates of Employment for each Employees in the Company. A class named, say, *List of Employment Dates* could be defined to encapsulate such a list with methods to:

- create a list,

- add a Date to the list (when someone joins the Company),

- delete a date from the list (when someone leaves the Company),

- iterate over the list (to allow Service Awards to be calculated),

- delete the list.

These methods do not need to know anything about the Date class objects which they are managing; in fact, the list does not even need to know what class the objects belong to. If a class was also needed to manage a list of Motor Vehicles then the *same* methods could be used. Without a "template" facility the same set of logic and data properties would have to be mechanically replicated to construct a class called, say, *List of Motor Vehicles*. Mechanically replicating a class definition can be prone to error and creates change control problems.

A language which supports Generics, or Templates, avoids these problems by allowing a class template to be defined in which the class of objects to be managed is specified as a parameter. Thus, the same class template could be used for *List of Employment Dates* and *List of Motor Vehicles*. An example of such a class template is shown in Figure 4.28, where the parameter is denoted by "<T>". Such a class template can be used to generate a real class definitions by specifying the name of the class that is to be given to the parameter, as also shown in figure 4.28.

This mechanism automatically generates the new classes from the template in much the same way as a macro processor would do. Whilst a macro processor would simply carry out a textual substitution of the parameter's name wherever it occurred in the body of the macro, a template instantiation has to understand the semantics (i.e. the meaning) of the template to ensure that the language system can still understand and check that its type

```
class List <T> is
function Add (Object: <T>) return Boolean;
function Remove (Object : <T>) return Boolean;
function Next return <T>;
-- ...
end List;
```

This can be used to generate real classes, thus:

```
class List <Employment_Date>;
        -- to define the class "List of Employment Dates"
```

```
class List <Motor Vehicles>;
        -- to define the class "List of MotorVehicles"
```

Figure 4.28   A class template

system has been applied properly. This understanding of a template and its instantiation is essential for an object oriented language to maintain its understanding of the types of all objects so that all the other object oriented features are maintained. Generics can be thought of as type-safe macros.

4.11   MEMORY MANAGEMENT

It was indicated in Section 4.5 that objects can have memory space allocated to them during the execution of a program. This allows objects to be created when they are needed and allows the logic in a program to model real world objects which spring into existence as the result of some event.

For example, when a person becomes an employee of a company a new Employment Record needs to be created. This can be modelled in a program by creating an Employment Record object when a new employee event is triggered. The creation of such an object will cause memory space to be allocated to it within the program. However, the Employment Record object will need to exist until the employee leaves the company, and this will probably be long after the program that created the object has completed its run. Objects like Employment Record that need to exist beyond the termination of the program which created them have to be given persistence by storing them in a   database; such objects are often called persistent objects. At some point in the program, these objects will have to be inserted into the database by copying the information held in the program's memory into the database. Once it has been written into the database it is possible that the object in memory will no longer be needed and can be discarded.

Programs also use transient objects, that is, objects which only exist during the life-span of the program that creates them. Examples of transient objects are the working variables used to support the logic of a program, such as the *Date* and *Days* objects created by our example code in figure 4.8.[1]

When an object is no longer needed by a program the memory space that it occupied should become available for use by a new object, otherwise it is possible that the program will eventually run out of memory space if it is continuously creating new objects. For example, every time that the procedure *Date_Example_5* shown in figure 4.8 is called, it will create two new *Date* objects and one new *Days* object by allocating new memory space for them. Similarly, an Employment Record object will be created for every new employee, and these objects will occupy memory space within the program until it completes its run; if the company has just employed several hundred new graduates these objects could consume a significant amount of memory which may need to be recovered and used for other new objects.

Languages that allow objects to be created dynamically, by allocating memory for them during program execution, also provide mechanisms whereby the allocated memory is recovered after the objects have ceased to exist. The recovered memory then becomes available for use in allocating memory to new objects. The management of the memory space occupied by dynamically created objects is called heap management and is either done automatically by the language system or it is left in the hands of the programmer.

A language such as Smalltalk or Eiffel that provides automatic heap management is easier to use than a language that requires the programmer to manage the heap. However, there is a cost associated with such automatic heap management; the language runtime system must be able to keep track of which objects are in use and which objects are no longer in use so that it knows when it is able to reuse the memory space. Keeping track of an object's use usually requires that a reference count is maintained for each object; when the count becomes zero the system knows that the object is no longer in use and can be discarded. Whether the memory space for a discarded object becomes immediately available for use by a new object will depend on the trade-offs made in designing the heap manager. From time to time, the heap manager must sweep up all the dead objects and amalgamate contiguous areas of memory so that new objects of any size may be allocated memory. If it is done too frequently the heap can become very fragmented because amalgamation will not occur very often; if it is done more infrequently the total memory requirements of the program will increase and the collection and amalgamation of dead objects will take longer. These algorithms are known as garbage collectors.

---

[1] We are referring here to objects that are created in a program's main memory, and not in a buffer pool which is used to cache objects to and from a database.

A garbage collector can make the performance of a program unpredictable because it may be activated at any time. This can make them unsuitable for programs that have hard realtime responses to meet.

The other approach to heap management is to insist that the programmer explicitly deletes an object when it is no longer required. The dangers, in this case, are that:

- an object may be prematurely deleted because the programmer over-looked the fact that another object is still using the object that has been deleted; subsequent access to a prematurely deleted object will usually cause the program to crash in an unpredictable fashion;

- an object, that is no longer being used, is not explicitly deleted; this leads to a phenomenon known as "heap leak" whereby memory space becomes unrecoverable and the program eventually runs out of space.

The C++ language does not provide an automatic garbage collector but leaves heap management as the responsibility of the class designer. However, it does provide several mechanisms that can be used by the class designer to minimise the above dangers.

C++ provides the operators **new** and **delete** to allow objects to be created and destroyed on the heap at runtime. These operators may be overloaded by individual class declarations so that the class designer can supply imple-mentations of them that match the needs of the application. This feature of C++ has been used by the object oriented database ObjectStore to add per-sistence to C++ objects.

When an object, or a reference to an object, goes out of scope, C++ auto-matically invokes a standard method of its class to ensure that such objects are properly discarded.

4.12 SUMMARY

This chapter has shown how all the object oriented logic features complement each other to support the set of programming language mechanisms that characterise an OOPL. We have shown that:

- Encapsulation of data properties is required by Abstract Data Types;

- Strong type checking is required for Function and Operator Overloading;

- Classes are a refinement of Abstract data Types;

- Inheritance is needed to allow classes to be reused;

- Polymorphism needs inheritance and strong typing to allow existing code to work with new derived classes;

- Generics, or template classes, allow further reuse of code and interfaces.

It has also been shown that there can be significant differences in the way that the memory storage allocated to objects can be managed, and the effect this can have on the meaning of the program's logic.

5

OBJECT ORIENTED PROGRAMMING LANGUAGES

This chapter describes:

- the evolution of object oriented programming languages from Simula,

- the ways in which, and the extent to which, the features, required of an object oriented programming language which were described in Chapter 4 are supported by the programming languages C++, Ada and Eiffel.

These languages have been chosen because they are statically typed and support the development, and evolution, of robust systems. Some other object oriented languages, notably Smalltalk, are dynamically typed and support the rapid evolution, and evaluation of, prototype systems. Space has precluded a detailed description of the latter languages but their major differences from statically typed languages has been indicated where appropriate.

5.1 EVOLUTION OF OOPLS

It is generally recognised that all object oriented programming languages are descended from Simula-67. The Simula-67 language was developed in the 1960s by Kristen Nygaard and Ole-Johan Dahl at the Norwegian Computer Centre (NCC) to support the modelling involved in discrete event simulation of scientific and industrial processes. It was a general purpose language that offered a simulation capability as an application of its own basic concepts. Simula was derived from Algol 60, which had established the benefits of block structure and nested procedures as mechanisms to control the visibility of component entities.

Simula-67 was the first programming language to bring together, in a single language, mechanisms to support the concepts of:

- *encapsulation and objects*,to group together data attributes and the processing actions (methods) on the data attributes,

- *static type checking*, i.e. checking that is performed during the language compilation process, to provide runtime safety for the external manipulation of the attributes of objects,

- *classes*, as templates for objects,

- *inheritance*, as a means of factorising the properties that classes had in common,

- *dynamic binding (polymorphism)*, to allow classes of objects that had identical abstract interfaces and properties to be used interchangeably,

- *coroutines*, to allow actions to be interleaved by enabling the simulation of asynchronous actions and the modelling of objects which can be active even when they have not received a message (autonomous objects such as a clock which will always be measuring the passage of time by "ticking").

The application of Simula-67 to the modelling and simulation of industrial and scientific processes also introduced an approach to software design based on modelling the direct representation of real world objects in a program.

It is no accident that to qualify as an object oriented programming language, a language must provide support for the set of concepts listed at the start of Chapter 4, that is, encapsulation, abstraction, classes, objects, methods, inheritance, message passing, polymorphism and genericity. That is not to say that it is only possible to practice an object oriented approach to software system development with an object oriented language; any general purpose programming language can probably be used in an object oriented fashion, with varying degrees of success, once the concepts of object oriented development are understood. In fact, one of the authors implemented several applications, in the C programming language, using the above concepts of object orientation during the 1980s but he had to implement and apply the concepts himself by a very disciplined use the C language; there was no built-in support from the language.

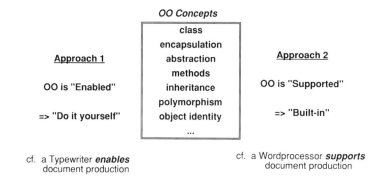

Figure 5.1 Programming approaches to object orientation

It is the degree to which a language *supports* the concepts of object orientation that identifies it as an object oriented language. A language may *enable* the use of an object oriented approach to system development without providing *support* for such an approach. This distinction between programming languages, shown in figure 5.1, is similar to the way that a typewriter *enables* the production of documents whereas a modern word processor actually *supports* the production of documents, because it has a model of what constitutes a document. A word processor supports the concepts of words, sentences, paragraphs, sections, headings, footnotes, etc. In the same way, an object oriented programming language supports the concepts of encapsulation, abstraction, classes, objects, methods, inheritance, message passing, polymorphism and genericity.

The evolution of object oriented programming languages (OOPLs) from Simula-67 is illustrated in figure 5.2, from which it can be seen that Smalltalk was also a major influence. Alan Kay, who created Smalltalk-80 at Xerox PARC with Adele Goldberg, had previously worked with an implementation of Simula. The concepts he found incorporated into Simula had a profound influence on the design of Smalltalk in which everything is an object of a class and all classes inherit from a single base class, called Object. Smalltalk introduced the term "method" to describe the actions performed by an object and the concept of "passing messages" as the means by which the "methods" were activated. It is also a dynamically typed language that binds a method to a message at runtime.

Bertrand Meyer, the designer of Eiffel, was also a user of Simula and one-time Chairman of the Association of Simula Users. Jean Ichbiah, the chief designer of Ada 83, led a team that implemented a subset of Simula and Bjarne Stroustrup, the designer of C++, used Simula and acknowledges its influence on the design of C++. These three languages are statically typed like Simula itself.

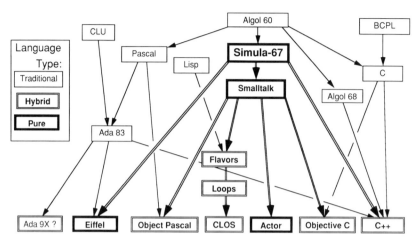

Figure 5.2   Evolution of object oriented languages

5.1.1   Static vs. dynamic typing

In a static type system a name or an expression identifying an object has a
type which can be determined and checked before the program is run.
Languages with a static type system are typically compiled into low level
machine instructions before they are executed. Early examples of such languages are FORTRAN and COBOL.

In a dynamic type system an object has a type which can only be
determined at runtime. Languages with a dynamic type system are typically
interpreted; that is, there is a program which "executes" the statements of the
language which are not translated into low level machine instructions. Early
examples of dynamically typed languages are Lisp and Basic.

Languages with a static type system are also referred to a strongly typed
languages since the programmer has to explicitly associate a type with every
name declared in a program so that the language compiler can verify that
the names, and expressions composed from these names, always refer to
objects of the specified type. The advantages of a statically typed language
are that errors in the use of the typing system are trapped before the
program is executed and the program can execute more efficiently since
there is no need to do any type checking at runtime.

Languages with a dynamic type system are often referred to as weakly
typed languages since the programmer does not have to specify the type of
object to which variables can refer when writing the program. Because each
object "knows" its own type when it is created the runtime system is able to
check that objects only participate in operations that they support. The
advantages of languages with a dynamic type system are that the programs

are more flexible and can cope with new types of objects which were not anticipated when the program was written. This flexibility is achieved at the cost of efficiency during execution of the program because of the need to maintain and check the type of all objects during execution.

It is really a misnomer to describe languages with a dynamic type system as weakly typed or, even worse, as untyped; such terms should be reserved for languages, like Assemblers and BCPL, which never apply type checking, either during compilation or during execution. As explained in Section 4.6.1, all OOPLs have to be strongly typed to support function name overloading; they also have to be strongly typed to ensure that objects only respond to messages for which they have had a method specified.

5.1.2 Pure vs. hybrid

There is much debate as to whether OOPLs should be "pure" or "hybrid". A pure OOPL is one that has been designed solely to support an object oriented paradigm in which everything must consist of classes, objects and methods. A hybrid OOPL, on the other hand, supports other programming paradigms in addition to supporting an object oriented paradigm. Hybrid OOPLs typically continue to support the features of the languages, such as C or Pascal, from which they were derived. It is therefore possible to use a hybrid OOPL in a non-object oriented fashion since the programmer is not constrained to use only classes, objects and methods. Figure 5.2 indicates which OOPLs are regarded as pure and which can be considered to be hybrid.

An advantage of a pure OOPL, such as Smalltalk or Eiffel, is that the power of object technology is not compromised and the programmer only has to master a single paradigm. However, most pure OOPLs are dynamically typed to deliver flexibility and simplicity of expression. As explained above this results in a loss of efficiency at runtime.

A hybrid OOPL, such as C++ or Objective C, will have maintained upwards compatibility with its base language which can have compromised some of its object oriented features, for example, by allowing data types to be declared without associated methods. The upwards compatibility of a hybrid OOPL with its base language will ease the transition of those familiar with the base language into the object oriented language but there is the danger that they will only partially adopt the object approach. Those unfamiliar with the base language of a hybrid OOPL will, in effect, have two languages to master before they can fully exploit a hybrid OOPL.

The relational 4GLs are being upgraded to provide mechanisms that allow data held in a relational data base to be manipulated in an object oriented fashion by, for example, allowing procedures to be stored with the data. These enhanced 4GLs are also a form of hybrid OOPL.

5.1.3   Overview of object oriented languages

This chapter describes some of the programming languages that support the concepts of object orientation.   The language C++ is described in some depth, as it is becoming the most widely used object oriented language and because it supports all the features that are necessary in an object oriented language; the mechanisms provided by C++ combine to create a very powerful and expressive language.   The growth in the use of C++ is illustrated by figure 5.3, from which it can be seen that the installed base of C++ users has grown exponentially over the last ten years.   This is partly as a result of C++ being designed to be upwards compatible with the C language, which itself is used very extensively in a very wide range of applications.   C++ was designed to maintain the efficiency of C so that it could also be used on a wide range of applications.   The efficiency is achieved by ensuring that its users only incur runtime overheads when particular features of C++ are used; if such features are not used there is no performance penalty at runtime.

The Ada language is also described because it is often assumed that it supports object orientation as a consequence of being the language that Grady Booch used to develop his object oriented design approach and the language that is used to implement designs constructed by the HOOD methodology.   In fact, Ada lacks some of the features required to enable it to completely support object oriented development; these shortcomings are described below.

The Eiffel language is looked at briefly because it was designed from scratch to support completely object orientation and other sound software engineering principles.   Its use of pre-conditions, post-conditions and invariants can significantly improve the robustness and documentation of programs developed in Eiffel.

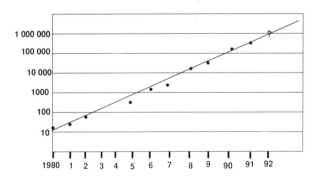

Figure 5.3   C++ growth of users/installations

5.2 C++

C++ was not designed to be a programming language which just supported an object oriented style of programming, but to be a general purpose programming language which, as Bjarne Stroustrup says, "makes writing good programs easier and more pleasant for the individual programmer." It was designed to build upon the strengths of C, to support data abstraction and to support object oriented programming. The following sections on C++ assume that the reader is familiar with the syntax of the C language as it is beyond the scope of this book to provide a description of the C language, for which many excellent books already exist.

5.2.1 C++ as a better C

Although C is not the cleanest nor safest programming language ever designed, it has become very extensively used for a very wide range of different applications because:

- it is flexible; it does not preclude the use of most programming styles,
- it is efficient; it maps onto machine resources straightforwardly,
- it is available on practically any machine you wish to use,
- it is portable; with care and thought porting is technically and economically feasible.

C++ was designed to provide better support for the styles of programming used in C by providing features that make the most common errors unlikely, by introducing:

- function prototypes to ensure the type safety of functional interfaces,
- inline functions to achieve the runtime efficiency of macros with the type safety of a functional interface,
- constant objects to allow constant values to have a known type,
- guaranteed initialisation of objects when they are created,
- reference variables as alternative names for objects.

Whilst these enhancements to the C language are not specifically features that are needed for objected orientation, they do provide a sound framework upon which the object oriented features of C++ are built; in particular, they allow C++ to be a statically typed language that ensures the type safety of all operations at compile time.

C++ introduced the use of function prototypes, which are now in ANSI C, to allow a compiler to check the argument types in function calls. In C++ all functions must be declared before they can be used and the declaration must provide a specification of the types of their arguments. In C, functions are often designed to accept a varying number of arguments which may also be of varying types. In addition to the use of the ellipsis (...) in a function declaration to inhibit argument type checking, C++ allows function names to be overloaded with signatures that have different types and/or numbers of arguments. It allows default argument values to be supplied which the compiler will use when that argument is left out.

In C, many simple and straightforward functions are defined as macros for efficiency and notational convenience. Unfortunately, macros do not provide a type checked interface. In C++ **inline** functions fulfil the need for efficiency whilst maintaining the type safety of a functional interface. Similarly, macros were used in C to define symbolic constants which were neither typed nor scoped. C++ introduced the keyword **const** to enable constant values of any type to be declared and whose "constantness" could be verified by the compiler. This feature is now part of ANSI C.

Another common source of error in C, and many other programming languages, arises from forgetting to initialise variables before they are used. This often occurs because variables have to be declared at the start of the block in which they are needed but no suitable value can be provided until some logic statements have been executed. Take, for example, the procedure in figures 4.6 and 4.10, expressed in C and C++ as:

```
void Date_Example_4( )             void Date_Example_6( )
{   // This is the C coding        {   // This is the C++ coding
    String S;                          String S;
    Date   Date1; // Not initialised!!
    Get (S);                           Get (S);
    Date1 = Date_from_String (S);      Date   Date1 = Date_from_String (S);
    // Now Date1 is initialised...     // Date1 is created and initialised
}                                  }
```

As can be seen from the example on the right, C++ allows declarations to be intermixed with statements so that variables may be declared at their first point of use where suitable values are more often available. In fact, C++

```
class complex {
private:
    double  real, imaginary;
public:
    complex ( double r, double i )  { real = r; imaginary = i; }
    complex ( double r )  { real =r; imaginary = 0; } //converts complex to float
    operator double ()  { return (re);}      // ignores Imaginary part !!
    complex operator + ( complex, complex );
    complex operator - ( complex, complex ); // binary minus
    complex operator - ( complex );          // unary minus
    complex operator * ( complex, complex );
    complex operator / ( complex, complex );

    // ...
}
```

Figure 5.4 A C++ abstract datatype

goes further than this by enabling a programmer to ensure that variables (i.e. objects) cannot be defined without being initialised with meaningful values, which is essential if objects are to be able to rely on their internal state.

C only provides "call by value" semantics for passing parameters to functions and "call by reference" has to be simulated by the explicit use of pointer values. Whilst this is adequate for the built-in types of C it becomes inconvenient for large objects and seriously limits the notational convenience with which user-defined types can be manipulated. C++ has therefore introduced the concept of a **reference** which acts as another name for an object. A reference object must be initialised and thereafter can be used as though it were the object it refers to. The user of an object can use a name for an object without needing to know whether it is the name of the object or the name of a reference to the object.

5.2.2 C++ support for abstract data types

C++ allows a programmer to define abstract data types that can be used as conveniently as, and in a similar manner to, built-in types. Numerical types are common examples of such data abstraction. A partial specification of the abstract data type for complex numbers is shown in figure 5.4. The declaration of the Abstract data type *complex*, as a **class** in C++, specifies the representation of a complex number together with the complete set of operations applicable to complex numbers. The representation is **private**, i.e. is only accessible to the functions declared in the definition of the **class** complex, but the functions are **public** to provide the methods available on objects of the class complex. In C++, methods are called member functions and are defined just like functions in C, for example:

```
complex operator + ( complex left, complex  right) {
    return complex ( left.real + right.real, left.imaginary + right.imaginary );
}
```

and used like this:

```
main()
{   complex a (2.3, 1);
    complex b (1, 4.5);
    complex c = a + b + complex( 1, 2.3 );
// ...
}
```

Since the representation is now hidden from the users of the type the only way variables of the type can be initialised is by use of some function declared for the type. If the use of such a function is the responsibility of the user it may be overlooked, and thereby cause the abstract data type to be created, and used, in an undefined state which undermines the integrity of the type. C++ avoids this problem by providing a specially named function to do the initialisation when an object instance of the class is created. This function is called a **constructor** which must have the same name as its class, e.g. the functions named *complex* in Figure 5.4.

When the construction of variables of a type is non-trivial, one often needs a complementary function to clean up variables after their last use. In C++ these clean up functions are called **destructors** which have names that are their class name prefixed with ~ (the one's complement operator in C and C++).

Whilst controlling construction and destruction of objects is sufficient for many types there are situations where it is necessary to control all copy operations, e.g. where objects contain pointers to their subcomponents and a "deep" copy is required. These pointers will usually represent a "has a" or "free form" semantic relationship; for example, an Employee object pointing at an Address object represents the fact that an Employee has an Address. A "deep" copy will ensure that when a copy of an Employee object is made it also makes a copy of its Address object whereas a "shallow" copy will leave the copy of the Employee object still pointing at the same Address object as the original Employee object.

There are *two distinct* circumstances when values of objects need to be copied:

- when a newly created object *is initialised* to the value of an existing object, for example, when an Employee becomes a new Star Performer,

- when the value of an object *is assigned* to another object, for example, when an Employee is promoted to a Manager and therefore replaces the existing object.

The initialisation case is handled in C++ by a special form of constructor called a **copy constructor** (or copy initialiser) which takes a single argument of a reference to an object of its type.

The assignment case is handled in C++ by allowing the assignment operator (= in C and C++) to be overloaded, i.e. redefined, by the class definition. The important characteristic of an assignment operation is that it can rely on the previous value of the object being assigned to whereas initialisation cannot. So, assigning an Employee object to a Manager object can rely on the Manager referring to an Address object, which may need to be discarded.

To allow abstract data types to be used as much like the built-in types as possible C++ allows all the standard operators to be defined for an abstract data type. Examples of overloading the +, -,* and / operators for complex are given in figure 5.4. The operators that may be overloaded include the subscripting operator [], the function application operator (), all the C compound assignment operators such as += and &= etc. and the prefix and postfix forms of the increment and decrement operators, ++ and - -.

User-defined type conversions, like the float to complex conversion implied by the constructor complex(*double*) and the *operator double()* in figure 5.4, can be defined and used explicitly. The C++ compiler will also apply them implicitly where necessary if they are unambiguous:

```
complex a = complex(1);
complex b = 1;              // implicit: 1 -> complex( 1.0 )
a = b + complex(2);
a = b + 2;                  // implicit: 2 -> complex(2.0)
a = 2 + b;                  // implicit: 2 -> complex(2.0)
double dd = b;              // implicit b -> double(b)
```

Conversion to a type can also be defined without modifying the declaration of a type, which is essential for conversion to built-in types, such as integer and character (which have no declarations), and "standard" user-defined types where the declarations are not generally accessible. This is achieved, in C++, by treating the names of built-in types and user-defined types as additional operators, as shown in figure 5.4.

5.2.2.1   Declaring classes in C++

The **class** is the key concept of C++ and provides the means by which user-defined types are defined. The **class** notation of C++ was developed as an extension of the C **struct** notation. A **class** has data members like a **struct**, but it may also have function members and it may be empty. A class declaration defines the complete set of characteristics of a user-defined type, in C++, in terms of the data members it contains *and* the operations (member functions) by which its data may be manipulated. Members (data and functions) cannot be added outside of the class declaration.

Members in a class may be data, functions, classes, enumerations, bitfields, friends and type names. No two members may have the same name unless they are overloaded function names and then their types must be sufficiently different. For example:

```
class Bad_Example {
    int error1;
    int error1;               // error: redefinition
    int f_example();
    int f_example();          // error: redefinition
    int f_example(int);       // OK
    int error1();             // error: same name as data member
    char y[];                 // error: number of elements MUST be given
}
```

Class members are accessed the same way as **struct** members in C; for example:

```
int Salary;
    class Employee {
    public:
    int Salary_of();
    private:
    int Salary;
    };
Employee Fred, * staff;    Salary = Fred.Salary_of();    Salary = staff >Salary_of();
```

A class is the unit of data hiding and encapsulation and supports data abstraction by allowing representation details to be hidden and accessed exclusively through a set of operations defined as part of the class.

A class also provides a unit of modularity by creating a separate name space for each class defined. If a class has only **static** data and function members then it is like a collection of objects and functions in their own name space, i.e. like a "module" in some other languages or a package in Ada.

A data or function member of a class may be declared **static** in the class declaration. There is only one copy of a static data member, shared by all objects of the class in a program; a static data member is a class variable rather then an instance variable. A static member is not part of objects of a class. For example:[1]

```
class Employee {
    static int number_of_Employees;
    static Employee *payroll_list;
// ...
};
int Employee::number_of_Employees = 0;    // Define & initialise class variable
Employee *Employee::payroll_list = NULL;  // Define & initialise class variable
```

The purpose of **static** members is to reduce the need for global variables by providing alternatives that are local to a class. A **static** member function or variable acts as a global for members of its class without affecting the rest of the program. In particular, its name does not clash with the names of global variables and functions or with the names of members of other classes. The association between the static members and their class is explicit and obvious, whereas the use of global variables and functions for similar purposes is neither.

5.2.2.2 Public, private and protected declarations

Public members of objects of a class are accessible to the class implementors and to any users of the class, i.e. by any function in the program. **Protected** members are only accessible to implementors of derived classes. **Private** members are only accessible to that class's member functions and its friends. These access controls are designed to provide protection against accidental

---

[1] The :: operator, used in the last two lines of the example, is used in C++ to qualify the name of a data or function member of a class by the name of the class to which it belongs. This allows the names of the members of a class to be chosen without the danger of them clashing with the names of members of any other class. Thus payroll_list could also be a member of the class Director, when it would be defined as Director::payroll_list.

misuse of members, not fraudulent misuse. Members of a class are **private** by default whereas members of a struct are **public** by default.

5.2.3 Member functions

A function declared as a member of a class is called a member function. The body of a member function may use the names of members of its class directly, even if the member is declared after the function body. Member functions whose bodies are defined in the class declaration are **inline**, i.e. the code in the body of the function replaces the function call. The benefit of inline functions is that, whilst the definition of the function provides for type safety in its use, the inline expansion of the code provides faster execution by removing the overhead of calling the function. For example:

```
int Salary;
class Employee {        // creates a new  name scope
public:                 // Body defined in class declaration & refers to Employee::Salary
int Salary_of() { return Salary; }  // return value of private data member
private:
int Salary;
};                      // end of new  name scope
```

is equivalent to, that is, it is as though it were written as:

```
int Salary;
class Employee {
public:
int Salary_of();
private:
int Salary;
};                      // end of new  name scope
                        // defined as inline outside of class declaration
inline int Employee::Salary_of() { return Salary;}
```

It is important to be able to inline member functions because, as in the above example, they often contain very little code and the cost, in execution speed, of calling the function could be comparable with the cost of executing the code the function encapsulates.

Member functions are always invoked with an implicit extra argument which points at the object of its class to which the member function is to be applied; the keyword **this** is used to denote the pointer to the object for which a member function is called. The type of **this** in a member function of a class **X** is **X* const** unless the member function is declared **const**; in this case, the type of **this** is **const X* const**. For example:

```
class Employee {
int Salary_of() const;
void Raise(int rise) { Salary += rise; }
void Deduct(int tax) const { Salary -= tax; }  // Error: const function cannot modify object
private:
int Salary;
};
int Employee::Salary_of() const { return Salary; }
void Trial_Use( Employee& x, const Employee& y ) {
```

x.Salary_of();	// OK; const function may be called for non-const object
x.Raise (100);	
y.Salary_of();	// OK: y is const and so is Employee::Salary_of()
y.Raise (200);	// Error since y is const and Employee;;Raise() is non-const

```
}
```

Static functions are called without a **this** pointer.

5.2.3.1 Friend functions

A friend of a class is a function that is not a member of the class but is permitted to use the **private** and **protected** member names from the class. A friend of a class is as much a part of the interface of a class as a member is. Friendship, like all other access, is granted by the class, and the friend must appear in the class declaration. However, the name of a friend is not in the name scope of the class. The C++ friendship feature is not an object oriented modelling facility but is a mechanism that can be used, very effectively, as an implementation technique to allow additional controlled access to **private** and **protected** members of a class, and to provide operations on an object of a class that would be inconvenient to invoke as proper member functions.

The major distinction between member functions and friend functions is that the former are declared with an implicit extra argument and called using the member access operators (. and ->), whereas friend functions have all their arguments specified and are called using the normal function calling notation. These differences are illustrated by figure 5.5.

```
class Employee {
    int Salary;
    friend void Profit_Share (Example*, int);
public:
    void Raise (int );
};
void Profit_Share (Employee* p, int bonus ) { p-> Salary += bonus; }
void Employee:: Raise (int rise) { Salary += rise; }

void Adjust_Salary() {
    Employee fred;
    Profit_Share (& fred, 2000);
    fred.Raise (500);
}
```

Figure 5.5   C++ member vs. friend functions

Friend functions can usefully be friends of two classes so that they have access to the private members of both classes. The standard example of this use of friend functions is for the operations between Vectors and Matrices as shown in figure 5.6.

By declaring **operator *()** to be a friend of Vector and Matrix it is able to access the elements of each of them directly and efficiently. If **operator *()** was just a normal global function then it would only be able to access the elements of the Vector and the Matrix through their public memberfunctions, such as Vector::element(int) and Matrix::element(int, int).

```
class Matrix;
class Vector {
    float v[4];
    friend Vector operator * ( const Matrix &, const Vector& );
    //...
public:
    element ( int );
};
class Matrix {
    Vector v[4];
    friend Vector operator * ( const Matrix &, const Vector& );
    // ....
public:
    element ( int , int );
};
Vector operator * ( const Matrix & m, const Vector& v ) {
    Vector result;
    for ( int i = 0; i<3; i++ ) {
        result.v[i] = 0;
        for ( int j = 0; j<3; j++ ) { result.v[i] += m.v [i] [j] * v.v [j]; }
    }
    return result;
}
```

Figure 5.6   Friends of two classes

This could be significantly less efficient, especially if the public functions were doing proper range checking.

5.2.4 Constructors and destructors

5.2.4.1 Constructors

A member function with the same name as its class is called a constructor. Classes with constructors ensure that objects of that class are initialised when they are created and before they are used.

The job of a constructor is to create the basic structure of the object, i.e. to construct the objects representing the base classes (if any), to initialise any virtual function table, to construct the objects representing non-static data members (if any), to lay down information that allows finding objects representing virtual bases (if any), and to execute the body of the constructor. Thus a constructor turns raw processor memory into an object to which the C++ type system applies.

Constructors are called whenever an object of a class with constructors is created:

- as a global object,
- as a local variable within a function,
- through an explicit use of operator **new**,
- through an explicit call of a constructor,
- as a temporary object,
- as a data member of another class,
- as an object representing a base class.

As a simple example, consider the constructors in figure 5.4, and repeated below:

```
class complex {
    double real, imaginary;
public:
    complex ( double r, double i ) { real=r; imaginary=i; } // Constructor for complex
    complex ( double r ) { real=r; imaginary=0; }        // float -> complex conversion
    // ...
}
```

These constructors would be called to initialise a,b and c thus:

```
main() {
    complex a = 2.3;              // a = complex::complex( double(2.3) );
    complex b  = complex(1, 2);   // b = complex::complex( (double)1, (double)2 );
    complex c(1,2);               // c = complex::complex( (double)1, (double)2 );
    // ...
}
```

A constructor can be invoked for a const object but they cannot be inherited. Constructors and copy constructors are automatically generated (by the compiler) if they are needed for assignment or initialisation but have not been included in the class definition. These automatically generated constructors apply a memberwise copy and a memberwise initialisation, which is often what is required and which would be tedious and error prone to have to write for every class definition.

5.2.4.2   *Destructors*

A member function of a class X with a name of the form ~X is called a destructor of the class; it is used to discard values of type X immediately before the object containing them is destroyed. A destructor turns a C++ object back into raw processor memory.

A destructor takes no arguments, no return type can be specified and it is not possible to take the address of a destructor. These restrictions are imposed so that the compiler writer has the freedom to implement destructors in ways that are different from ordinary member functions, e.g. by passing additional arguments to destructors to control memory deallocation.

Destructors are invoked implicitly:

● when an automatic or temporary object goes out of scope,

● for constructed static objects, at program termination,

● through explicit use of the **delete** operator for objects allocated by the **new** operator,

● when explicitly called.

The destruction of objects is done in the reverse order to construction.

5.2.5 Function name and operator overloading

As noted above, only member function names may be replicated within a class declaration, but only if their arguments differ in number and/or types; this is known as function name overloading. It can also be applied to global functions, i.e. functions defined outside of a class declaration.

When an overloaded function name is used the compiler selects the correct function by comparing the types of the actual arguments with the types of the formal arguments. Basically, it must be possible for the C++ compiler to distinguish between overloaded functions by being able to differentiate between the possible actual arguments they can accept, i.e. the formal arguments must accept different sets of initialiser values. It should be noted that C++ does not allow functions that only differ in the return type to be overloaded. Consider:

Salary **operator** + (**const** Salary &, **const** Wages &);

Wages **operator** + (**const** Salary &, **const** Wages &);// *Error: functions only differ in return type*

void Pay (Salary s, Wages w) {

      Salary s1 = s+ w ;// *Error: which operator + should be used?*

      Wages w2 = s+ w ;   // *Error: which operator + should be used?*

}

Whilst a human reader may be able to deduce, in the simple situation above, that s1 should be initialised by calling the first operator + and w2 by calling the second, in general it is not that simple to determine what was really meant. Implicit conversions, which, for example, could automatically convert a Wages value into a Salary value can complicate the situation and it would not be possible for a C++ compiler to analyse expressions bottom up by looking at only a single operator and its operands at a time if overloaded functions could differ only in their return types.

The abstract data type, Date, used in Chapter 4 to explain the features of object logic, is an example where overloading operators provides a very convenient notation for manipulating objects of the type. The pseudo type definition developed in Chapter 4 into that shown by figure 4.11 could be expressed in C++ by the definition shown in figure 5.7. Note that all the overloaded operators are specified to be **const** functions; this enables the compiler to ensure that these operations do not modify the objects on which they are invoked or supplied as their arguments. The assignment operation, denoted by **operator =()** is different, since it must modify the Date object on which it is invoked; however, the **const** Date argument specifies that the

```
class Date {
public:
        Date (String);
        Date (Years, Months, Day_in_Month);
        Date (const Date &);                // Copy Constructor
        Date operator = (const Date);      // Assignment operator
        Date operator -  (Days) const;
        Date operator +  (Days) const;
        Days operator -  (Date) const;
        int   operator == (Date) const;
        int   operator <= (Date) const;
        int   operator >= (Date) const;
        int   operator <  (Date) const;
        int   operator >  (Date) const;
        String String() const;
        ~Date();
private:    // ... representation of Date
};
```

Figure 5.7   Date as a C++ class

assignment operation will not modify that argument, that is, it will not modify the object which it is copying. The ability, in C++, to specify that functions and data values are constant helps to document, in a way that can be verified by the compiler, important characteristics and assumptions of a program.

5.2.6   Efficiency

C++ provides a single declaration that defines both the private implementation details and the public interface for a class that is used as the interface to the users and the implementors of the member functions. This means that the compiler knows the size of every object which it uses when allocating processor memory for object instances. A C++ program therefore requires recompilation even when there are only changes to the **private** or **protected** parts of a class declaration.

The reason for this approach in C++ is that it allows the compiler to allocate memory storage for objects rather than having to delay memory allocation until runtime and therefore requiring that access to all objects is via a pointer. This approach means that C++ objects need only occupy the storage needed for their members and objects do not all have to be allocated in free store, as is the case with Smalltalk. The design of C++ was aimed at maintaining the efficiency, in terms of both space and time, of C; by avoiding the use of heap management for all objects C++ programs can be 3–10 times more efficient in time and space than systems that always use heap management for user defined objects.

Another benefit of C++'s approach is that it makes abstract data types, i.e. classes, behave more like built-in types. As explained in Section 4.5 and figure 4.5, built-in types use copy semantics when an object of a built-in type is assigned to another object of the same built-in type. This interpretation is maintained in C++ for abstract data types and classes.

The "cost" of this consistency and runtime efficiency is the overhead of needing to recompile a program after changes to a class's representation.

5.2.7   Defining class hierarchies in C++

This section describes how C++ supports inheritance of classes as the mechanism that allows common properties to be factored out into super-classes, and allows class derivation to be used to specialise behaviour by addition rather than by modification of existing code and data. *Inheritance is the mechanism which programming languages have to provide to support object oriented programming.*

In C++ a class can be *derived* from another class which is called its *base* class. A base class is sometimes called a *super*-class and a derived class is sometimes called a *sub*-class in other programming languages. It has been found that these terms cause confusion, since the sub-class actually contains its super-class as well as the additional data and function members of the sub-class, i.e. the sub-class is, in some sense, more than its super-class.

A class is derived from another, in C++, by specifying the base class in the derived class's declaration, thus:

```
class Employee {
public:
  int Age, Bonus;              // some properties of an Employee
  int Salary_of()
};
class Star_Performer : public Employee { // inherit the properties of an Employee
public:
  int Bonus, Star_Bonus;       // new properties of a Star_Performer
};
void Use_of_Star_Performer() {
  Star_Performer SP;
  SP.Salary = 20000;
  SP.Employee::Bonus = 200;// access Employee's Bonus member
  SP.Bonus = 300;              // access Star_Performer's Bonus member
  SP.Star_Bonus = 400;
}
```

In a derived class's declaration the base class may be **public, protected** or **private**. If the base class has a **public** access specifier then the **public** members of the base class become **public** members of the derived class and the **protected** members of the base class become **protected** members of the derived class; this is sometimes called *interface inheritance* or *sub-typing* since objects of the derived class respond to the methods of the base class.

If the base class has a **protected** access specifier then the **public** members of the base class become **protected** members of the derived class. If the base class has a **private** access specifier then the **public** and **protected** members of the base class become **private** members of the derived class; this is sometimes called *implementation inheritance* since the inheritance is an implementation detail not accessible to the users of the derived class.

If no access specifier is given then a base class of a derived class declared as a **class** is taken as private, whereas if the derived class is declared as a **struct** the base class is taken as public.

A derived class inherits all the members of its base class; all the non-static data members are concatenated. No information is stored in an object about non-virtual member functions; the compiler keeps track of which member functions apply to which class of objects using its access rules.

Declarations in a derived class may adjust the access to individual members of its base class:

```
class Employee {
    int Salary;
public:
    int Age, Bonus;
    int Salary_of();         // can use Salary, Age, Bonus, and Salary_of
};
class Broker : private Employee {
    int Commission;
public:
Employee::Age;  // adjust access to Employee::Age to be public; N.B. no type is
                //specified
    int Portfolio
    int Profit_Shared();    // can use Employee::Bonus, Age & Salary_of
};
    int Uses (Broker &)     // can use Broker::Age, Broker::Portfolio
                            //& Broker::Profit_Shared
```

The above example demonstrates the use of private, or implementation, inheritance. As can been seen, the user of a Broker object is not aware that a Broker has inherited the properties of an Employee even though they have access to Broker::Age which is actually the Age attribute of an Employee. Furthermore, a Broker does not support the method Salary_of() although the implementation of Broker::Profit_Shared() could use Employee::Salary_of().

5.2.8 Virtual functions and polymorphism

If a base class and a class derived from it both define a function with the same signature there will be no ambiguity as the correct function to call can be deduced from the types of the objects making the call. For example, if we introduce the function Salary_of() into a class derived from the Employee class above:

```
class Employee {
public:
    int Age, Bonus;              // some properties of an Employee
    int Salary_of()
};
class Star_Performer : public Employee { // inherit the properties of an Employee
public:
    int Bonus, Star_Bonus;       // new properties of a Star_Performer
    int Salary_of();             // Declare a new version of Salary_of
};
void Use_of_Star_Performer( Star_Performer & Sp) {
    Employee * E1; Star_Performer *Sp1;
    Employee   E2; Star_Performer Sp2;
    Sp1 = &Sp;     Sp1 -> Salary_of();     // calls Star_Performer::Salary_of()
    Sp2 = Sp;      Sp2 . Salary_of();      // calls Star_Performer::Salary_of()
    E1 = &Sp;      E1 -> Salary_of();      // calls Employee::Salary_of()
    E2 = Sp;       E2 . Salary_of();       // calls Employee::Salary_of()
}
```

The above situation depicts the normal compile-time binding of a function name to the code that represents it; in a statically typed language, like C++, the typed context is sufficient to identify which function should be invoked.

If the functions being called are not defined the program will not link successfully.

C++ supports the concept of virtual functions to allow the binding of member function calls to be delayed until runtime without compromising the typing system. If a member function of a base class is specified to be **virtual,** then that member function may be overridden in a derived class so that the derived class's member function will be called even if the access is through a pointer or reference to its base type. The effect of making the method Salary_of() a virtual function is highlighted, in italics, below:

```
class Employee {
public:
  int Age, Bonus;            // some properties of an Employee
  virtual int Salary_of();   // Declare Employee::Salary_of to be a virtual function
};                           // for which an implementation must be defined
class Star_Performer : public Employee { // inherit the properties of an Employee
public:
  int Bonus, Star_Bonus;     // new properties of a Star_Performer
  int Salary_of();           // Declare a new version of Salary_of
};
void Use_of_Star_Performer( Star_Performer & Sp) {
  Employee * E1;  Star_Performer *Sp1;
  Employee   E2;  Star_Performer Sp2;
                  Sp.Salary_of();     // calls Star_Performer::Salary_of()
    Sp1 = &Sp;    Sp1 -> Salary_of(); // calls Star_Performer::Salary_of()
    Sp2 = Sp;     Sp2 . Salary_of();  // calls Star_Performer::Salary_of()
    E1 = &Sp;     E1 -> Salary_of();  // calls Star_Performer::Salary_of()
    E2 = Sp;      E2 . Salary_of();   // calls Employee::Salary_of()
}
```

If a virtual function, defined in a base class, is not redefined in a derived class then a virtual function call on that derived class will automatically invoke the function defined by its nearest superclass. This is why a virtual function must have a definition in the base class that introduces it.

It is this ability to select the member function that corresponds to the actual object type that exists at runtime that differentiates `object-oriented` *programming from traditional programming.* The same interface is used to select from a set of functions *at runtime* so that as the object being referenced or pointed at

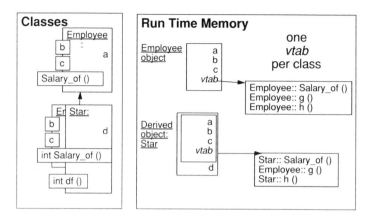

Figure 5.8   How C++ polymorphic functions work

changes dynamically the function being invoked may also change; this dynamic binding of an interface to a variety of functions is also known as *polymorphism*.

In C++ this dynamic binding of virtual functions does not violate the static (compile-time) type checking. Whilst compiling a call of a member function, C++ will check that a function with the correct signature exists in that class, or one of its super-classes. If it finds that it was declared to be **virtual** then it generates code to invoke the function indirectly through a table that it associates with every class that declares or inherits virtual functions; this table is called *vtab*. If the member function is not virtual then C++ generates a direct call to the function defined for the type of the class seen by the compiler.

The way that C++ achieves polymorphic calls for virtual functions is depicted in figure 5.8. A class which defines one or more virtual member functions will contain a hidden data member, called *vtab*, which points at a table that is automatically constructed for such a class. This table contains the address of each member function that is defined to be virtual. Figure 5.8 shows that the class named *Employee* defined three virtual functions Salary_of(), g() and h(). When the class named *Star* is derived from the class named *Employee*, it will inherit all the data and function members of the base class, including the hidden data member *vtab*. However, the compiler constructs a new version of the *vtab* table for the derived class but initialises it to contain the addresses of the base class's virtual member functions. When a virtual member function is invoked through a pointer to an object the compiler generates code to invoke the function through its address stored in the *vtab* table; this is possible for all classes derived from *base* because the hidden data member, *vtab*, will always appear in the same place in all objects derived from the base class as it is a data member of the base class. Although each *vtab* member points at a different table, the member function addresses they contain will all be the same unless a derived class redefines the virtual member function. In this case, the compiler records in the *vtab* table for that derived class the address of the redefined virtual member function. In figure 5.8, the derived class *Star* has redefined the virtual functions Salary_of() and h(). Now, at runtime when the code accesses the hidden data member *vtab* from a pointer to an object of the base class, it will reference the derived class's vtab table and invoke the derived class's virtual member function if the pointer to the base class object actually points at an object of the derived class.

The "cost" of C++'s support for polymorphism is the additional hidden data member in every object of a class with a virtual member function, the vtab table that is needed for each such class, and the extra code needed to invoke a virtual member function through this table rather than directly by name; this extra code will only involve one or two additional memory references. It should be noted that with this approach to dynamic binding the execution overhead of the extra code is constant; it does not matter whether a derived class has redefined a virtual method or not. Classes that do not define any virtual member functions incur none of these overheads.

This approach is different from, for example, that used by Smalltalk, which applies dynamic (runtime) type checking. In Smalltalk one may write code to invoke a member function on an object (send a message to an object) without knowing whether the type of that object actually supports a method with that signature; an error message will be produced at runtime if the object cannot service the message (function). To achieve this checking at runtime Smalltalk has to work its way up the class hierarchy, when an object

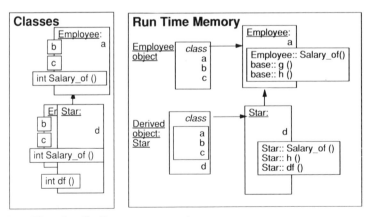

Figure 5.9   How Smalltalk messages work

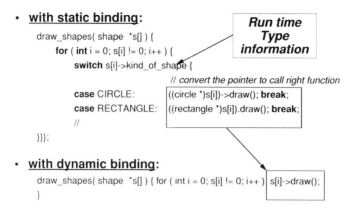

Figure 5.10 Date as an Ada package

receives a message, to locate a class that supplies an implementation of the required method. The approach of Smalltalk is depicted in figure 5.9. There are obvious performance overheads at runtime with this approach from the need to search up the class hierarchy; the search time will be longer for objects of a derived class that has not overridden a method defined in a superclass. There is also the space penalty associated with retaining the class hierarchy as a set of meta-objects in the execution environment. As C++ has type checked the code during compilation it does not need to retain the class declarations as meta-objects in the runtime environment.

The "benefit" of Smalltalk's way of supporting runtime binding is the freedom it provides to easily, and quickly, modify the class hierarchy and add methods to the classes. It makes Smalltalk an ideal environment for rapid prototyping and exploratory programming, as described in Chapter 7.

C++ could have implemented all member function calls indirectly through a function table, as it does for virtual functions. This would have created an overhead on all C++ programs even when the program did not need to use polymorphism. In addition, each object would have to include the space needed to contain the pointer to the function table which would have made all C++ data structures incompatible with C. These overheads on all objects and all member function calls would also have violated one of the design objectives of C++ that you only pay for what you use, or put the other way round, if you don't use it you don't pay for it.

To overcome these runtime overheads C++ requires the class implementor to specify when runtime binding should be employed by declaring a function to be virtual. There is, of course, a cost associated even with this approach in that changing a normal member function into a virtual member function after a class has been used will require all users of that class to be recompiled.

The classic example of the power and benefits of runtime binding is the development of a class to represent graphical shapes which provides a member function to draw itself. From such a base class one could derive classes to represent circles, ellipses, rectangles, triangles, etc. Each of these derived classes would supply its own implementation of the draw function. Now, suppose an array of pointers to objects of class shape is passed to a function which is expected to get them all drawn. Without polymorphism this function would have to discover which type of shape each element of the array contained as is shown at the top of figure 5.10.

The statically bound implementation has to type convert each pointer into the type which it has identified through the use of a switch statement on a public member of all the classes; this implies that this implementation aspect cannot be encapsulated (nor hidden behind a member function interface since only the base class's member function would ever get called in the above function). The major problem with the above solution is that when a new type of shape, say a hexagon, is derived then the function *draw_shapes* has to be modified to add an extra **case** to its **switch** statement and then be recompiled (and tested?).

If the draw member function is made **virtual** so that dynamic binding is applied the *draw_shapes* example becomes that shown at the bottom of figure 5.10. Not only is this simpler and more straightforward logic, it also continues to work, without change or even recompilation, when new types of shapes are derived after *draw_shapes()* has been written and compiled.

With dynamic binding one can write programs that will handle objects of derived classes that did not even exist when the program was written and compiled.

5.2.8.1   Abstract classes

In the example shown in figure 5.10, the base class for shape would need to declare *draw()* to be a virtual function, thus:

```
class point;
class shape {
    centre point;
    // ...
public:
    point where() { return point }
    void move (point p) { centre = p; draw(); }
    virtual void draw() { cerr << "Can't draw a base shape\n"; }
    // ...
};
```

Since *draw* is **virtual** it must have an implementation in the base class but, for the above base class it cannot do anything useful since there is no shape to draw, and so it just reports an error. The implementation of *draw*, in the base class, could do nothing, but then any derived class that forgot to provide its own implementation of *draw* would silently fail to draw itself.

To avoid these problems, C++ introduces the concept of an abstract class as a class that can only be used as a base class from which other classes can be derived, that is, an abstract class is a class for which no objects can be constructed as simple instances of that class. The abstract base class defines an interface for which each derived class may provide an implementation.

A class becomes an abstract class if its declaration contains at least one **pure virtual function**. A pure virtual function is defined by replacing its body by the text: = 0; thus:

```
class point;
    class shape {                       // an abstract class
    centre point;
    // ...
public:
    point where() { return point }
    void move (point p) { centre = p; draw(); }
    virtual void draw() = 0;            // pure virtual
    // ...
};
```

An abstract class can have member functions, constructors and destructors like any other class; the latter will be needed during the construction and destruction of the derived class objects. A pure virtual function is inherited as a pure virtual function so one may have derived classes that are themselves abstract classes.

5.2.9 Class inheritance and class composition

When a class D uses **public** derivation from another class B it can be said that D *is a* B, or more precisely D *is a kind of* B. If, on the other hand, a class C contains as one of its members an object of class B, it is said that C *has a* B. Thus inheritance satisfies an *is a* relationship whilst membership, or composition, satisfies a *has a* relationship.

For example, in figure 5.11 the type Garage contains a data member v of type Vehicle; this models the *has a* relationship that a Garage has a Vehicle.

```
class Vehicle {
public:
    virtual void start ();
    void move ();
    colour painted;
}
struct Garage {                          struct Garage : private Vehicle {
    Vehicle v;  // Garage hasa Vehicle
    void start ();                       void start (); // overrides Vehicle::start ()
}                                        }

void Use_Garage( Garage * pG ) {
    Vehicle * pV = pG;      // error: no Garage* to Vehicle* conversion
    pV = &pG->v;           // so set pV to point at the v member of pG
    pV->move ();           // calls Vehicle::move ()
    pG->move ();           // error: Garage does not have a member move ()
    pG->v.move ();
    pV->start ();          // calls Vehicle::start ()
                           // (not overriden by Garage::start () )
    pG>start ();           // calls Garage::start ()
}
```

Figure 5.11   Garage has a vehicle

A similar effect could be achieved by deriving a Garage from a Vehicle using **private** derivation, as shown in the box in figure 5.11, except that this would have overriden the virtual member function Vehicle::start(). Apart from a derived class's ability to override the virtual functions of its base class **private** derivation is equivalent to membership or composition.

To model the fact that a Car *is a kind of* Vehicle public inheritance should be used as shown in figure 5.12.

5.2.9.1   *Initialising base and member classes*

In figures 5.11 and 5.12, consider how the member Garage::v and the inherited base class part of Car could be initialised. An obvious approach is to expect that the constructors for classes Garage and Car should call a constructor of the class Vehicle from within their bodies, although it raises the question as to how the Vehicle class member is named. In figure 5.13 the constructor for Garage actually creates a local object of type Vehicle and initialises that rather than Garage::v; this local object will be destroyed when the constructor has finished without initialising Garage::v. In the same figure, the constructor for Car would also create a local object, if it were legal C++. The crux of these problems is that constructors are expected to be invoked when an object of its class is created, so invoking a constructor from within another constructor will create a local or temporary object within the scope of the invoking constructor; it will not initialise any part of the object being created by the invoking constructor. Whilst the concept of ensuring that objects are always initialised on creation is straightforward, actually achieving it takes some care in C++.

```
class Vehicle {
public:
    virtual void start ();
    void move ();
    colour painted;
}
class Car : public Vehicle {      // Car isa Vehicle
public:
    void start ();                // overrides Vehicle::start ()
    int passengers;
};

void Use_a_Car ( Car * pC ) {
    Vehicle* pV = pC;             // ok:  implicit Car* to Vehicle* conversion
    pV -> move ();                // calls Vehicle::move ()
    pC -> move ();                // calls Vehicle::move ()
    pV -> start ();               // virtual call of Car::start ()
    pC -> start ();               // calls Car::start ()
}
```

Figure 5.12   Car is a vehicle

Initialisers for the immediate base classes of a class and for members declared in a class can be specified in the definition of a constructor for a class by specifying their use <u>before</u> the body of the constructor. So, in figure 5.14, the constructor for *Garage* specifies that its member *v* is to be initialised by applying *v(color)* before the constructor's body is executed. Similarly, the constructor for *Car* specifies that its base member, *Vehicle*, is to initialised by applying *Vehicle(color)* before the constructor's body is executed.

Note that in the case of a member variable its initialisation uses the name of the member, whereas in the case of a base class the initialisation uses the base class name. The members are always initialised in declaration order, irrespective of the order they are given in an initialisation list; the

```
struct Vehicle {
    virtual void start ();
    void move ();
    colour painted;
    Vehicle ( colour c ) { painted = c; }
};

struct Garage {
    Vehicle v;
    void start ();
    Garage ( colour color ) {Vehicle v ( color ) }
                             // Does not set Garage::v.painted
};

struct Car : public Vehicle {
    void start ();                 // overrides Vehicle::start ()
    int passengers;
    Car ( colour color ) { Vehicle ( color ) } // Illegal C++

};
```

Figure 5.13   Initiating members and bases (the wrong way)

```
struct Vehicle {
    virtual void start ();
    void move ();
    colour painted;
    Vehicle ( colour c ) { painted = c; }
}
struct Car : public Vehicle {
    void start ();                    // overrides Vehicle::start ()
    int passengers;
    // Should be written as:
    Car ( colour color ) : Vehicle ( color ) { Passengers = 0; }
};
struct Garage {
    Vehicle v;
    void start ();
    // Should be written as:
        Garage ( colour color ) : v( color ) { Passengers = 0; }
};
```

- **Can only initialise immediate bases**

Figure 5.14   Initialising members and bases (the right way)

initialisations in a list are separated from each other by commas and introduced by a semicolon.

One is only allowed to initialise immediate base classes in a derived class' constructors; one is not allowed to initialise an indirect base class[1] in this way; they will have been initialised by their immediate descendants. This avoids the possibility of specifying multiple initialisations of a single base or member.

5.2.10   Multiple inheritance

Version 2.0 of C++ introduced support for multiple inheritance, i.e. the ability to derive a class from more than one base class as illustrated by figure 5.15, where the class *Hovercraft* is derived from both of the classes *Car* and *Ship*. This example also shows that it is possible for the same *indirect* base class to be inherited more than once; in this example objects of class *Hovercraft* will have two sub-objects of class *Vehicle*. It is illegal for a *direct* base class to occur more than once since references to its members would be ambiguous.

There can still be some ambiguity with multiple instances of the same indirect class but most of them can be resolved by explicit qualification, e.g. to access Vehicle::painted one must specify which sub-object is required, as shown in figure 5.16. In addition, figure 5.16 shows that converting the types of objects that can be pointed at in such situations has to be done with care.

---

[1]   An indirect base class is a base class that is higher up the inheritance tree than the immediate parent class.

```
class Vehicle { colour painted; /* ... */ };
class Car :  public Vehicle { int passengers; /* ... */ };
class Ship : public Vehicle { int tonnage ; /* ... */ };
class Hovercraft : public Car, public Ship { int i; /* ... */ };
```

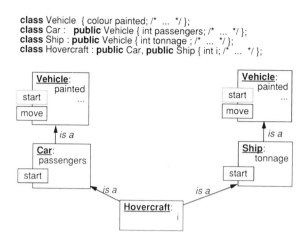

Figure 5.15   Multiple base classes

5.2.10.1   *Virtual base classes*

To avoid classes that are inherited more than once from creating multiple subobjects in the derived classes, C++ allows a base class to be defined as **virtual**, as in figure 5.17. This causes a single sub-object of the base class to be shared by every base class that specified the base class to be **virtual**. In figure 5.17, objects of the class *Hovercraft* only has one sub-object of class *Vehicle* whereas, without the use of virtual base classes there would be two as in figure 5.15.

An important aspect of multiple inheritance as compared to single inheritance is that classes within the inheritance network produced by multipleinheritance can share information without forcing that information towards

- **by qualification:**

Hovercraft::f() { if (Ship::painted == Car::painted) { // ...;};

- **casting between pointers in such situations has to be done with care:**

```
Hovercraft *pH = new Hovercraft;
Vehicle *pV = pH              // error: ambiguous
pV = (Vehicle *) pH           // error: ambiguous
pV = ( Vehicle *) (Car *) pH;   // OK since casting to Car's Vehicle
pH = ( Hovercraft *)( Car *)pV   // OK: casting to Hovercraft with Car's Vehicle
```

Figure 5.16   Accessing multiple base classes

```
class Vehicle { colour painted; /*  ...  */ };
class Car :  virtual public Vehicle { int passengers; /*  ...  */ };
class Ship : virtual public Vehicle { int tonnage ; /*  ...  */ };
class Hovercraft :  public Car, public Ship { int i; /*  ...  */ };
```

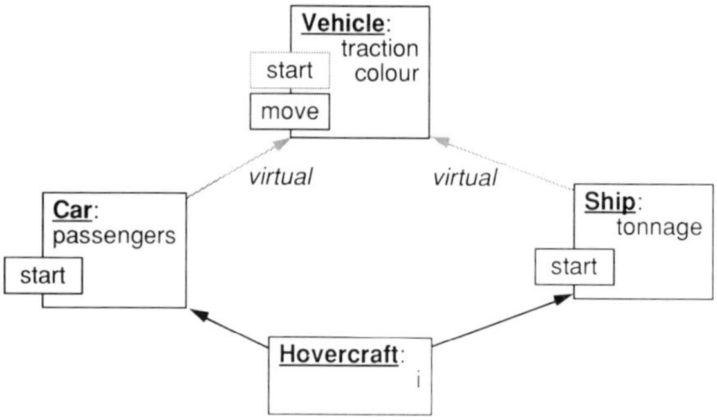

Figure 5.17   Virtual base classes

the single root of an inheritance tree. With multiple inheritance in general, and virtual base classes in particular, it is possible for sibling classes like *Car* and *Ship* to share information in a common base class like *Vehicle*, without affecting other classes in an inheritance lattice. This can overcome a problem with single inheritance systems whereby information that needs to be shared tends to drift towards the common root of the tree which acts as a pool of common, but often unrelated, properties.

A very powerful way to use multiple inheritance is to use an abstract class to define an interface and to combine it with a concrete[1] class which provides an implementation for that interface. For example, we could define an abstract class that provides an interface to a set of objects of type T which supports the notion of iteration over its elements:

```
class set {
public:
    virtual int insert( T*) =0;
    virtual int remove( T*) =0;
    virtual int is_member( T*) =0;
    virtual T* first() =0;
    virtual T* next() =0;
    virtual ~set() {}
};
```

---

[1]   A concrete class is the opposite of a abstract class. A concrete class provides an implementation of all its methods and objects of a concrete class are expected to be created.

We can then have several classes that provide alternative implementations for this interface, such as a single linked list class or an array class; these are the concrete classes.

Consider a **class** array that implements a fixed sized array of objects of type T:

```
class array {
    int size;                       // size of the array
    int last;                       // index of last element used
    T *vector;                      // pointer to array of integers
public:
    array (int n) { size = n; last = 0; vector = new T[n]; }  // construct array of given size
    ~array();                       // destructor
    array (const array&);           // copy constructor
        // ...
};
```

If this class was derived from **class** *set* then all the pure virtual functions of the base class would have an implementation in the derived class:

```
class array : public set{
    // as above
    int current_index;              // to support first() & next()
public:
    // as above
    int insert (T* t) { if (last == size) return 0; *vector[last++] = *t; return 1; }
    T *first() { current_index = 0; return next(); }
    // ... the other virtual functions
};
```

This way of providing an implementation for an abstract class is depicted on the left hand side of figure 5.18. This refinement of an abstract base class directly into an implementation class has several implications:

● the <u>implementation</u> in the derived class has to reflect the <u>interface</u> of the abstract class so that we now have two mechanisms intermingled,

● the implementation in the derived class may not be the most efficient for the concept supported by that class,

- the derived class is no longer reusable without its implementation of the base class.

These are overcome by defining the class *array* separately with its own implementation of appropriate member functions (including, for instance, the operator [ ]) and to use multiple inheritance to derive a new class, say array_set, from set and array:

```
class array_set : public set, private array {
    int current_index;
public:
    int insert (T *);
    int remove (T *);
    int is_member (T *);
    T * first() { current_index = 0; return next(); }
    T * next () { return vector[current_index]; }
    array_set (int s) : array (s), current_index (0) { }
};
```

This approach is depicted on the right hand side of figure 5.18. Note that the concrete class *array*, which provides the implementation, is a **private** base class so that none of the implementation details of the concrete class are accessible to the users of *array_set*. Now the concrete class *array* will have its

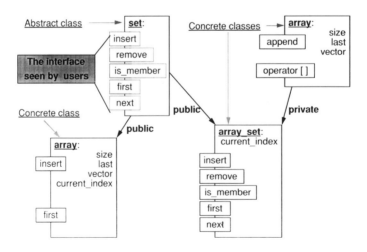

Figure 5.18   Abstract and concrete classes

own appropriate implementation, and the class can be reused to support other abstract classes such as an iterator, and also directly for efficiency. The users of the abstract base class need not be aware of the concrete class nor of the class derived from them both. In fact one could provide several derived classes without affecting, or recompiling users of the abstract base class.

This use of multiple inheritance is an elegant way to combine separately developed abstract base classes, that define an interface for a single concept, and concrete classes that provide efficient and particular implementations of specific mechanisms.

5.3 ADA

The Ada language was commissioned in the late 1970s by the United States Department of Defense (USDOD) to be their language of choice for realtime and embedded military computer systems. Three languages designs, known as Red, Green and Blue, were produced by separate design teams and subjected to extensive expert review from which the Green design emerged as the winner. This was refined and implemented and resulted in Ada being published as a standard, ANSI/MIL-STD-1815A, in 1983.

Ada made several significant contributions to the evolution of programming languages and to the software development environments in which they are used. It supports many of the facilities needed to allow good software engineering practices to be applied, and incorporates the concept of an Ada Programming Support Environment (APSE). The APSE manages inter-modules dependences through the use of an Ada Library System and provides a complete and self-contained software development environment which enhances the reliability, robustness and tracebility of software developed in Ada.

The Ada language incorporates support for:

- **encapsulation** through the use of Ada packages,

- **information hiding** with private and limited private data types. Instances of these data types can only be manipulated by the subprograms specified in the package that defines the private data type; an Ada private type is an abstract data type,

- **re-use** of generic subprograms and packages,

- **inheritance** through the definition of derived data types which, however, cannot have additional data properties, or modification of the existing data properties,

- **reliability** through the application of static type checking and constraint checking at runtime. The Ada Language provides support for realtime operations with its tasking primitives based on the concept of a rendezvous between two asynchronous threads of control within an Ada program.

5.3.1   Ada support for data abstraction

An Ada package construct constitutes a name scope in Ada. It controls the visibility of the names of a set of data types, subprograms (procedures and functions) and entities (program variables). An Ada package consists of two parts:

- **the package specification** which declares the names of the types, subprograms and objects which are to be visible to the users of the package; in the case of subprograms their signatures are also specified,

- **the package body** which contains the implementation logic of any subprograms or tasks made visible in the specification part. The body may also contain further declarations of types, subprograms, tasks, packages and entities that are needed to support the implementation of the visible interface; such details are hidden from the users of the package specification.

Ada allows subprogram names to be overloaded with signatures that have different types and/or numbers of parameters or return values, and allows default argument values to be supplied which the compiler will use when an argument is omitted. All the operators supported by Ada can also be overloaded except for the assignment operator (the := symbol), the inequality operator (the /= symbol) and the equality operator (the = symbol); the = operator can only be user-defined for limited private data types.

An Ada package can be used to define an abstract data type. The Ada form for an abstract data type for complex numbers is shown in figure 5.19 for which a number of characteristics, and differences from the form in C++, shown in figure 5.4, are described below. The Ada form has been written to provide the same functionality as the C++ form.

It is the Ada package that groups the operations (the procedures, functions and overloaded operators) with the data type on which they operate rather than the data type declaration itself, as in C++. This grouping is only enforced, in Ada, for data types which have been declared to be private or limited private. An Ada package may contain any number of declarations of types, subprograms and entities which need not be related or associated in any way other than they will all become visible when that package is made visible.

```
package Complex_Type is
    type complex is private;
    function becomes ( r : float; i : float := 0.0) return complex;
        pragma inline (becomes);
    function Real_Part (This : complex) return float;
    function "+" ( left, right : complex ) return complex;
    function "-" ( left, right : complex ) return complex;
    function "*" ( left, right : complex ) return complex;
    function "/" ( left, right : complex ) return complex;
    function "-" ( right : complex ) return complex;
private
    type complex is record
        re : float := 0.0;
        im : float := 0.0;
    end record;
end Complex_Type:
```

Figure 5.19   An Ada abstract data type

The characteristic of an Ada private data type is that its representation and composition is not accessible to users of the type. Instances (called entities in Ada) of a private type can only be manipulated through the operations that have been specified in the package that contains the definition of the private data type. The instances can be compared and copied just like basic data types because an equality and an assignment operation is automatically provided by Ada for every data type but these operations only support a bitwise, that is a "shallow", comparison and copy. These automatically supplied operations cannot be overriden by the implementor of a data type, as is the case with a C++ class.

An Ada data type has to be declared as limited private to inhibit the automatic support for equality and assignment of instances of a data type. An instance of a limited private data type can only be copied into, or compared with, another instance if the necessary operations have been specified and implemented by the package that declares the limited private data type. There is no default implementation that is automatically supplied by the Ada compiler, as is the case in C++. As indicated above, Ada does not allow the assignment operator to be overloaded so a user's implementation of this operation, for a limited private data type, has to be specified as a a named procedure. This means that instances of limited private types cannot be manipulated with the same degree of notational convenience as other kinds of Ada data.

The only mechanism in Ada that ensures that an entity is initialised when it is created is the provision of default values against the components of a record type declaration as has been done for the declaration of the record

```
package Date_Type is
    type Date is private;
    function A_Date (Text: String) return Date;
    function A_Date ( Year   : Years;
                      Month: Months;
                      Day   : Day_in_Month) return Date;
    function "-"  (Left : Date, Right: Days) return Date;
    function "+"  (Left : Date, Right: Days) return Date;
    function "-"  (Left, Right: Date) return Days;
    function "<=" (Left, Right: Date) return Boolean;
    function ">=" (Left, Right: Date) return Boolean;
    function "<"  (Left, Right: Date) return Boolean;
    function ">"  (Left, Right: Date) return Boolean;
    function Make_String (From : Date) return String;
private
-- ... representation of Date
end Date_Type;
```

Figure 5.20   Date as an Ada package

type *complex* in figure 5.19. Whilst functions can be declared which return values of a private type, of which the function *becomes* in figure 5.19 is an example, there is no mechanism in Ada, like constructors in C++, that can ensure that such functions are automatically associated with the creation of entities of the type. It is therefore quite possible, in Ada, for an instance of an abstract data type to be created in an undefined state and accessed before it has been initialised.

The abstract data type, Date, shown in figure 5.5 as a C++ class declaration, is shown in figure 5.20 as an Ada package specification as another example of the differences between the two languages.

5.3.2   Ada support for inheritance

Ada supports a form of inheritance, in that an Ada data type declaration can specify that the data type is derived from an existing data type. From the type *complex* declared in figure 5.19 a derived type, called Another_Complex_Type, could be declared, thus:

```
with Complex_Type;
package Example is
type Another_Complex_Type is new  Complex_Type.complex;
end Example;
```

An Ada derived type inherits all the operations declared for the base type and these may be redefined for the new type and additional operations

```
type A_Shape (kind_of_shape: shape_kind) is record
     case kind_of_shape is
     when CIRCLE          => A_Circle;
     when RECTANGLE   => A_Rectangle;
     // ...
     end case;
  end record;
  type shapes is array (positive <>) of A_Shape;
procedure draw_shapes (shape : shapes ) is
begin
     for I in shape'Range loop
         case shape (I).kind_of_shape is
         when CIRCLE =>
                 Draw (shape (I).A_Circle);
         when RECTANGLE =>
                 Draw (shape (I).A_Rectangle);
         // ...
         end case;
     end loop;
end draw_shapes;
```

Figure 5.21 Drawing an array of shapes in Ada

specified. However, if the base type is private the only way to implement any redefined or additional operations is through the use of the operations of the base type; there is no concept, in Ada, of protected access, as in C++.

It is not possible to specify new data properties for a derived type in Ada, and consequently, all types derived from a base type have exactly the same representation. Therefore, Ada allows any type in a derivation tree to be explicitly converted into any other type in the same derivation tree. The only form of implicit type conversion in Ada is between subtypes of a base type. An Ada subtype is either simply another name for a type or it imposes a constraint upon the set of values of the base type that may be used as values for the subtype.

Ada's support for inheritance cannot be used to capture generalised abstractions, as a base abstract data type, from which specialised or refined abstract data types can be derived, in the way that an object oriented class model requires. Neither does Ada support any form of dynamic binding or polymorphism.

The only way to implement, in Ada, the classic example of the interface to an array of shapes is shown in figure 5.21. This shows the essence of the Ada form of the traditional approach illustrated previously by the example in figure 5.10. If the set of shapes is extended, then both the variant record type *A_Shape* and the procedure *Draw_Shapes* have to be modified, to include the new type of shape, and recompiled. Both the data type and the procedure are dependent upon the representations for the type definitions of all the shapes which they are designed to process unless these types are private types which are implemented as Ada access types.

108

• **Ada supports:**	+ *Genericity*
	+ *Overloading (not completely)*
	+ *Static type checking*
	+ *Encapsulation*
	+ *Information Hiding*
• **BUT does not support:**	
• **Inheritance (fully)**	- no specialisation & refinement
• **Polymorphism**	- no dynamic code binding
	- subprograms not 1st class objects
• **enforced initialisation**	- unreliable
• **extensibility**	- fixed execution model
• **A complete typing model**	- no reference objects to static data

Figure 5.22   Ada: shortcomings for OOP

5.3.3   Ada support for object orientation

The limitations of Ada's inheritance model and its lack of support for polymorphism does not allow it to be used as an object oriented programming language. At best, Ada can be classified as an object-based language in that it does provide support for abstract data typing. A more complete list of the shortcomings of Ada as an object oriented programming language is given in figure 5.22.

It is unfortunate that a program design method based on the use of Ada is called Hierarchical Object Oriented Design (HOOD), as it causes confusion between its hierarchical decomposition of objects and the construction of truly object oriented class hierarchies which support abstractions through generalisations and specialisations.

The Ada 9X project is addressing the known shortcomings of Ada, and expects, at the time of writing, to define a new Ada Standard by 1994. It is to be hoped that Ada 9X will provide much better support for an object oriented approach for the development of realtime and embedded computer systems. It will be interesting to see whether the present investment in Ada-83 by Ada-based companies and the need for upwards compatibility will allow Ada 9X to become sufficiently object oriented to challenge other object oriented languages such as C++, which will have several years of widespread use and experience behind them by the time that Ada 9X hits the market place.

5.4   EIFFEL

Eiffel, supplied by Interactive Software Environments Inc., is a highly regarded rival to C++ which, as yet, has not achieved a significant degree of commercial acceptance. It uses C as an intermediate language, but the

```
deferred class   LIST[T]   export empty, present, insert,...

feature  present (x:T):BOOLEAN is do   -- present is a method of the class
                  from
                        if not empty then start end
                  until
                        finished or else found
                  loop
                        move
                  end;
                  Result := found

        end; -- present
  start is  require not empty  -- Pre-condition which must be true for feature to work
        deferred
           ensure position = 1  -- Post-condition which will be true on completion of the feature
        end; -- start
  position: INTEGER;
  -- Declarations for empty, found, over,...
  invariant                        -- Conditions which are always true for objects of the class
        empty implies finished;
        position >= 0; position <= size + 1
end  -- class LIST
```

Figure 5.23   Eiffel: sample code

syntax of Eiffel itself is completely different from that of C, as can be seen from figure 5.23, which lists a short piece of Eiffel code.

Efficiency is stated as one of the principal design objectives of Eiffel, but not to the extent that the essential object oriented concepts are compromised. It is a statically typed language like C++, but all objects are created on the heap at runtime and the use of this memory is managed by an automatic garbage collector, as described in Section 4.11. This is a major differences from C++, in which efficiency is a major objective of its design and object orientation is subsidiary to this objective. In this sense, Eiffel is a pure object oriented programming language which ensures that everything must consist of classes, objects and methods.

Eiffel development tools and compilation techniques are comprehensive and flexible and encapsulation is well handled with mandatory hiding of data.

5.4.1   Pre- and post-conditions and invariants

One of the more novel features of Eiffel is its support for the concept of a "contract" between the supplier of a class and the user of a class. The supplier, or implementor, of a class is able to specify, as part of the class's definition in the Eiffel language, under which conditions objects of the class will behave correctly. These conditions are expressed, in Eiffel, in the form of:

- Pre-conditions that must be satisfied <u>before</u> a method is invoked,

- Post-conditions that are guaranteed to hold <u>after</u> a method has executed,

- Invariants that are <u>always</u> true for all instances of a class.

The "contract" between the supplier and the user of a class expects that:

- the <u>user</u> of a class will ensure that the pre-conditions on a method are satisfied before the method is invoked. This allows the implementation of the method to assume that its pre-conditions are satisfied so that logic to verify the pre-conditions need not be included in the method.

- the <u>supplier</u> of the class will guarantee that the post-conditions are satisfied after the method has been applied. This allows the user of the method to assume that the method has behaved as expected so that the user does not need to include logic to cater for the possibility of erroneous behaviour by the method.

The Eiffel language system can check, during system development, that these assumptions about the characteristics of a class and its methods are satisfied. The checks are applied by automatically incorporating code, into the system under development, which tests whether the pre-conditions, post-conditions and invariants are true and, if not, reports the failure to the programme developer.

Examples of the use of pre-conditions, post-conditions and invariants are illustrated by the piece of sample Eiffel source code in figure 5.23. The method called *start* has a pre-condition, introduced by the word **require**, which states that the object must not be *empty* when the the *start* method is called. This method also has a post-condition, introduced by the word **ensure**, which states that *position* will always to equal to 1 after the *start* method has been applied. The invariants for a class are given after the word **invariant** at the end of a class's definition. In figure 5.23, the invariants state that if the method *empty* is true then so is the method *finished*; also, the value of *position* is always between zero and one more than the value of *size*.

It is possible to provide similar facilities in languages that do not <u>support</u> them as language features, but it could only be done by a disciplined use of special conventions. The benefit of Eiffel's built-in support for pre-conditions, post-conditions and invariants is that their use becomes an integral part a class's definition in Eiffel and an integral part of the documentation of the class which can be automatically produced, processed and verified by the language system.

5.5 SUMMARY

This chapter has shown how all OOPLs have evolved from Simula into:

- statically or dynamically type languages,
- pure, or hybrid, object oriented languages.

The hybrid language C++ has been described in some depth because of:

- the extensive range of mechanisms it supports,
- its flexibility and concern for efficiency,
- its breadth of applicability and extensive adoption as an object oriented language.

The Ada language has been shown to lack some of the features needed by a fully object oriented language to support the evolution of a software system by addition rather than by modification.

Eiffel's support for pre-conditions, post-conditions and invariants were described as valuable additions to an object oriented language that add rigour and documentation to systems implemented in this language.

6

OBJECT ORIENTED STRUCTURED DESIGN METHODS AND TECHNIQUES

There are various "battles" occurring in the structured methods market place for object oriented information modelling, and in the techniques to be used for modelling information in an object oriented way. The leading methods are assessed, as are the best techniques for object oriented information modelling. It will be seen that none of the new methods claiming to be object oriented are particularly impressive, all suffering from substantial sins of omission and commission.

Unlike these structured methods the authors have developed objectively based rules for the building of a class model and for the normalisation of logic to the classes in the class model. The rules are described in detail, with worked examples.

6.1 THE CURRENT POSITION

Currently there is no widely used structured method for the logical and physical design of application systems in an object oriented way. New methods specifically developed for object oriented analysis and design are appearing on the marketplace, such as those by Booch (1991), Schlaer/Mellor (1992) and Coad/Yourdon (1990). Certain other methods have been developed for a specialist part of the object oriented market, such as HOOD for realtime systems using the Ada programming language. But there has been no general or widespread market penetration of these new products.

All the new structured methods the authors have seen are, in their view, significantly deficient. This is not surprising given that the development of such object oriented methods is in its early stages. Even the long established structured design methods for "conventional" systems by no means get "10 out of 10". And reflecting this early and incomplete state of affairs, the requirements for logical and physical object oriented design and development techniques described in this chapter do not address all issues.

The book describes a set of extremely good and proven in practice object oriented design techniques that could well be used for the development of an excellent object oriented structured design method and would get high marks out of 10, but not a total score. This book takes the science of object oriented information modelling further forward by:

- filling in most of the missing gaps, such as the logic that remains at the event level;
- most importantly, basing the information modelling on a set of mechanistically applied and objectively based rules.

There are still gaps which the authors fully acknowledge. There is, for example, no understanding yet of how the physical facilities function name and operator overloadings can be used for the logical modelling of information in an object oriented way.

6.2   THE "BATTLES"

There is a series of battles taking place over the development of structured methods for object oriented design and development.

Which approach should be used—new structured methods or enhancements to the existing methods?   Just as there are specialist vendors of object oriented programming languages and file handlers, so there are specialist developers of object oriented structured design and development methods. Such methods include those mentioned above, but there are also long established existing structured methods for batch and online centralised processing, and for real-time systems, that are widely used. These methods include SSADM, Information Engineering, MERISE and Yourdon, these being the leading methods in terms of market penetration.

Most of the vendors of these leading structured methods have announced object oriented enhancements to their products.   Clear statements of direction have been made by the vendors of Information Engineering and MERISE regarding the early enhancement to support object oriented design, but there is no such position regarding the SSADM method in the United

Kingdom. A large question mark hangs over the SSADM. The design "ownership" of the method belongs to the CCTA department of the UK Government Treasury, but the significant fundings for the development of the method are stopping, such that the announcements for major developments of the method with broad timetables, including the enhancement to be object oriented, have been withdrawn. Indeed, there are rumours that the CCTA is passing the ownership of SSADM to the User Group for them to plan the method's future and raise the funds necessary to develop the method to be object oriented. The future development of SSADM is currently very unclear.

Given:

- the poor techniques of the new object oriented structured method;

- the rigorous rule based approach described in this book with the rules applied to the key based data and event based logic paradigms used by the long established "traditional" structured methods;

there is much to be said for applying the traditional methods and then adding on object orientation by applying the OO information modelling rules. That is the approach advocated in this book.

Which approach to object oriented information modelling should be used?

- build the information model in an object oriented manner from the outset. To do this there are two approaches:
  — just identify the methods[1] of the classes that require to be invoked and link them at run time through the sending of messages, this being one of the approaches for class modelling. There are no fixed relationships between the classes.

    Structured methods of this type do not require to be as sophisticated as the other approaches—there is, for example, no need to build an object model of the static relationship between classes as the relationships are established at run time. This has been the approach of the developers of the HOOD (Hierarchical Object Oriented Design) method.
  — build a class model followed by the other object oriented information modelling techniques, such as object state modelling.

    This is the approach used by such methods as Shlear/Mellor, Rumbaugh *et al.* and Coad/Yourdon.

---

[1] It is unfortunate that the term methods has two meanings—a structured design and development method and logic process (methods) normalised to object classes. Both terms will be used in the chapter without explanation, the context in which the term is being used defining which meaning is intended

- enhance the existing structured methods originally developed for batch and online processing and then apply the object oriented   information modelling rules described in this book to convert key based data and event based logic of the traditional logical designs into an object oriented design.

Should one migrate immediately to the new methods or wait for the existing methods to be enhanced to support object orientation?
It is certain that the enhancement of existing structured methods to be object oriented will be the approach that ultimately dominates object oriented design techniques. In the long run the early established object oriented structured methods will be "ground into powder" by the long established but object oriented enhanced traditional methods. The reasons for this are:

- there is no way the current vendors of structured methods are going to surrender the methods marketplace to the new object oriented entrants;

- there is no way that the users of these existing methods and their supporting CASE tools are going to throw away all their skills and experiences of the methods. They will wait for the methods to be enhanced;

- object orientation is an extension of existing technology (see Chapters 1 and 2), and that what is true of the technology is also true of the design techniques. Enhancement of the structured methods is by extension, by addition to the existing techniques, rather than their modification. The object oriented information modelling rules of this book follow this principle.

It is not necessary to throw away existing skills in existing structured methods—keep the skills and the structured methods and add object orientation to them.

Method/process driven or data driven?   This issue is the same as that argued over when the current structured methods were being developed. For these methods the question is should one identify the business processes of the application first and from this ascertain the data items required to support the process, and from this build the logical data model? Or should one identify the "things" of interest to the application, the "things" being entities about which data can be recorded, from this build the logical data model, match the business requirements against the model to ensure the model supports the requirements and then specify the logic of the processes that support the requirements?
   The same question is valid for object oriented design. Should one identify the object classes and their relationships via the sending of messages between the methods and bind the data objects to the methods at runtime (the process driven approach) or model the class model, identify the business requirements, normalise the logic of the business requirements into

methods, and from this model the object oriented application programs (the data driven approach)?

It is probable that the data driven approach will be adopted most widely. One can see this with the object oriented enhancements to Information Engineering and MERISE, and with the ease with which SSADM can be made object oriented. And many of the emerging methods, such as Coad/Yourdon, are data driven. The reason is not just the inertia from the existing techniques, but because of the inherent soundness of the approach:

- identify the classes and then normalise the data and logic properties to them. The classes and their relationship have to be modelled, otherwise it is not possible to normalise the data or logic. *The object oriented concept of the normalisation of information requires the data driven approach.*

- there are fixed relationships between the classes of an application system. The approach adopted whereby classes are standalone, with the relationships between the class objects established only at runtime by the sending of messages (the HOOD approach), ignores the fact that there are fixed relationships between class objects (Orders always relate to Customer, for example).

Building the process model first and then identifying the data properties required to support the processes is a valid approach (it works), but it cannot be the basis of the normalisation of information without having to adopt an iterative approach, build the process model and from this the class model, and then normalise the processes to the model. It is the wrong way around for most business applications.

The process driven approach is useful for realtime applications that use less persistent and much transient data.

At a seminar given recently by one of the authors, the benefits of the data driven approach was put forward and it was noisily argued against by one of the delegates. I totally disagree with your argument! We regard all objects as standalone features that directly match those "things as perceived by the users (no problems with this) which we link with messages when we prototype the methods". And that's it.

But that's fine for the definition of the objects and their processing when the application program runs, but what about the creation and maintenance of the objectbase, referential integrity, the semantic description of the relationships, and the state of the objects so that you can test the state as pre- and post-conditions? What do you mean? asked the delegate. It eventually emerged that they were still in the prototyping and testing stage, and were entering discussions with the objectbase designer. He was asking questions about the messages and the keys of the objects and using these to model the fixed relationships between the objects, ascertaining any commonality of the data properties and from this modelling any further class abstractions. So the objectbase designer does recognise that there are fixed relationships between the classes that can only be ascertained by the data driven approach, the formal modelling of the class object model. No answer. Might not the objectbase designer identify commonality in a way that is not perceived by the user and from this abstract additional classes? No answer. How can you normalise the logic to the object classes without having a class model? No answer. With the data driven appproach the sequence is:

— build the traditional logical data model and identify the business requirements and the events

— apply the class data abstraction rules, to build the class hierarchies

— apply the rule of the role of the data to the role of the object class

— apply the rules of logic normalisation to third normal form to model aggregation abstraction and build aggregation hierarchies

— apply the other techniques of object oriented information modelling.

There is no question that ultimately one has to recognise the soundness of the data driven approach. The process driven approach is fine for prototyping, but the full application of the data driven approach is required for the full implementation of an object oriented application system.

"Top Down" or "Bottom Up"   The traditional approach has been top-down analysis and design—start by high level identification of data and process requirements, even in the information system strategy stage, and progressively decompose both into more and more precise detail as one progresses through the various stages of the structured method—the so-called "Waterfall Approach". The problem with this approach is that there is no concept of information reuse built into the structure of the stages, tasks, techniques and products. The bottom-up approach is tailor-made for object orientation—construct as much of the required system from the objects of the current system, and where they are deficient in data or processing add both as sub-classes onto the objects of the current system. The information requirements for and testing of the system required can be undertaken by prototyping, which, as discussed in Chapter 7, is also ideally supported by object oriented technology. However, the problem with the bottom-up approach is that there is no concept of ensuring that the information requirements are based on the business objectives of the company.

The likely future structured methods scenario is a blend of the top-down approach to the completion of the analysis stage and the use of the bottom-up approach for the design and the construction stages.

Add object orientation to the back end of the existing methods or integrate object orientation into the methods   The basis of the addition approach is that the user thinks in terms of key-based entities and event-based processing, this being the information modelling paradigm used by the existing structured design methods. They think in terms of Customers (with the key of Customer Number) and Orders (Order Number) and events/business requirements such as Create Customer, Mark Customer as Non-Credit-Worthy, Accept Order, Close Order. And they will continue to think in this way, object orientation or no object orientation—that is the way they run their business.

The "conventional" information technology of today's database file handlers and programming languages have recognised this fact and are also based on keys for the data and events for the programs. And object orientation needs to do the same or it will not be accepted. Chapters 2 and 3 show that object oriented technology includes information modelling facilities that the users do not use in the running of their business, such as the facilities of class behaviour, and the normalisation of logic to identify aggregation. They are not interested that Employees and Brokers have common behaviour— Employees and Brokers are considered as separate entities performing different business functions such as getting promoted and brokering a deal. The fact that some clever information modellers are able to abstract common data and logic information is fine if that helps the systems design, development and maintenance process, but let me, the user, still think in terms of Employees and Brokers. You designers design your object oriented system, but I will continue with my user allocated keys and user triggered business events.

It so happens that object orientation has not abandoned keys for the data and events for the logic. Classes that represent Employees and Brokers still have keys, and there are still object oriented application programs for accepting and closing an order. The crucial thing is that the object oriented facilities are added to the underlying technology of yesteryear—there is nothing wrong with it.

Given this object oriented "add to" technical relationship with "old" but valid technology, the question of should this be the approach for the design techniques for object oriented information modelling arises. Why not continue to apply the standard techniques used by traditional structured design methods and then convert them to object orientation by adding the object oriented modelling facilities? Why not build a logical data model and then identify class and aggregation properties, and from this abstract new super and sub classes as appropriate. This is the approach the authors have used on a number of object oriented design projects. The benefits gained from this approach are that:

- a comparison of the logical data model with the class model can be most informative, as the greater the degree of difference the greater the benefits offered by object orientation;

- the skills of users of existing structured design methods are wholly preserved;

- users participating in the logical design will use techniques and produce deliverables that are only based on keys and events. They will not have to learn concepts and design techniques that are irrelevant to the running of the business;

- experienced specialists in object oriented design can undertake the conversion process to object orientation.

These benefits are not minor.

The alternative approach is the use of object oriented design techniques from the beginning of the logical design process. This is the approach used by the new specialist object oriented design methods and, when the existing traditional methods are enhanced to object orientation, by these methods. The tide of development is moving, perhaps inevitably, to this approach, possibly without thinking about the impact on the user participating in the design process.

6.3   NEW OBJECT ORIENTED METHODS

It is inevitable that new structured methods specifically tailored for the object oriented environment would appear. There is an increasing number of them, the leading ones being Booch (1991), Shlaer and Mellor (1992), Rumbaugh *et al.* (1991), HOOD and Coad and Yourdon (1990). A few initial comments can be made about them, with a brief assessment of each method.

6.3.1   Initial comments

The non-method specific comments are:

- *Disappointment*
  All the methods have significant sins of omission and commission. There is an excuse for this given the early state of the development of object oriented structured methods and the issues of object oriented information modelling still to be resolved. It is to be hoped that when the long established traditional structured methods of SSADM, Information Engineering

and MERISE are enhanced to support object orientation, that the sins of omision are not present. Given the much better understanding of the requirements of object oriented information modelling, it is to be hoped that the sins of omission will be progressively omitted. Examples of this better understanding include that described in this book, such as the rules for class and aggregation abstraction, the event process modelling and polymorphic modelling.

The sins of omission are:

— None of the methods have any rules for the identification of classes or for the class and aggregation abstraction of information from the initially based key based entities. The best that is offered is guidance with examples. These rules are defined in Section 6.4.3.2.

— None of the methods have any rules for the normalisation of logic to the object classes. These rules are defined in Section 6.4.4.2.

— None of the methods have any techniques for object oriented dialogue design. How to do this is described in Section 6.4.9.

— None of the methods have any advice on the different object messaging strategies, and which of the strategies is based on good object oriented design principles. This described in Section 6.4.11.

— None of the methods show how to model polymorphism or genericity.

— Some of the methods (Booch, for example) contain no advice on objectbase design.

— Most seriously of all, none of the methods have any serious techniques for the modelling of event processing in an object oriented way. This technique is the basis of object oriented application program design.

This is a substantial list of omissions.

The sins of commission are:

The use of the widely applied state transition diagramming technique for the modelling of object states is, in the authors' opinion, inadequate.

State transition diagrams were developed for the realtime requirement to synchronise synchronous events, that is events to which the computer system responds as the event occurs, hence the term realtime. There is a need to bring order out of chaos when the synchronous events do not occur in the sequence in which they should, and for which the computer system is designed. For example, a synchronous event is the monitoring of radar returns as the radar aerial rotates. Assume that the correct order is that an aircraft appears on the radar screen in a flying condition. The next event is that the aircraft prepares to land, and not take off. If the take off event occurs next it needs to be corrected.

These are synchronous events, for which the simplistic state transition diagramming technique is fine.

The problem is that non-realtime systems, such as administrative applications for the commercial marketplace, deal with asynchronous events, that is is events occur and the computer system deals with them later, perhaps one second later or a few hours or days later. An order is received in the post or by telephone and is entered into the computer system one minute later with online processing, or a few hours later with batch processing. The life of asynchronous events can be much more complicated. The order of the events as far as the computer system is concerned could be completely non-rational (so could realtime systems, the authors hear being muttered by readers who like the STDs), events can be totally random and the events can process differently depending upon the iteration in the total iteration cycle, to mention but some of the added complexities (that snookered you devotees of the STD technique). There is no doubt that the STD technique could be enhanced to support these requirements, but the STD technique as described in the manuals of the above methods is not able to support the requirements of the object states in the non-realtime market place.

It also needs to be realised that there are two states to model. The methods named above define an object state as the data properties of the objects together being in a specified set of values. The state of the aircraft object taking off is that its data properties are that the engines are running at "full blast", the flaps are "lowered" and the pilot is "awake". That's fine for realtime systems.

But it is not adequate for online and batch systems. When an order is received one cannot state that the values of the invoice data properties are to be such and such values. The Received Date of the order could be any date value, the Product on Order could be any value and the Delivery Address could be any value.

For this requirement one needs to add a state variable to the object, the value of which is appropriate to the last event that changed the object. How to do this is discussed in Section 6.4.6. The state transition diagram has no concept of a state indicator—its state indicator is the value set of the attribute set for a given object state. Something quite different.

- *Narrow focus*
  The first three named methods are extensions of the Yourdon method developed for the realtime market.

6.3.2   Hierarchical object oriented design (HOOD)

HOOD has evolved from the work done by CISI Ingénrie and Matra Espace for the European Space Agency, and was tailored for realtime object based systems using the Ada programming language. This limits its general applicability and its object orientedness. It was released in 1988, and being first on the market it obtained an early lead in penetration.

The method is a process driven one, with processes being decomposed until the methods for the classes can be established. The relationships between the classes is established by sending messages to the classes to be acccessed in support of the business requirement at runtime. There is no technique in the method for establishing the fixed relationships between the classes. There is therefore no technique for building class models, and from this establishing whether the relationships are class, aggregation or business. There is thus no modelling mechanism for establishing property inheritance/information reusability.

The diagramming notation for the object is given in figure 6.1. It can be seen that the object diagram includes a portion to contain operations of a method as well as the messages that are passed to the methods of the other objects. It must be appreciated that HOOD models the method to be invoked for a given event/business requirement, so that only the methods relevant to the event/business requirement for the class object being messaged is modelled. The class, if it contains user data in reality may, probably will, have n attached methods. What is being modelled is the runtime structure of the class methods being messaged from the event level class containing the logic specific to the triggered business requirement.

This can be seen in figure 6.2. The arrows represent the messages being sent from the event level class object to the other methods in the classes containing the methods to be invoked in support of an event/business requirement.

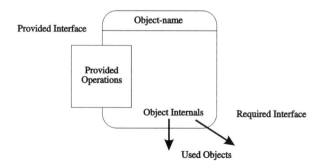

Figure 6.1   HOOD object notation

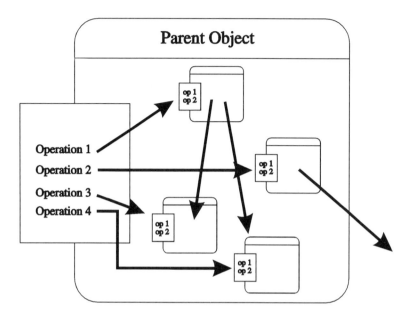

Figure 6.2 HOOD structure of a business process

This process modelling has a number of deficiencies in addition to the general failures of the new methods detailed above. It has no techniques for modelling or advice on:

- class models;
- object state models.

Of the "big three" of the object oriented information modelling techniques (see section 6.4.1) HOOD only really supports the event process modelling, although there is no concept of central policeman messaging.

It has been said, perhaps unkindly, that the only thing that is object oriented about the method is what is between the H and the D.

6.3.3   Shlaer/Mellor

This method is an extension of the Yourdon method, and is heavily oriented to realtime applications.

Many of the design products are specifically for realtime rather than object orientation—for example the Object Communication Model is for asynchronous event communication, and the Object Access Model is for synchronous event communication. The Timer and the Threads of Control are also for realtime. Given their non-relevance to object orientation they are not discussed.

A particularly attractive feature of the method is the facility of the domain. This is not the relational domain of a data property having a value range. A Shlaer/Mellor domain is based on the idea that there are groups of information objects which are not related to each other. An example of this could be the object classes about windows (buttons, sliders, canvas). These classes have nothing to do with the classes of the invoicing domain (purchase orders, products, customers and invoice). One produces all the design deliverables for each of the domains.

The method is able to support the building of only two of the three main design deliverables of object orientation—the class model (the Information Model) and the object state model (the State Model with an Action DFD for each of the states). There is no event process model.

The method has all the general deficiencies detailed above.

One of the authors has recently been advising a client on the use of the method. Substantial changes and improvement have been required. The main ones were:

- the inclusion of "has a" relationships between objects—the information model does not include aggregation;

- the need for the Event Process Models. The method contains no technique for the modeling of event level logic and the sending of messages to other objects that require to be accessed for the event/business requirement.

- the inclusion of rules for class and aggregation abstraction and the normalisation of logic;

- the modelling of polymorphism and genericity;

- advice on the messaging strategies.

A large question mark as to the usefulness of the Action Dataflow Diagrams:

- To say that they are Dataflow Diagrams is a complete misnomer; There is virtually no data flow, as the diagrams are modelled on a single object based datastore and then only for one state change of the object class.

- The level of process decomposition is too low and is inconsistent. The action processes are to the lowest level of detail of any structured design method the authors have ever seen. First of all, the processes are at the operation level so that they are not really processes merely logic statements: for example, they contain condition and iterative logic—and proper dataflow diagrams are not designed to show logic, merely processes that pass data between each other. If one studies the action processes sometimes they are a single operation of logic "Set Status = "controlling" (Figure 6.2.7/TR.9)(see book references below), sometimes they contain condition logic "Determine if hot enough" (Figure 6.2.7/TR.10) and sometimes they contain whole processes which, when modelled to the same level of detail as the two previous action processes, will contain many operations, such as Create Temperature Ramp (Figure 6.2.4/TR.1). There is therefore no consistency in the action processes. *What the Action DFDs have become is logic flow diagrams, not dataflow diagrams.*

- This level of processing detail goes beyond the normalisation of logic to the classes, the level required for object oriented design. The *n* actions in the Action Dataflow Diagrams are all to one class based datastore, so the logic for the state change is already in third normal form. There is no need to have *n* action processes for one class based datastore. Object oriented design does not need modelling to the even lower level of detail modelled in the Action DFDs.

- There are aspects of bad object oriented design in the examples of Action Dataflow Diagrams. Consider diagram 6.2.4 of their book "Object LifeCycles—Modelling the World in States" Yourdon Press 1992). The object being supported is the Temperature Ramp. The diagrams contains actions that require access to other classes. The actions for the Temperature Ramp therefore contain logic pertinent to other classes The actions require to know about the information contained in the other objects. This breaks object oriented information hiding, encapsulation, where one class based process knows nothing of the information contained in other classes.

- What new information does the Action Dataflow Diagram give us? There is a heavy degree of duplication of modelled information between the Object State Models and the Action DFDs. This can be seen in figures 6.2.2 and 6.2.4 where the logic for state 1 of the Temperature Ramp is defined in the Object State Model *and* the Action DFD. The Object State Model defines the logic as textual operations, whereas the Action DFD merely draws the same logic operations as bubbles. For example, the OSM operation 1 = Action DFD action TR1, 2 = TIM3, 3 = TR4 and so on. There seems to be total duplication.

It was decided to not use the Action Dataflow Diagramming technique on the project.

6.3.4   Rumbaugh et al.

This method is also an object oriented extension of the Yourdon method, and oriented to realtime applications.

The method can support the building of the three main design deliverables of object orientation—class object model (the Object Model), the object state model (the Dynamic Model) and, to some degree, the event process model (the Functional Model).

The Object Model is particularly sweet. Not only does it model the three types of relationships between classes but it also models the fact that there is class sitting on top of keys—that is, that underneath the class model there is a traditional data model with key-based entities/objects and one-to-many cardinalities between the objects. The other methods do this but through the use of textual explanation. An example of a Rumbaugh class model is illustrated in figure 6.3 The triangle shows the "is a" generalisation class relationship, the diamond the "has a" aggregation composition relationship, with the absence of either notation showing the standard free form association relationship. The black ball indicates a one-to-many cardinality relationship—the absence of the ball a one-to-one relationship.

The Dynamic Model is based on the state transistion diagramming, but in nested form—a given state can itself be composed on n states. This does not solve the deficiencies of the technique.

The Function Model is based on dataflow diagramming, a somewhat old fashioned way of modelling the processing of a system and one that does not show the sequence of messaging between classes for an event/business

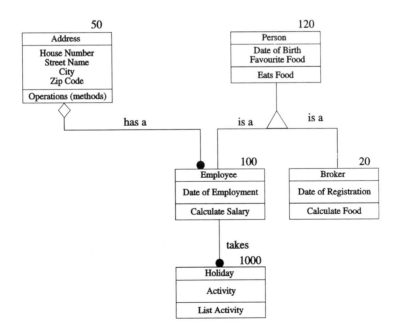

Figure 6.3   Rumbaugh object model

requirement, unless the processes are nicely normalised as methods to the class and aggregation objects. Advice as to ensuring this is not provided.

The method has all the general deficiencies detailed above.

6.3.5 Booch

This method is also an object oriented extension of the Yourdon method and oriented to realtime applications.

The method can support building of the three main design deliverables of object orientation logical information modelling—class model (the Class Diagrams—static semantics), the object state model (the State Transition Diagrams) and, to some degree, the event process model (Object Diagrams—dynamic semantics).

The physical design of programs is included in the Module Diagrams, with the allocation of processes to processor modelled in the Process Diagrams. The requirements of realtime are included in the use of the Timing Diagrams. There is no advice as to objectbase design.

The Class Diagram has an unusual notation in that the classes are modelled in the form of clouds.

The method has all the general deficiencies detailed above.

6.3.6 Coad/Yourdon

This method is not designed for realtime applications, and is not an

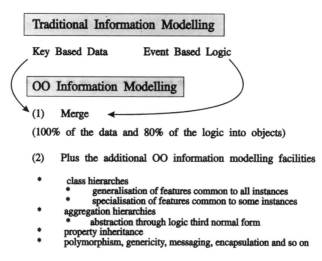

Figure 6.4 Object Oriented information modelling

extension of the Yourdon method, in spite of the authorship.

The method is not able to support building of the three main design deliverables of object orientation logical information modelling. In a sequence of five layers it supports the building of the class model (first three layers) and its populating with data (attribute layer) and logic properties (service layer), and also relates the objects together by the sending of messages, this being a sort of halfway house for the event process model, but there is no relating of the messages to the events/business requirements in model form. There is also no technique for modelling the states of objects.

The method has all the general deficiencies detailed above and in the authors' opinion, is the weakest of the methods reviewed.

6.4   STRUCTURED DESIGN IN AN OBJECT ORIENTED ENVIRONMENT

What is described here is not an object oriented structured method but a set of techniques that an object oriented structured method will have to use, along with the rules for object oriented information modelling. In line with the fact that object oriented technology is a set of added facilities to existing file handler and programming technologies, so it is with the design techniques. All the design techniques have been taken from traditional structured methods, principally SSADM version 4 and Information Engineering. It will be shown that it is easy to add the requirements of object oriented information modelling to the techniques used by the long established "traditional" structured design methods. This is particularly the case with the techniques of SSADM as version 4 is already beautifully object-based. Add such facilities as class and inheritance and you are virtually there. There is very little change, almost all of it is one of addition.

The basic approach to be adopted is illustrated in figure 6.4. This shows that, in line with the traditional separation of data from logic, the object oriented design techniques are based on key-based data and event-based logic. Everything concerning object oriented information design ultimately hangs from these two features of current information design.

With object orientation there is the underlying concept of the normalisation of information (both data and logic). This concept underlies all the object oriented infor-mation modelling techniques. The separation of data and logic is still preserved in the techniques but, with the additions to the techniques to cater for the normalisation of logic as well as data, the result is that the logic is modelled to the object class to which it "sensibly" belongs, just as for the data. There is thus a normalised merging of 100% of the data and some 80% of the logic to the class-, aggregation- and key-based objects to form a common object oriented information-base.

6.4.1 The base situation

The authors believe that three information modelling techniques and their derivatives will dominate the logical design and physical development of object oriented application systems. The techniques are extensions of existing techniques long used in a variety of current structured methods. All the leading methods of SSADM, Information Engineering and MERISE use variations of the techniques detailed in this chapter. They are:

- *the object class model*
  This is based on the traditional binary logical data model but with the additions of class and aggregation abstractions, property inheritance, the three types of relationship semantics and property instantiation of abstract objects.

  The model shows the classes, their fixed relationships, the level of abstraction from the most general to the most particular, the type of the relationship between the class objects with the "is a", the "has a" and the free form semantics, class and aggregation property inheritance, the methods to the classes containing user data and the method only class[1].

  There is a battle for the modelling of object oriented logic. The two leading modelling techniques are the Jackson model and action diagraming. Both are perfectly valid and, as will be shown, it is very easy to convert a Jackson model into an action diagram, and *vice versa*. The authors firmly believe that the Jackson modelling technique will win the day—it is beautifully object based, it is diagrammatic, making it easier to understand, with the diagram of itself containing design information, and the definition of the operations on the diagram makes it easier to identify commonality of operations across potential class methods, and from this the need to generalise the common logic as a super-class common procedure containing the generalised logic. The Jackson approach is therefore used for the modelling and specification of object oriented logic. The techniques and the deliverables for logic are:

- *the object state model*
  This is based on the Entity Life History (ELH) technique used in SSADM, but with the addition of the logic operations of the methods.

  The model shows the methods that update the object instances, the state of the object instance prior to and following the execution of a method that changes the state of the object instance and the sequence in which the methods need to be invoked during the life of each object instance, the operations of the methods and the generalisation that can be achieved from common operations in the methods.

---

[1] The binary data model is much more popular than the n-array data model developed by P. Chen and used by such methods as Shlaer/Mellor.

- *the event process model*
  This model is based on the Process Model technique used in SSADM.
  The model shows the methods that have to have messages sent to them from the event level class, the sequence in which the messages need to be sent, the logic of each of the invoked methods to which the messages are sent, and any commonality of the operations in the methods that enable further generalisations of the logic to be modelled as a super class common procedure. The model builds the structure of object oriented application programs.

This technique is not supported by any of the current object oriented structured design methods. It is a major omission.

The Jackson modelling approach is also the basis of modelling other parts of the object oriented logical design requirements, specifically the Human/Computer Interface (HCI):

- *the menu and dialogue models*
  It is extremely easy to model the HCI screens and the processing that is associated with the screens. This screen processing becomes method only abstract classes for the HCI in the class model.

6.4.2 The class model

The facilities that are modelled in a class model are:

- object classes (containing user data and methods and method only abstract classes);

- abstract classes (classes with no instances);

- class abstraction (common behaviour between objects);

- aggregation abstraction (complex objects broken down into their individual properties)

- class and aggregation property inheritance hierarchies;

- the three types of relationship between the objects—the "is a" for class inheritance, the "has a" for aggregation inheritance and the free form for the business relationships and no inheritance;

- the methods (logic properties) in the classes.

The model is structured on the basis that information at the top of the model is more general (super-class generalisation) than information at the bottom (sub-class specialisation). The Company class in figure 2.21 is more general than the Star Bonus class.

This deliverable is mandatory for object oriented design.

6.4.3 Building the class model

The class model is to object orientation what the logical data model is to current database technology. But the class model is more than this, as it also models the structure of the application and systems logic. The processing logic of the application is normalised as appropriate to the classes containing user data, and the system processes are also included in the building of the class model.

The basic approach of this technique is to build a logical data model, as done with current structured design methods, and from this to extend the model through abstraction to include object oriented features. The merits of this approach are its objective starting point and mechanistically produced, and hence objectively based, finishing point, the class model. This is not like the guidance by example approach of other object oriented structured methods. The objective starting points are the key to the entities, to which are applied mechanistic rules of class and aggregation abstraction. The result is a correctly designed class model: nothing "wishy washy" here. The approach is data driven so as to conform with the requirements of the object oriented concept of information normalisation.

The tasks for this technique are:

- build the logical data model of the key based entities;

- identify class and from this any class objects with common behaviour of the data properties to be abstracted from the key based entities of the logical data model. Identify any additional class objects containing only methods;

- abstract the data properties that need generalisation for the aggregation modelling of complex objects;

- define the class, aggregation and free form semantics as appropriate to the relationships between the classes;

- define the data properties for each of the classes and instantiate those with a value if the value is applicable to all instances of the class;

- add the event/business requirement classes;

- add common procedures and the human/computer interface classes;

- add the Class Libraries.

There is a school of thought that believes that the first step is not required and that one should build a class model from the beginning. The problem with this line of reasoning is that it is not possible to apply the rules of abstraction unless one has key-based entities of a logical data model from which to identify the need for class and aggregation abstraction If there is no logical data model then the construction of the class model has to be based on the flair and experience of the practitioner. Flair and experience are not the hallmark of a structured method.

6.4.3.1   Build the logical data model

The first step is to build a logical data model. The model is shown in figure 6.5, along with a set of data attributes and volumes to some of the entities. All the entities are based on keys, such as the key of Employee Number to identify the Employee entity and Broker Number to identify the Broker entity. The arrow of the relationship points from the master entity to the detail entity; thus Commission is a detail entity of Broker.

The technique for building the model is not described here as it is well known and described in numerous manuals of numerous structured design methods. The important point to realise is that the initial identification of class is based on keys, as with the traditional structured methods. The logical data model and its key based entities is the starting point for the building of an objectively based class model.

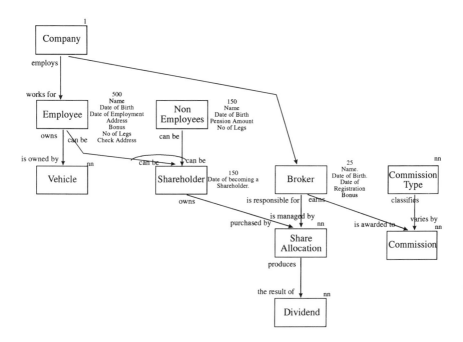

Figure 6.5   The logical data model

Many of the books that have been written on techniques for the identification of objects have stated that the identification of objects is an art form flair of the skilled practitioner. The authors very much disagree with this notion. The authors believe that the application of a set of rules should be used for the mechanistic identification of objects and the construction of the class model. These rules are described below.

The logical data model is now to be converted into a class model.

6.4.3.2 Identify and model class and aggregation hierarchies

Class is the facility that models common behaviour between objects. Sets of objects with common behaviour have a common class. Common behaviour is identified as data or logic properties that are common to more than one class. In figure 1.7 the class objects of Employee and Broker contain many properties that are common, such as Date of Birth and Warm Blooded. The classes therefore have common behaviour which needs to be modelled through abstraction.

Rules have been developed by the authors which will enable any common behaviour of the data properties to be identified, and the degree of abstraction to be ascertained. The approach is that the data properties are tested to identify and model class abstractions. To this are then tested the logic properties, which when in third normal form, will create abstractions of aggregation classes. Data abstraction produces class hierarchies, logic abstraction produces aggregation abstractions. The data abstraction rules are:

- *The Behaviour Rule*
  Is the data property common to more than one class?
  If it is then there is common behaviour between the classes, and abstraction of the common data property is required, the abstraction being either generalisation or specialisation.

- *The Data Generalisation Rule*
  Is the property common to all instances of the class?
  If the answer is yes then the data property is to be generalised to a super class of the source class. An example of this is the property of Date of Birth—it is common to both Employee and Broker, and all the 100 instances of employees and the 20 instances of brokers have birthdays. Date of Birth therefore needs to be generalised to a super class. And the same is true of Favourite Food, all 120 instances of Persons having favourite foods.

- *The Data Specialisation Rule*
  Is the property common to only some of the instances of the class object?

If the answer is yes then the property is to be specialised to a sub-class object of the source class. The property of bonus is common to Employee and Broker but not all employees and brokers get bonuses, only 12 employees and 3 brokers being so entitled. Bonus therefore requires to be specialised to a sub class.

- *The Information Role Rule*
  This rule relates to the question of how far should the data properties be generalised and specialised? The rule is that a property is abstracted to the level in the class object model appropriate to its role. This rule is also appropriate to the normalisation of information for abstract objects, i.e. objects with no user defined keys. The role of the data or logic property is related to the role of the object class.
  The role rule is that of the practiced eye[1].
  Because this is not a mechanical rule, the best way to explain this is by example. The common data properties to all instances of both Employee and Broker of Date of Birth "sensibly" belongs to a super class of Person, No. of Legs "sensibly" belongs to a super class of Man, and Warm Blooded "sensibly" belongs to a super class of Mammal. This "sensibleness" in the placement of properties to the classes matches the "role" of the data property to the role of the class. Date of Employment is not a data property common to many of the classes and is not abstracted. It is relevant to the role of employment and remains as a data property of Employee. Being warm blooded matches the rule of being mammalian.

- *The Logic Abstraction Rule*
  The rule is the normalisation of logic to the abstracted class objects containing user data.
  This rule can only be applied after the data properties have been abstracted into class hierarchies. What this means is that, if you accept the argument about object orientation requiring the normalisation of logic, then object oriented logical design has to be data driven—data normalisation precedes logic data class abstraction precedes logic abstraction through logic normalisation. The position for the logic properties is different from the data properties. Almost without exception, the logic properties, the methods, are defined at the class level, there being only occasionally logic at the instances of the class objects. This latter point is certainly true when the application system is being analysed and designed, as the object instances which could contain methods have not been created and entered in the objectbase. The instance objects of the

---

[1] To describe role as being based on a rule is perhaps an exaggeration. Rules need a mechanism to apply mechanistically, the practiced eye requires art, skill and intelligence.

application are not yet known, so it would be impossible to have different versions of logic at the instance level. The data abstraction questions "Is the property common to all instances of the class object?" and "Is the property common to only some of the instances of the class object?" are therefore not relevant to the logic properties.

The mechanism for the abstraction of the logic into methods and the placement of the methods to the class is based on the rules for the normalisation of logic. What the rules are and how to apply them is described in Section 6.3.4.2. But the logic component also follows the same principle of abstraction/specialisation as the data.

The public method Calculate Salary is relevant at the Employee class level, as all instances of Employees need to have their basic salary calculated. This was the original event-based logic called Calculate Salary. It contained all the logic for the calculation of all forms of employee remuneration. But the application of the rules for logic normalisation shows that the logic of Calculate Salary needs to be split, as some of the logic has nothing to do with Employees but with the data abstracted super and sub classes. There is a specialised method of Calculate Bonus for the sub-class Star Performer. The logic in this method follows the principle that it is more specialised than the more general logic in the method in the super-class Employee object—it is an extension of, an addition to, the general Calculate Salary logic. It is a specialised abstraction from the base logic of Calculate Salary, the residue of the base logic being Calculate Salary. The more specialised logic would be for the calculation of the Star Performers's bonus, whereas the more general logic would be for the calculation of the Employee's basic salary. And the logic for compensating for the loss of a leg is even more general than the original base logic and is a generalised method to the Man class.

The normalisation of logic therefore produces the same results as the abstraction rules for data in first and second normal form. The rule of third normal form produces aggregation classes.

The application of the practiced eye is useful to confirm the correctness of the normalisation of logic. The process Calculate Lost Leg Compensation is appropriate to the role of the class Man (it accesses the object instances to see if the value is less than 2, and if it is calculates the appropriate compensation), Calculate Salary is appropriate to Employee and Calculate Bonus is appropriate to Star Performer. And a process called Calculate Commission would be appropriate to Broker.

If Calculate Salary was also appropriate to Broker, then it would be good design to create a sub class to Person of Employed Person.

The generalisations and specialisations of the logical data model are shown in figure 6.6. The arrow on the lines of the relationship point from the master classes to the detail classes of concrete objects and from the

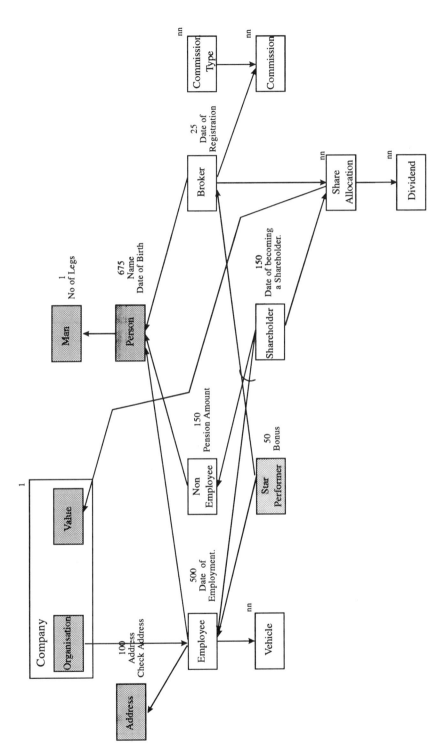

Figure 6.6 Build class, aggregation and sub-type hierarchies

sub classes to the super classes where there has been class and aggregation abstraction.

The resultant structure of the final class model from the application of the data and logic abstraction rules is illustrated in figure 6.6. This shows that the core of the class model is the logical data model and is the source of all class and aggregation abstractions, with the class and aggregation creating super classes and class also creating sub classes.

As part of the class modelling it is necessary to identify which of the class objects are abstract in that they support no instances of the class. In the class object model in figure 6.6, Man is an abstract class object, there being only a definition of the class object in the objectbase schema.

6.4.3.3 Create sub-type classes

Consider the Company class object in figure 2.21. Some of the data properties are not relevant to all the detail classes. The data about the Company Organisation is relevant to the company's Employees, but this is of no concern to the other detail entities of the Company entity. Likewise, the value of the company has nothing to do with the Employees but is decidedly of relevance to the Share Allocation as the value of the Company affects the value of the Share Allocation.

This business context sensitive data needs to be specialised as sub-types of the base class object, and the correct relationships to the sub-class objects of Company established. This is illustrated in figures 6.6 and 2.21, so that the Employees relate to the Company/Organisation and the Share Allocation to the Company/Value.

6.4.3.4 Identify abstract and concrete classes

Mark the classes that define no instances. These become abstract classes. Any data properties they contain must be instantiated with a value. The property No. of Legs for the Man abstract class has a value of "2". This is illustrated in figure 6.7. The other classes are concrete objects. The abstract classes are identified by the absence of the bifurcated lines of the bottom of the class rectangles.

6.4.3.5 Add the relationship semantics

This is a simple matter of defining the appropriate semantics to the relationships of the class model so far constructed, as it is the semantics

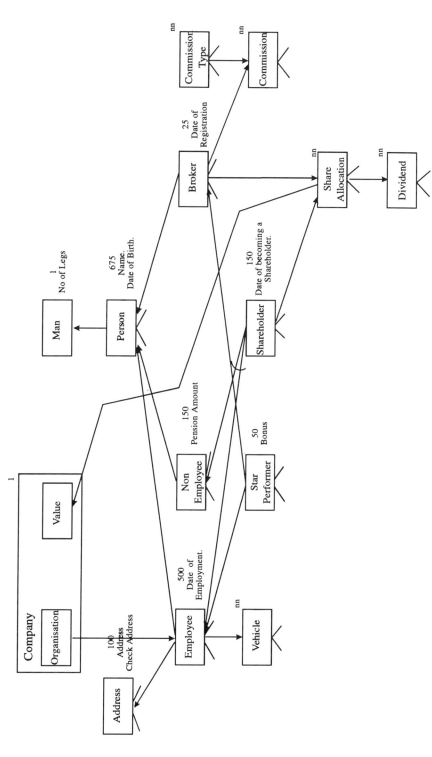

Figure 6.7 Identity abstract and concrete objects

that define class and aggregation hierarchies. This can be seen in figure 6.8, where the "is a" semantic description models class hierarchies, the "has a" semantic the aggregation hierarchy, and the free form the relationships that are not class or aggregation based but business based.

The top super classes to a class hierarchy is the Man class, and from this the sub classes of the Man class hierarchy can be seen, bifurcating in the middle to include Employee, Non-Employee and Broker, and coming together in the Star Performer.

The aggregation semantic to the Address abstracted data property for the Employee class can be seen. An Employee "has a" Address.

The remaining semantics are the free form semantic, describing the business purpose of the relationships between the classes. An example is that an Employee "works for" a Company and a Company "employs" Employees.

6.4.3.6 *Define and instantiate the data properties*

This is a simple matter of defining the name, format and length of the data properties and any instantiation if a property has a value that is generic to all instances of the class, this being true for all abstract classes. An example of instantiation could be a value of "2" for the data property of No. of Legs for the class Person.

6.4.3.7 *Add the event classes*

There are, from a modelling point of view, two types of events: those that are internal to the company and are triggered by users in the company and those that are external but are of interest to the company and triggered by persons not in the company's employment.

The need for this distinction is that the information in the class model is more general as one goes up the class model and more particular as one goes down the class model. Events that are external to the company of their nature are more general than those that are triggered within the company. Events that are external to the company are generic to n companies, and therefore more general than the company class. They therefore need to be modelled as super classes to the company.[1]

An external event could be the raising of interest rates. The company is interested in that it will now have to pay more on its borrowings.

Internal events are specific to the company and are therefore modelled as

---

[1] From a physical development point of view, there is no difference in the treatment of the external and the internal events—both are developed into application programs.

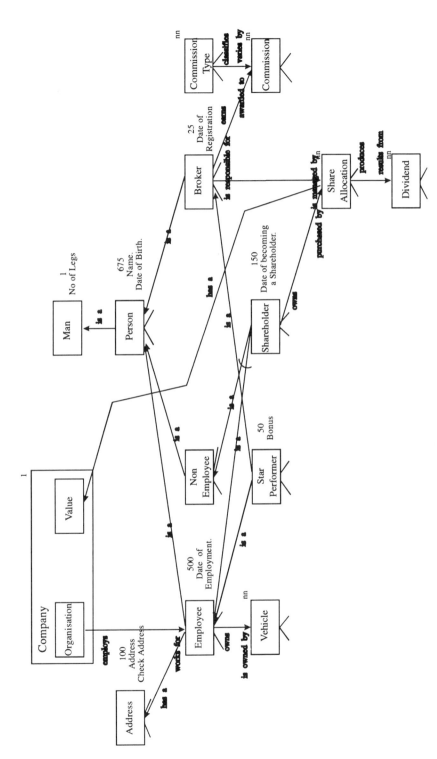

Figure 6.8 Specify class, aggregate and business semantics

sub classes to the company class. An example of such an event is Calculate Dividend. Others are Raise Invoice, Make Payment and Create Customer.

Both kinds of events are illustrated in figure 6.9.

6.4.3.8   Add common procedures and the human/computer interface

Any logic that is found to be common to n methods can be abstracted and defined as a more general class. The placement of the class Common Procedure classes follows the same principle as the event classes. This is also the same for the classes that support the human/computer interface— dialogue and menu screens can be specific to a company or generic to the computer industry. There are two kinds of menu screens—those for windows technology with their slide-off and pull-down menus and those for the selection of business requirements. The former are super classes to the Company class if they are screens from windows packages, such as Hewlett Packard's New Wave and Microsoft's Windows, but would be sub classes if developed in-house. And the same would be for the dialogue screens, screens for the display of information pertinent to a business requirement once selected from the menu screens. If the screen

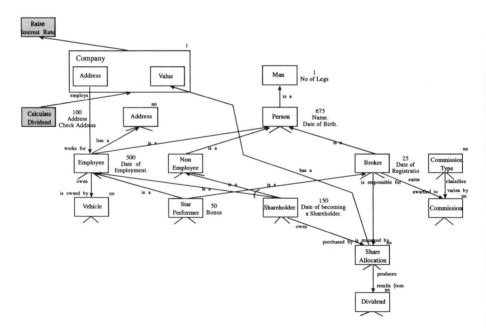

Figure 6.9   Add the event classes

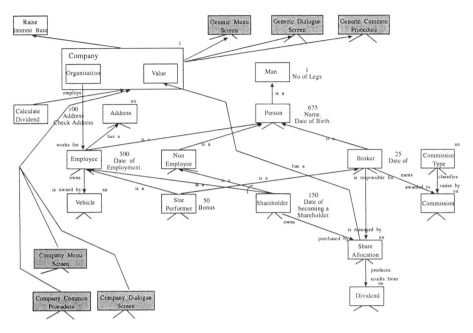

Figure 6.10 Add common procedure, menu and dialogue classes

was unique to the company it would be a sub class of the Company class—if it was generic/bought in then it would be a super class to the Company class. This is illustrated in figure 6.10.

6.4.3.9 Add the class libraries

These are the libraries of generalised system classes that are obtained with many of the object oriented programming languages and from specialist software vendors. They can, of course, also be developed in-house. Being of a general functional nature, such as print and sort objects, they are modelled as super classes to the Company class. This is illustrated in figure 6.11.

6.4.4 Information normalisation (formerly relational data analysis)

The term relational data analysis is no longer adequate because it no longer is appropriate to relational technology or to data. It should be replaced by the term "Information Normalisation", because it is now realised the rules of normalisation that have for so long been applicable only to data are now realised to be equally applicable to logic. *The result is that all information can be normalised.*

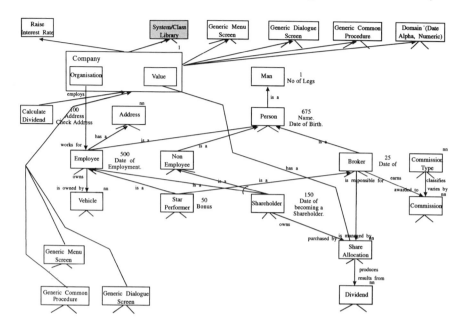

Figure 6.11   Add the system classes

This section will not repeat the technique of the normalisation of data: many textbooks are available on the subject. All that will be described is the definition of the data normalisation rules and their redefinition, with examples, for the normalisation of logic, both declarative logic and procedural logic.

The rules of data normalisation are:

- *First Normal Form*—"Take out Repeating Groups", that is any data property that has many values for a given value of the key. Remove them and create a new relation of the repeating group.

- *Second Normal Form*—"Test for Part Key Dependence", that is if a data property is dependent on only part of a multi-part key relation, remove it and create a new relation of the part key dependence.

- *Third Normal Form*—"Test for Inter Data Dependence", that is if any of the data properties in the second normal form relation are dependent on any of the other data properties. If they are remove them and create a new relation of the dependence.

There are two aspects to consider for the normalisation of information, both data and logic, in an object oriented environment:

- the introduction of the concept of the role of the information that is being normalised;

- the normalisation of logic.

6.4.4.1 The normalisation of object oriented data

Given that a logical data model needs to be built as the beginning of a class model, the rules for data normalisation to third normal form developed by Dr. Codd require to be applied unchanged.

The rules for data normalisation do not, however, support the concept of the role of the information to be normalised. This is an omission that needs to be rectified for object orientation.

Consider the classes Man, Person and Employee and the data property of Date of Birth in figure 6.12. With a relational approach to data modelling the Date of Birth could happily reside in the Employee entity and not break the rules of data normalisation—is the data dependent on the key, the whole and nothing but the key? Yes. But with object orientation this is not adequate. Is Date of Birth relevant to the role of Employee? No. Date of Birth has nothing to do with employment. But the Employees are Persons, and therefore the class of Person is abstracted as a more general super class to Employee. Should the Date of Birth be defined as a data property of Employee, Person or Man? From the role point of view, the data property is relevant to Person and not to Employee—Date of Birth has nothing to do with employment.

But what about putting Date of Birth as a property of Man? Notice that Man is a class with no instances—it is an abstract class. Man is a

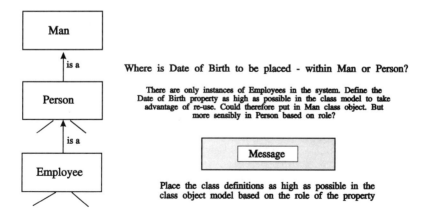

Figure 6.12 The role of data

Logic First Normal Form Rule
"For a given class is there more than one possible version of the logic?"

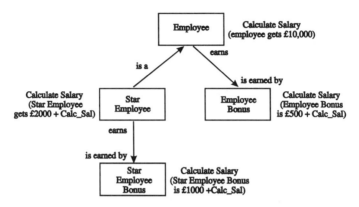

Figure 6.13   The normalisation of logic (1NF at the class level)

generic "thing" with no instances, but containing information that is generic to any sub class, to all instances of Person and Employee. This means that any data properties are instantiated with a generic value relevant to all the instances of the sub classes. To instantiate Date of Birth with a generic value would clearly be nonsensical as each instance of a Person could have a birthday on a different date. Date of Birth is a property that describes individual instances of Person and thereby, through property inheritance, Employee. Notice that Person is a class with instances, because there are individual Persons who might also be Employees. Date of Birth "sensibly" belongs to the role of a Person, not with the role of Man, to a concrete and not an abstract class. Thus all the instances of Person and Employee can have individual birthdays.

Consideration of the role of the data properties needs to be applied after the standard normalisation rules have been used to build the standard logical data model and the rules of class abstraction to add the class hierarchies.

6.4.4.2   *The normalisation of object oriented logic (procedural) for concrete objects*

The work of Dr. Codd defined the rules for the normalisation of data, and the rules have been widely accepted and applied. The rules are applied to user defined keys and are thus appropriate to concrete objects. *The authors believe that the rules for data normalisation are as relevant to logic as they are to data and can be applied to object oriented concrete objects.* Why not—it is just information. All that needs to be done is to alter the phraseology of the rules to cater for logic.

An example of the normalisation of logic up to first normal form is given in figure 6.13. The rule of first normal for data is "Take out repeating groups". The test for repetition is "For a given value of the key is there more than one possible value of the data?" Suitably rephrased for logic, the wording becomes "For a given class is there more than version of the logic?" There is no concept of a key as well as dealing with a class

Figure 6.13 shows the normalisation of the logic for the business requirement of calculating salaries, the logic of which varies, is relevant to, different objects. The logic varies depending on whether the object is an Employee, Star Employee, Star Employee Bonus or Employee Bonus. The base logic for the event/business requirement is in the event class Calculate Salary, with the remaining logic "normalised" to the classes containing user data to which the logic is pertinent. All Employees receive a salary of £10,000; the Star Employees receive an additional £2000; the Star Employee Bonus is a further £1000 and the Employee Bonus is £500 on the basic salary. There are therefore n polymorphic versions of the logic Calculate Salary.

The logic for calculating the bonus of £1000 is appropriate to Star Employee Bonus, and is therefore normalised to the Star Employee Bonus class. *It can be seen that the sub class contains the logic that is additional to the logic of the method of the super class.* Thus the calculation of the Star Employee Bonus is the combined logic of the Star Employee Bonus (£1000), Star Employee (£2000) and Employee (£10,000). The sub class methods inherit the logic of the more general case super-class methods.

What is obtained here is:

- the repetition of different versions of the logic for one occurrence of the original base logic appropriate to the Employee

- a set of polymorphic processes. What was one process named Calculate Salary is now four processes called Calculate Salary, each with different versions of logic dependent on the object class instance being accessed

Wherever applied, the rule of first normal form of logic will produce polymorphic processes.

Figure 6.14 shows an example of logic that has to be normalised to second normal form. The rule of second normal form for data is "Test for part key dependence". The test is "Is the data dependent on the whole key or part of the key?" Again suitably rephrased the test would be "Is the logic dependent on the whole key or part of the key?"

The key of the stock class is a compound key of Product Code and Depot Code, as it contains the stock of a particular product at a particular depot. The method Calculate Stock Value is in second normal form in that it is calculating the value of the stock of a product at a depot. The method Increase Product Price is not in second normal form in that it is only relevant

Logic Second Normal Form Rule
"Is the logic depedent on the whole key?"

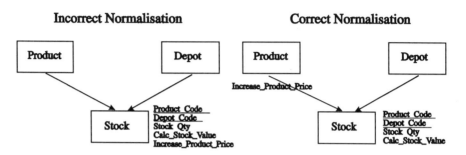

Figure 6.14   The normalisation of logic (2NF at the class level)

to product—it is calculating the increase in the price of a product and has nothing to do with the stock at a depot. The method is in the wrong class, and needs to be moved to Product, so that the logic of the method is now appropriately related to the class it is relevant to.

Figure 6.15 shows an example of logic that needs to be normalised to third normal form. The third normal form data normalisation rule is "Test for inter data dependence", that is: are some of the data properties dependent on each other rather then the prime key? Suitably rephrased, the rule becomes "Is the logic dependent on a data property that is not the prime key?"

The method Check Name Range is a logic property of the class

Third Normal Form rule
"Is the logic dependant on a data property that is not the prime key?"

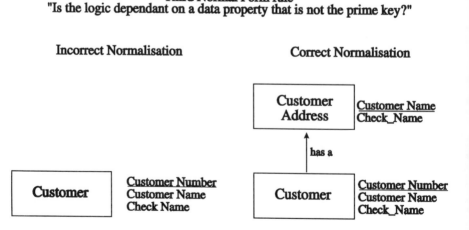

Figure 6.15   The normalisation of logic (3NF at the class level)

Customer. The logic needs to access the Customer Name and retrieve customer details if the name of the customer is within the specified range. The company markets shirts emblazoned with personalised names and wishes to supply a free set for a given set of customers with specific surnames. The logic is dependent on a data property of the class object that is not the prime key, in this case the Customer Name. In the example of Calculate Stock Value, the logic was dependent on the prime key of Product. But Customer Name is not the prime key, Customer Number is. The method needs to be abstracted with the Customer Name data property and generalised as a super class.

The rule of third normal form for logic is the basis of the aggregation objects. This was first discussed in section 2.2.2. The result will be aggregation objects composed of a single data property with one or more methods that process that single data property. There is a problem with this rule of logic third normal form. Since each data property requires an edit routine to ensure that input values are correct the net result of third normal form logic modelling is that each data property would become a class with an edit method and one or more other methods processing against the data property for other business purposes. This is decomposition of object classes to too fine a level of detail, rather like Smalltalk where everything is an object. A suggested third normal form compromise is to abstract into logic third normal form aggregation classes. The logic is other than an input edit process. This would result in the aggregation classes containing one edit method and one or more other methods serving business purposes.

The examples given so far are to business objects that one would see in a traditional logical data model. The normalisation of logic is also appropriate to the system objects and other objects not normally found in a traditional logical data model as well, *such as*:

- the Object class. The Object class contains logic that is universally applicable. For a chemicals application the chemical formulae convert into methods which contain logic that is universally recognised to be laws of chemistry, and therefore universally true. The logic for these chemical formulae would become method properties in the Object object.

- The logic contained in the system classes, typically for system type procedures such as numeric editing, storing an object and string handling. Being generally applicable, the objects would be defined as sub classes to the Object class.

- The logic is contained in the event class, that is the logic that is specific to the business requirement. This event level logic by its nature cannot be normalised to a business class, as the logic is not relevant to any key of a business class. Typically the logic would be the issuing of the messages to the other classes, the synchronisation of the message responses received from the classes and any final processing before the information is output and screen formatting.

6.4.4.3   *The normalisation of object oriented logic (procedural) for abstract objects*

Object orientation is able to model abstract classes, i.e. classes without user-defined keys and object instances. Dr. Codd's rules for data normalisation, being based on user-defined keys, are therefore not suitable for abstract classes. Another new rule requires to be defined.

Since keys cannot be used for information normalisation it is necessary to relate the data and logic properties to the role of the class, the role of the properties matching the role of the abstract class. The rule is the very simple one of "Does the role of the property match the role of the class?" Using the examples in figure 1.7 with the abstract class of Man the data property of No. of Legs and the logic property of Calculate Lost Leg Compensation (to be invoked if one or more legs have been amputated), both properties are relevant to the role of being a man, a *homo sapiens*, and are therefore correctly related to the class Man. If the data property was Date of Employment this has nothing to do with being a man but an employee, and the same would be true for the logic property of Calculate Salary. To place these properties within Man would be wrong; they relate to the role of being an Employee and would therefore be correctly placed within the class of Employee.

6.4.4.4   *The normalisation of object oriented logic (declarative)*

Rules are usually in the form of "If condition A then conclusion B". Each rule is a declarative statement of some universal or application domain truth. Each rule therefore has value in its own right. A rule can therefore be standalone. A rule can also be linked with other rules relevant to an application task to form a ruleset. A ruleset is a group of rules for a particular application domain task (a problem-to-solve process in centralised data processing) for which domain relevant advice is sought. A domain could be how to service a car. Domains can be decomposed into many tasks and sub-tasks, and hence rulesets within rulesets. Car servicing tasks could be how to change a tyre, check the oil and maintain the electrics, each requiring expertise and advice and their own ruleset.

The issue of the normalisation of declarative logic has caused the authors much thought, and the answer is still not certain. There is no reason why declarative logic cannot be normalised like procedural logic—it is nothing more than another way of representing logic, but that reasoning is the simple part. The dilemma is this: given that each rule is a statement of some truth and is therefore a piece of logic that can be standalone, does one normalise each rule on a standalone basis or as a set of rules in the ruleset (for the purposes of this section, the nearest equivalent of an application program in declarative logic) and, if the normalisation is to a single rule, does one normalise to the condition of the rule or to the conclusion if the two relate to different "things"/objects?

Consider the problem of normalising a rule on a standalone basis. The situation is all too often that the condition is usually about a "thing" of A and the conclusion about a "thing" of B. To which object, A or B, should the rule go? And what if there are n conditions about A, B, C and D and there are n conclusions about E, F and G? An extreme example could be "If the world is round and Joe Bloggs is big and the President of the United States is on the campaign trail, then it is raining and necessary to get your car repaired". N conditions and n conclusions each relating to different classes and instances of the class. Where does one start with that rule?

How about normalising the rules to the query to which they are providing advice—that is at the ruleset level? This seems to be the most plausible approach. The approach of normalising rules on a standalone basis does not seem to be viable, even though rules have value in their own right. Thus the ruleset rules appropriate to changing a tyre would normalise to the tyre class, and the rules in the ruleset for maintaining a car electrics would normalise to the electric sub class of the super class of car. This is normalising declarative logic in the same way as procedural logic—and this approach is therefore the more attractive because it is common.

But what if the ruleset has rules that are to be found in multiple rulesets? There could be a ruleset of rules about purchasing a computer with a printer. There could well be another for selling a computer with a printer, and some of the rules in the purchasing ruleset are also in the ruleset for selling. No problem. They are common functionality and should be generalised as a super class containing part of the ruleset for both purchasing and selling.

If declarative logic is combined with procedural logic then both need to be normalised as standard. This most frequently occurs with the use of rules as the mechanism for defining the pre- and post-conditions for method processing of the application class objects. "If colour of car is non-blank then print error message 55" could be a pre-condition rule for a method Paint Car. The rules for information abstraction can be applied here. If the rule is specific to painting a car then it is not abstracted. If the rule can be used elsewhere then it is abstracted. There is no problem with intermingling procedural and declarative logic.

6.4.5 Dataflow diagrams/process decomposition diagrams/process dependency diagrams

These three techniques are considered together because they model information about the decomposition of high level processes to lower level more detailed processes, and how data is passed from one process to the other. Dataflow diagrams tend to model decomposition and dataflow in one deliverable, whereas process decomposition and process dependency diagrams separate these two modelling features. The technique of dataflow modelling is considered but the points made are relevant to the two other techniques.

The technique is unchanged regarding object oriented modelling, the only addition to consider being the decomposition of the processes.

One of the decomposition problems is that most of the structured methods which use dataflow diagramming do not provide very good advice as to how to decompose the processes and what level of decomposition to go to. Advice such as "Decompose until you get to a satisfactory level of detail" and "Lower level processes contain more detail" is not very helpful.

Object oriented processing provides the answer to one of these questions—the level to which you decompose. *What the authors have found most practical is to decompose the processes to the "do something" titled event/business requirement level, and then to normalise the logic to the classes to which they appropriately belong.* Examples of event level processes would be "Send Invoice", "Pay Insurance Premium" and "Produce Monthly Status Report".

There is thus no point in decomposing processes below the event level for object oriented use of the dataflow modelling technique. The event level logic is normalised to the event class and the remaining logic, some 80%, to the business classes as appropriate.

6.4.6   The object state model

The technique is based directly on the Entity Life History technique of the SSADM structured design method and suitably renamed the object state model. The purpose of the technique is to ensure that events which affect an entity in a logical data model occur in the right order. It is therefore impossible to delete an entity before it has been inserted into the objectbases, and is ideal for modelling the state of the objects in an objectbase. The technique is only to be used against the concrete objects containing user data in the class model. An object state model is produced for each such class. There is no need to model the life of abstract classes. They are created with instantiated data properties and that's it—or should be.

The business classes can have many different events affecting them, they can occur in sequence, iterate and be selective, incur quits and resumes, and they can occur in parallel, all in a potentially highly complicated manner. This state is monitored in a state variable data property which has a specific before and after event value.

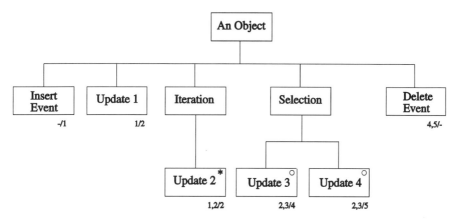

Figure 6.16   An entity life history/object state models

Consider the Object State Model in figure 6.16. The model is Jackson-like in form. It shows the simple life of a class, the class being the box at the top of the model and the boxes at the bottom the processes which affect the class. In the Entity Life History model the processes are at the event level. In the Object State Model the processes are the methods which affect the life of the business classes being modelled. The object state model process boxes are therefore at a lower level of detail than the event level processes of the Entity Life History.

The sequence of events is from left to right, so that the first event is the insertion of an object instance into the objectbase, followed by update event 1, an iteration of n updates 2 (which can be an iteration of zero), a selection of updates 3 or 4, and a deletion. The sequence in which the events that affect the class is monitored by the state indicator facility, a data property in each object instance. There is a predecessor state value and a post-succesor state value for each event that affects the object instance, the state that an object instance must be in before a method can change it, and the state the object instance must be in after the method changes it. The state indicator value after the insertion is 1, so the predecessor state for update 1 is a value of 1 (if the indicator value is not 1 send an error message), to be set to a value of 2 after update 1 has completed. When the event/business requirement update 2 occurs the value of the state indicator data property of the object instance being accessed should be "2", this stating that the last event that updated the object instance was update 1. If this is the value, processing can continue as the correct predecessor event to update 2 occurred. If the value was not "2" then another and incorrect event occurred previously. An error message needs to be issued and processing stopped until the error is corrected.

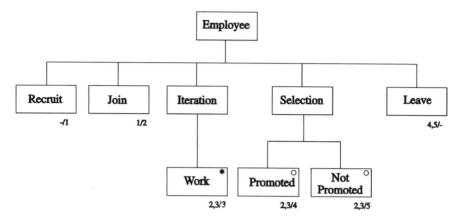

Figure 6.17   An entity life history/object state model example

A worked example is illustrated in figure 6.17, which shows that an Employee is recruited into the objectbase. Some time later the employee joins the company and undertakes many iterations of work. Some time later there is or is not promotion, and after that the employee leaves the company and the objectbase. The fact that the employee does not do any work after being promoted is neither here not there.

Methods that merely retrieve the data properties are not modelled as they do not change the state of the object instance and can therefore be invoked in any order. Such methods are often called observers.

What is the purpose of this standard technique for traditional entity state modelling in an object oriented environment? The usefulness of the object state model to object orientation is that it models:

- *the methods that affect a class object*
  In figure 6.18 there are five methods for both class objects 1 and 2.

- *the operations of the methods*
  From this the commonality of operations across the methods in different object state models shows those which can be generalised and made common procedures. The residue of the operations become methods in the class.

  Figure 6.18 needs detailed interpretation. Operation 1 is common to method 1 for class 1 and to method 4 for class 2. It is an object instance insert operation. Being common it represents common behaviour of some logic across more than one class method, and so can be generalised. It becomes a common procedure/class library class. Operation 7 is a common operation for methods 3 and 7, being a delete object

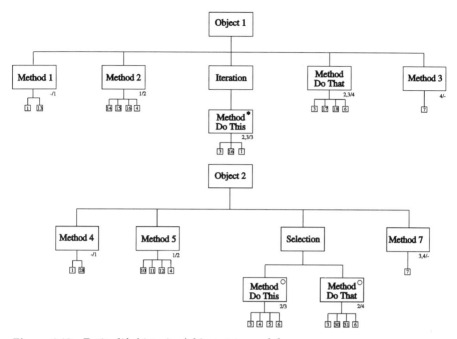

Figure 6.18 Entity life histories/object state models

instance process. It can likewise be generalised. Operation 6 is common to methods Do That and Do This. Operations common to several methods include 4 and 16 (common to two methods for the same class). Such common operations can also be generalised as common procedures.

The residue of the operations not generalised become the source method attached to the class being modelled. Thus, method 2 for class 1 has operations 14 and 15, and method Event Do That for class 2 has operations 30 and 31.

- the sequence in which the class methods that affect the class's instances must be invoked by the receipt of messages, mostly from the event class, is based on the sequence of the methods in the Object State Model.

  For class 1 in figure 6.18, the sequence which the methods that affect the object instances is method 1, 2, Do This, Do That and 3.

- *the pre- and post-conditions that must exist prior to and following execution of the method affecting the object instance. It is a most useful mechanism for ensuring that the logic of the method executes correctly.* It is also the basis of a "contract" between the class sending the message and the class receiving the message.

This can be done either crudely or in detail. The crude way is to check the value of the state indicator in the logic of each method. For method Do This for class object 1 the method logic would start as a precondition by checking that the value of the state indicator was either 2 or 3 and if not valid send an error message and stop processing. If the state indicator was OK, then to accept the message and invoke the method. At the end of processing there would be logic to set the state indicator value to 3. The post condition would check the state indicator was 3 and if OK send the response.

The more detailed approach is to check those values of the data properties that are pertinent to the business function of the method. Assume that the object is a car and that the method Do This is to paint the car. The data properties of car colour would need to be checked as a pre-condition to ensure that the colour is blank. As a post-condition the logic would be to check that the colour is non-blank. There could, of course, be a range of data properties that need to be checked in the pre and post-condition testing. Pre and post conditions are discussed further in section 6.4.7.4.

6.4.7   Modelling object oriented application programs

Object oriented processing is still event level triggered. The sending of messages between the objects to be accessed for the event are all initially triggered when the event/business requirement occurs. As we have seen in non-object oriented systems, application programs should be pitched at the event level and the constituent modules at the problem-to-solve level. What is true of traditional batch and online centralised processing is also true of object oriented processing. Once again, it is a case of the facilities of centralised processing being generic, with the facilities of object orientation being add-ons.

Application programs in object oriented systems are also event based but, instead of being composed of problem-to-solve modules, are composed of a set of normalised class based methods. The "program" is triggered from the event class for the business requirement. The succeeding application objects are "chained" in the sequence required to be accessed for the processing to proceed, as in conventional processing. The other classes could be system classes for common routines, menu and dialogue screen processing and common procedures.

There is a "battle" going on over the best way in which to model the structure of object oriented application programs. The two leading techniques are the Jackson approach and Action Diagrams. With the Jackson approach there is another battle as to whether to use the object state or the event process models as the basis for designing object oriented application programs.

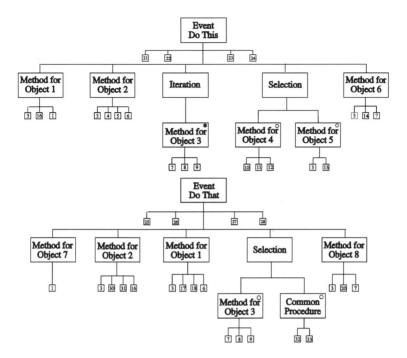

Figure 6.19 Process models/event process models

Both techniques are widely used, and both can be easily tailored to support object oriented logical design of event processing.

While both methods are equally valid, the authors believe that the Jackson approach will "win the day" because it is very diagrammatic, with the diagram beautifully modelling the structure of object oriented processing. The technique is also already object-based.

6.4.7.1 The event process model

The object state model looks at the events/business requirements that alter the state of the object during its life. It is the object's view of the world. The event process model is the opposite view, the view of the objects that an event accesses through the sending of messages. The same Jackson-like modelling of logic should not confuse the reader that the purpose of the state and the event models are quite different.

The event process model models:

● the structure of an object oriented application program;

- the methods that need to be messaged/invoked for an event/business requirement that the application program is supporting;

- the logic that is to be executed against the data in the objectbase as required by an event/business requirement. [1]

The technique is based directly on the Process Modelling technique of SSADM version 4, and suitably renamed the event process model for object oriented process modelling.

An example of the business requirements/events Do This and Do That process model is illustrated in figure 6.19. The model shows the sequence, selection and iteration of the methods the events need to send messages to invoke the processing required by the event.

The rectangle at the top of the model is the event/business requirement. Operations are also detailed at the event level. This event level process is, in effect, the main procedure of an application program, with the messages to the methods fulfilling a similar role as program calls to procedures. This part is the 20% of the business logic that is application dependent.

The rectangles at the bottom of the model represent the methods in the class objects containing user data or class objects containing only a method (typically, a class library or common procedure) to be invoked. Operations are listed against each of the methods to detail the logic to be executed. The methods at the bottom of the event process models are application independent.

The usefulness of the event process model to object orientation is that it models:

- the methods to be invoked by the event/business requirement classes;

- the sequence, iteration and selection of the methods to be invoked for the event/business requirement

   In effect, what one is modelling is the access path of the business requirement to the object instances in the objectbase. In figure 6.19 the access path for Do This is class 1 (a specified Customer), then class 2 (the latest Order for the Customer), class 3 (all the Order Lines for the

---

[1]   Booch (1991) argues that finding the right classes and then organising them into separate modules are entirely independent design decisions. The authors do not accept this argument. The identification of classes, their abstraction and placement in the class model, the normalisation of logic into methods are based on the rules defined in this chapter. The technique of Event Process Modelling is then based on the classes and the normalised logic, and the model is then used *directly on* a one-for-one basis as the structure of an object oriented application program. There is a continuous trace of the techniques and their products from the beginning of the identification of classes and ultimately the modelling of the object oriented application programs.

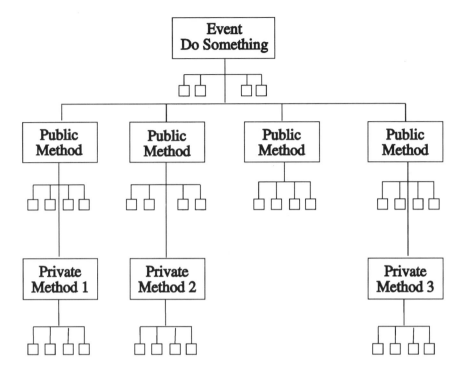

Figure 6.20 The public methods triggering private methods

Order), class 4 or 5 (either an Invoice or a Payment Request) and class 6 (a specified Product).

The method does not have to be defined for an application class object containing user data, as implied by the above example. For the event Do That there is a Common Procedure method which is invoked and is defined in an abstract class that contains no user data, just the method.

- specification of the logic in the methods, both at the event level and for the methods defined for the application classes with user data and method only classes;

The operations can be interpreted in exactly the same manner as for the object state model. Operation 3 is a read for update and is common to several methods. It can be generalised as a common procedure. Operations 1 and 7 are the same, being inserts, and deleted of object instances, and can likewise be generalised. And so on. The residue operations become the methods of the classes the methods are operating against. Thus 30–31 are the operations of the method for class 2.

Figure 6.21   System triggered private methods

- the structure of an object oriented application program

    The "program" for the event/business requirement Do That is composed of:
    — the event level processing of operations 25–28, these being concerned with the sending of messages to the methods modelled in figure 6.19, and processing the replies and any other needs as appropriate;
    — four methods defined for the business classes containing user data and one common procedure method.

6.4.7.2   Private methods

If the public method being modelled requires to invoke a private method in the class being accessed then this has to be modelled separately, as is illustrated in figure 6.20. This shows that the public methods send messages to and expect responses from the private methods in exactly the same way as the event level object communicates with the public methods. For figure 6.20 the private method 1 is for objectbase referential integrity checking for an object instance insert, private method 2 is for a business condition test (the stock level is too low so place a stock replenishment order) and private method 3 is for ensuring that there are no detail/sub-class instances in the objectbase before the super class is deleted.

    The private method can be invoked by:

- the triggering of a system event such as the need to check for objectbase referential integrity (thus when an Order is being inserted the private

method Check Order Referential Integrity is fired to ensure the Customer and Product object instances for the Order are present). These methods could also be explicitly invoked by the public methods maintaining the objectbase;
- the occurrence of a business condition occurring, as described above;

- the passage of time, such as end of month processing.

The last two types of events can be unpredictable as to when they occur. When this occurs, they therefore require to be modelled as random events outside the standard object state model. When this situation occurs then the modelling of the private method can be as illustrated in figure 6.21.

6.4.7.3   Action diagrams

Action diagrams can quite easily be made object oriented. An example of this is shown in figure 6.22. The event/business requirement is Do This as for figure 6.19, this enabling a direct comparison of the Jackson and the Action Diagramming techniques to be made.

The action diagram symbols show well the aspects of sequence, iteration and selection of the methods to be invoked, and the operations within the methods.

The interpretation of the action diagrams is the same as for the event process models.

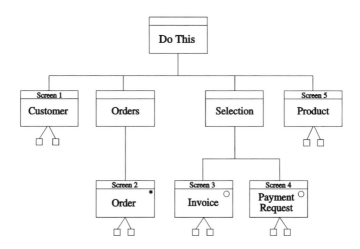

Figure 6.22   Event object Do This in action diagram form

6.4.7.4 Modelling pre and post conditions

This is becoming a much more commonly used facility in object orientation, particularly with the Eiffel programming language, which provides facilities for it. It is a most useful facility, as it enables the state of the object instance being accessed to be correct before a method is triggered, the execution of the named method to be guaranteed as being correct and the state of the object instance to be correct when the method has completed its processing. The changes to the object instances are thus probably correct. The facility thus enables a "contract" to be obtained between the method that sends a message and receives a response and the method that receives the message and sends the response. The sending method can send the message knowing that the named method will not be triggered if there is anything "wrong" with the object instance being accessed by the named method and knowing that the response contains valid information because the named method has executed successfully and done what it is functionally supposed to do, with the object instance being in the correct new state.

There are two ways in which the pre and post conditions of an object instance can be tested—by checking the values of the data properties of the object instance as set by the last update process or by checking the state indicator of the object instance as set by the last update process. The former approach is required for realtime applications and the latter is often used for batch and online processing, using the object state modelling approach illustrated in section 6.4.6.

Either way, the use of declarative logic is being increasingly used for pre and post condition testing. Declarative logic is quite different from the long practised procedural logic. Procedural logic is positional logic with each line of code only relevant in the context of the line of code that precedes it and succeeds it. A line of procedural code has no value in its own right. There are also many programming constructs for procedural code, the main ones being sequence, selection, iteration and branching for data processing and read, write, update and delete for data access.

Declarative code is quite different:

- it is not positional, as the lines of code are symbolically related.

- Declarative logic is in the form of rules. The rules are in the form of "If condition A then conclusion B". There could be rules "If condition A then conclusion B" and "If condition B then conclusion C". These two rules relate in that the conclusion of one rule matches the condition of another rule. The rules chain together on the basis of the value of the conditions and the conclusions. This means that the rules do not have to be positional and can be written in any order.

The great benefit of this freedom is that pre and post conditions can be added to an object method at any time without affecting the condition testing already in place. This greatly aids maintainability.

- There is only one construct—"if condition then conclusion".

  This single construct contains both process and access logic. The one construct of such functional power substantially reduces learning curves.

- Each rule is a statement of some truth so it has value in its own right.

  The rule could be "If today is Monday (fact) then tomorrow is Tuesday (fact)" or "If today is sunny (a fact) then go sunbathing" (a command), the meaningful association between the facts and command being the "if... then... clause". Both of these statements are meaningful as standalone rules.

  So we have a situation where a rule can be:

  —if a fact(s) is(are) true then some more fact(s);

  —if a fact(s) is(are) true then do something;

  Both forms of rules are useful for condition testing but particularly the latter. The condition of the rule can be used to test the state of the object instance and if it is OK the conclusion can be drawn and the appropriate class method invoked, with a command being the named method as

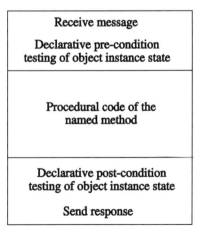

Figure 6.23   Pre and post condition testing

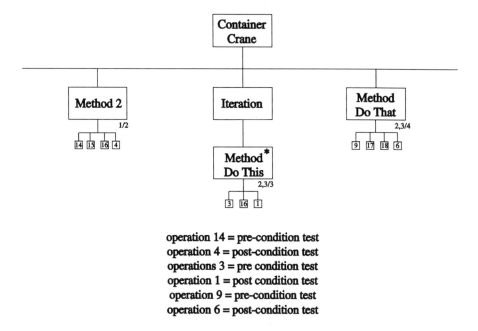

Figure 6.24   Pre and post condition testing

a procedure call. The pre condition test could be "If object instance "123452. State_Indicator = "3" then call method "Do This", this being the named method in the newly received message. The post condition test could be similar to the pre condition test but would test the updated state indicator updated by the invoked method. The post condition test would be "If object instance "123452. State_Indicator = "4" then send response with value "whatever".

The great benefit of this for condition testing is that it is conducted only against known positions of truth/validity, this being an excellent basis of a contract between the sender and the receiver of a message. The pre condition is the contract as far as the named method is concerned—it only operates when the object instance it is processing is in the correct state. The post condition is the contract as far as the sender of the message is concerned—it only receives a valid response because it can be proved that the named method has executed successfully and processed correctly.

There is also a further benefit of this approach. The command based conclusion is an excellent way in which declarative logic can be linked with procedural logic, thus combining the best of both forms of logic.

Procedural logic has the advantage of efficiency and declarative logic has the advantage of flexibility. The conclusion command in the declarative statement invokes the procedural code of the named method in the command.

An example of the structure of pre and post condition testing is shown in figure 6.23 with an example of the way that the object state model can be used for modelling the test conditions in figure 6.24.

An example of the alternative approach to the testing of the state indicator of an object instance is given below, this approach being the testing of the values of one or more of the data properties.

Method Fly_Aircraft
Check pre-condition such as:
    "Select Engine_State, Fuel_State, Aircraft_Height
    From Aircraft
    Where Engine_State = "Full blast", Fuel.State = "Full" and
    Aircraft_Height = "100"
    If OK then Execute Fly_Aircraft;
    Do whatever......
Check post_conditions such as:
    If Engine_State = "Idle", Fuel_State = "Empty" and
    Aircraft_Height = "0"
    Then send response "ABC, EFC. HIJ, etc
    End Fly_Aircraft;"

6.4.7.5 Message strategies

There is a serious issue that fundamentally affects the correctness of the normalisation of the logic to the methods. It is the strategy to be used for the sending of messages between the classes. There are two basic strategies that can be used, Central Policeman and Long Chain[1]. The strategies are illustrated in figure 6.25.

One of the central concepts of object orientation is the normalisation of logic. The benefit is that all logic that can be normalised to the business classes in the class model is application independent and therefore much more stable than the residue of application dependent logic at the event level.

The Central Policeman messaging strategy is based on the principle that all messaging to the business classes is done from the event class. The

---

[1] The authors are grateful to a business colleague, Peter Fletcher, for pointing out the advantages of the Long Chain approach to messaging over the previous Round Robin approach that the authors used to use.

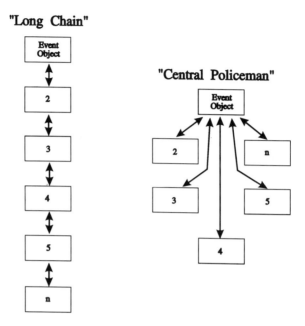

Figure 6.25   Messaging strategies 1

messages are, in fact, mostly data access calls to the object instances that contain the data pertinent to the event/business requirement (there could be messages to method only classes) but, because of encapsulation, the calls have to be in the form of messages to public methods in the classes to be accessed. The messages are therefore logic that is relevant to and conditional on the business requirement, the event. Thus, it is correct from a normalisation point of view to place all messages to the business classes at the event level. The event knows what classes it needs to message. Each of the accessed instances of the classes containaing the relevant data is completely unaware of the other classes instances to be accessed for the event/business requirement. Business object class A does not know that the next object class to be accessed for the event/business requirement is object class B. This enforces encapsulation. All business access logic to the business classes is at the event level with the Central Policeman messaging strategy.

   The Long Chain messaging strategy is based on the principle that the business classes containing user data can send a message to the next business class to be accessed for the event/business requirement the method is supporting. Thus, using the above example, the method in the class number 2 would send a message to class 3 for the event. The business classes being messaged require to know which is the next class to be messaged for the event/business requirement and therefore are not independent of the other classes. The methods in the business classes require to contain access logic pertinent to the event/business requirement regarding access to the next business class. The business classes therefore contain logic in the methods that is pertinent to the event/business requirement and not just the class. The rules of the normalisation of logic are therefore being broken. Notwithstanding this, this practice has been followed on many object oriented design projects.

The practice of object orientation is indicating that the Long Chain messaging strategy is wrong under all circumstances, that the central policeman access strategy should always be used and that *object messaging should be centred on the event class.*

It is also being realised that there is a need to base object messaging on the base classes of class and aggregation hierarchies, the source object classes of a set of "is a" and "has a" relationships to the derived class and aggregation object classes. The need for this additional central policeman basis for messages is that the user of the system should not require to know that the designer of the system, because of some esoteric rules for class behaviour abstraction and third normal form logic normalisation for aggregation composition abstraction, has made classes understood by the user, a Person and a Car for example, as the basis of abstraction into things called Person, Man and Mammal and decomposition into an aggregate structure of a set of classes, that the Car in actuality is made up of this, that and the other. Users think in terms of key based entities as in the logical data model from which the class model is derived. All the user (and the application programmers) knows is that there is an employee and a car which includes all sorts of facilities, such as a carburettor and an engine. Look, you can see them—what's all this nonsense about behaviour abstraction and logic normalisation leading to aggregation abstraction?

One needs to isolate the user from the abstractions the object class model has derived from the logical data model. *One has to encapsulate the user from object oriented information modelling.* The basic structure for an object oriented application program where there is a need to message abstracted classes is shown in figure 6.26. *There is central policeman messaging from the event class and from the base class to any class and aggregation hierarchies.* Thus in the above examples, the user would send a message to an employee and customer without realising that object orientation has derived all sorts of other object classes from them. The user would send a message to the Employee and Customer classes with all the details of the customer, including in the message argument list details of such abstracted things as the customer name and customer address or whatever for the Customer, if that is required to be accessed. The invoked method in the Employee and Customer classes would send the messages, unseen by the user, to the Person, Man and

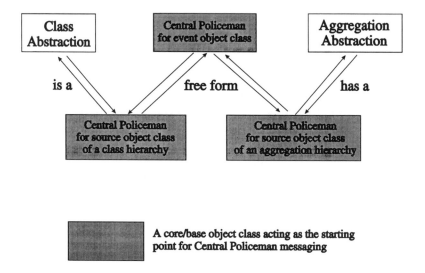

Figure 6.26   Messaging strategies 2

Mammal and the Customer Name and Customer Address classes as appropriate. This basing messages on the base class of a class and aggregation hierarchy enforces encapsulation of the multi-class structure of what is just an employee and a customer as far as the user/event programmer is concerned.

In figure 6.27 there is central policeman messaging from the event to the first classes to be messaged in support of the business requirement and from there long chain messaging. Reflecting the class structure in figure 1.7 there is a message to a method in the Employee class and from there to the appropriate methods in the super classes of the class hierarchy. And for the Customer class the messages from Customer Name to Customer Address reflect the need to go from Customer to Customer Name and to Customer Address for a business requirement that wants to access some data properties from the Customer class and the aggregation classes related to Customer. The classes Customer Name and Customer Address have been abstracted because of there being methods that process Customer Name and Address. The problems with this long chain approach to messaging are that:

- the logic in the methods is not in third normal form, as there is logic pertaining to the structure of the class model and the event in that a message has to go to this object class next for this event.

    What should have been done is to put the messaging to the object classes as much as possible into the event class, this acting as the controlling central policeman for the business requirement/object oriented application program.

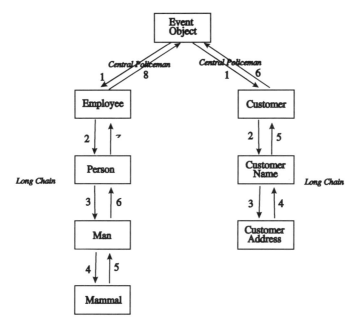

Figure 6.27 Messaging strategies 3

- the class and aggregation abstractions in the class model are not hidden from the user/event level programmer.

  What should have been done is to adopt central policeman messaging as in figure 6.27, with the source classes from which class and aggregation abstraction has been obtained; also the point from which messages to the class and aggregation hierachies can be sent. The user and event programmer would thus only see the data to be processed in terms of the key based objects/entities as in a logical data model. This would facilitate migration to object orientation.

- There is a ripple effect of change because there is not total information hiding. For example, if the business requirement changes and there is no need to access Customer Name then three methods require to change their code with the long chain approach, the method in Customer not to send a message to a method in Customer Name, the Customer Name method to disappear and the Customer Address method would require to be messaged from Customer.

  The methods to be invoked to access the aggregate classes would only be those appropriate to the business requirement. In the example in figure 6.27 there is a need to access the aggregation classes of Customer Name and Address and no other aggregation classes. The access requirements of the business requirement to the aggregation classes

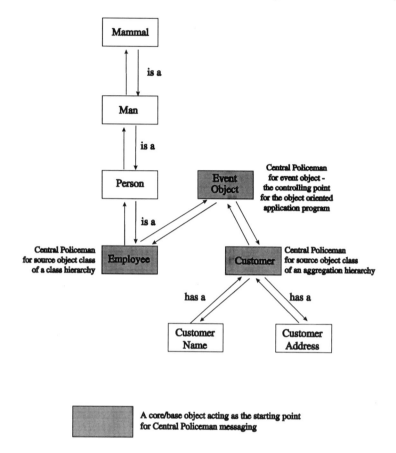

Figure 6.28   Messaging strategies 4

would be defined in the message to the Customer class.

Should there be the same change in a business requirement as detailed above the messaging approach of central policeman would be to alter the appropriate methods in the two object classes only, the Customer, the central point for the sending messages to the abstracted aggregation objects and the affected aggregation classes. This a 30% improvement to the above example.

The same is true of the round robin messaging from Employee to Person, Man, Mammal and back to Employee.

Figure 6.28 shows the full encapsulation of the user from the object oriented abstractions from Employee and Customer. The event process is to access certain employees who have been dealing in some way with customers. The user would enter the search keys in blind ignorance

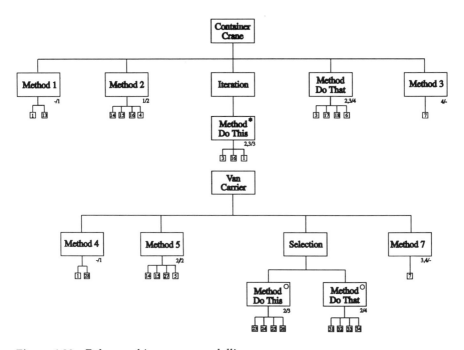

Figure 6.29 Polymorphic process modelling

that there have abstractions for both object classes to be messaged. And the application programmer of the event class does not need to know the abstractions—so object orientation information modelling is hidden/encapsulated from the programmer as well as the user. Central policeman messaging is obtained from the event class and from the two base classes from which abstractions have been made. Both the Employee and the Customer methods supporting this event would require to send messages to the other methods in the abstracted classes containing information pertinent to the event/business requirement.

The added beauty of this encapsulation of object orientation is that it supports a change to the objectbase. There could be a later need to add further abstractions to the existing class model. This would not affect the event class processing as it is isolated from the abstracted classes. The event class process would continue unchanged to send messages to the Employee and Customer classes.

6.4.7.6 Modelling polymorphic processes

There is a good way to ascertain if a process is polymorphic. If the logic is of the kind that states:

"If object instance is X then do...."

"If object instance is Y then do...."

this is a clear indication that the logic is dependent on which class instance of an object is being messaged. One then has to name a common polymorphic name for the processes with the instance variations on the lines of figure 6.29. The recognition of a polymorphic process is best achieved by studying the Object State Diagrams. If there is a commonly named process that updates several classes with many, but not all, the operations being the same then the processes are candidates for polymorphism. There is the method, Method 2, that is common to two classes, Container Crane and Van Carrier, but as can be seen from their operations they have a common set of operations 14 and 16 but thereafter differ. There is therefore some common processing with some different processing in each of the similarly named processes. Very much polymorphic processing.

The methods Do This and Do That should be named as different processes. Although they both support the two events/business requirements Do This and Do That they are, in fact, different processes and should be named differently, such as Do This.Update Container Crane and Do This.Update Van Carrier as appropriate.

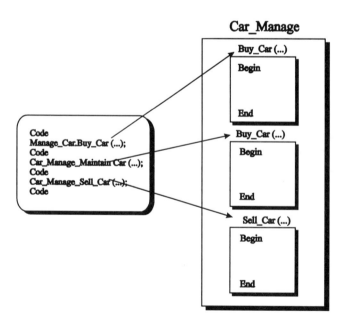

Figure 6.30   Genericity (parameter modelling)

6.4.7.7 Modelling genericity

This is parameter driven software. This supports the facility of describing a class in terms of parameters, with the object class to be processed specified as a parameter. In the context of SSADM genericity is very useful for supporting the facility of the functional level process. There is a general function for the management of a motor vehicle, this covering the different types of vehicles of car, trucks and buses. There is a common process which does not know which class is to be supported when it is triggered. This is decided by the parameter that is passed to the method Manage Vehicle, say a parameter of the value "C" for car and so on. A model of generic functions is illustrated in figure 6.30.

6.4.7.8 Human/computer interface design

There are two types of screens for the Human/Computer Interface—menu and dialogue screens. Menu screens support the man/machine interface for the selection of a business requirement, and dialogue screens the man/machine interface of the selected business requirement.

Menu screens

The menu screens are not pitched at the event/business requirement level. They contain options for/are generic to the selection of many business requirements. The menu selection logic is therefore not normalisable to a business object in the class model: they should be normalised to their own

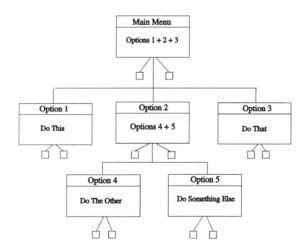

Figure 6.31 Menu screen structure model

classes. If the menu screens are bought-in software, such as pull-down and slide-off menu construction facilities or whole screen formats, then the classes are super classes to the Company class. If the menu screen designs are specific to the company, then the classes are sub classes to the Company class.

Most of the structured methods rightly pitched the menu screens at the user role level. One could design a user role class object and put the menu selection logic for the user role into the appropriate user role class. The authors have tended to create a separate menu class that fulfils a similar function, but a more accurate approach is to build a structure diagram, as illustrated in figure 6.31. The diagram is à la Jackson but without iteration or selection. The logic/operations for each screen are defined in the same way as for the event process models, and become method only classes. There would be a method only class for each of the option screens and the main menu screen of figure 6.31.

Dialogue screens

The same Jackson-like structure diagram can be used for modelling the dialogue screens for each event/business requirement of the application.

An example is illustrated in figure 6.32, where the dialogue screen for the event/business requirement Do This has five screens in sequence, with iteration and selection. The operations for the screen processing (editing an input screen attributes, processing the values in the screen input) are specified as in the event process model, and are interpreted for common processing in like manner. Any common operations can be generalised as

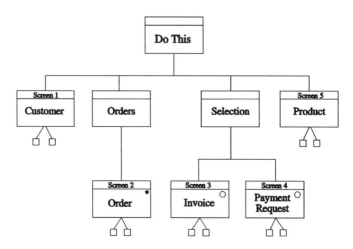

Figure 6.32   Dialogue structure model

super-class method only classes. The residue operations become the methods for the dialogue screens.

If the logic for dialogue screen handling is generic to many business requirements then the logic should be normalisable to a common procedure class.

A failure of some structured methods, such as SSADM, is to recognise that with the advent of the client-server hardware architecture the processing of the man/machine operations can be done on the front-end client processor, with the database processing operations of the business classes being done on the back-end mainframe type server processor. No operations are specified on the dialogue or menu structure diagrams. There is a simple solution. The database operations on the server are defined in the event process models, and the client processing is defined in the Dialogue Structure Models.

6.4.7.9   The structure of object oriented application programs

Given all the above techniques for the modelling of logic in an object oriented way the structure of object oriented application programs is modelled in figure 6.33. The event class is the controlling process for the application program, being the initiator of messages and the final receiver

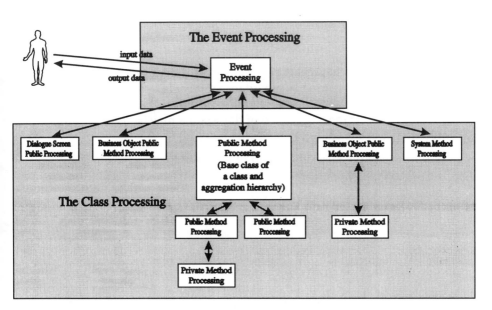

Figure 6.33   The full structure of an OO application program

of messages to the business classes containing the user data to be accessed prior to any final processing, dialogue screens if the event is online, the business objects that are the source object classes from which class and aggregation hierarchies have been abstracted being the other centres of central policemen messaging and private methods being invoked from the public methods as required.

6.4.8 Objectbase design

In line with the concept of logical design = physical design, objectbase design has already been done in the class object model. Each class object in the model becomes a class object in the objectbase. Abstract class objects are only definitions in the objectbase schema, whereas class objects with user keys and data properties are also object instances in the objectbase.

The rules of objectbase design have not changed from those long applied for database design. Such design aspects as clustering the detail object in the same page/block as the most frequently accessed master object, storing the object instances in a key sequence if that is the most frequent access for a given class object and a larger page/block for a class object and its instances if the bulk of access is serial rather than direct are as true for objectbase design as for database design. But an objectbase is more than a traditional database. It contains additional facilities, including:

- definitions of the methods, either as properties of the class objects containing user data or as method only class objects;
- the schema needs to be part of the locking mechanism of the objectbase. Given the need for property inheritance if there is a change in the schema definition, the schema needs to be locked while the changes are being made, otherwise the old version of the schema may be used for property inheritance as the changes are being made;
- the storage of the methods as part of the objectbase.

6.4.9 Object oriented program design

The basic mechanism of program identification and batch program sequencing is unchanged for object oriented design. In a practical world, module identification in an object oriented design is simple. The processing at the event level is within the application program event object. Typically, this logic is concerned with the initialisation of program variables, the synchronisation of the message responses, any processing dependent on the synchronised responses, and any transaction screen formatting. The "modules" are the normalised logic in the public and private methods within the other system and business objects. Methods can in turn issue further messages to other methods in the same or other objects, thus creating the classic program structure chart. The format of the messages and their returned information can be defined as in conventional programming.

Program structure charts are perfectly valid in object oriented programming.

6.5 SUMMARY

The chapter shows that:

- most of the current leading structured designs methods for object oriented information modelling are for realtime applications and are extensions of the Yourdon method;

- all of these methods have major deficiencies, such as no techniques for dialogue design, the normalisation of logic, with the use of the State Transition Diagram technique for modelling the state of objects being considerably deficient in capability;

- there are three main techniques for modelling information in an object oriented way—the class object model, the object state model and the event process model. The first shows the class, composition and business objects and the associated relationships between them. The state model shows the state of the objects when a message invokes method and the sequence in which the methods that update the class object should be invoked. The event process model shows the 20% of logic that is at the event level, the 80% of logic that normalises to the class objects, the sequence of messaging to the class objects for the event, and any commonality of operations in the methods for generalisation into common procedure methods;

- the Central Policeman message strategy is the most object oriented. It does not need access logic pertinent to the event to be in the methods in the class objects. It assists in keeping the logic in the methods in normalised form. The "root" objects from which central policeman messages should be based are the event objects, the base objects of the composition and the aggregate objects. The base object of the composition object is that from which methods are to specific data properties, and hence require abstraction to composition objects on the basis of third normal form logic normalisation. The base object for the aggregate object is that which has mandatory relationships to other objects.

7

MANAGING OBJECT ORIENTED PROJECTS

This chapter explores the issues that management must address before adopting object orientation as the basis for the future design, development and maintenance of their application systems. Each factor needs to be understood and its impact on the present organisation assessed so that all the potential benefits of object orientation can be realised and the risks, inherent in change, can be adequately controlled. The factors addressed in this chapter are:

- choice of products and applications,
- new development opportunities,
- prototyping and evolutionary development,
- project team roles and activities,
- project evaluation,
- costs and benefits.

7.1 MANAGEMENT ISSUES

Object oriented technology was primarily created and has evolved to support the program coding phase of a software development project where the application consisted of potentially complex relationships among the software elements. From its research laboratory inception object oriented technology has been extensively adopted by individuals and small groups initially to provide support for three narrowly focused activities of programmers:

- customising existing applications to meet personal preferences,

- managing the specification of complex information models,

- composing innovative graphical user interfaces.

It now faces its most significant test: general acceptance by software development organisations for all commercial and industrial operations. Technologists can believe that object oriented technology will be accepted simply because it provides the right solutions for the design and development problems that the software industry faces. But the design and development changes that object orientation brings require an organisation to resolve many issues before the technology can be successfully adopted.

Object oriented technology impacts:

- various levels of management in an organisation, as well as each member of the software development team,

- the technical rules for all programming team participants: the application analysers, the system designers and documentors and the code implementors, documentors, testers and maintainers,

- the design techniques that are applied,

- the user's expectations of new kinds of applications designed to let the user express opinions at the desktop,

- the structure of the software development process, changing the roles that must be fulfilled in the development team as well as its evaluation and reward.

7.2   COMMERCIAL ADOPTION

7.2.1   Choice of products

Another question for management considering the adoption of OO technology is "What type of OO product should be used for the OO development of application systems?" There are two basic choices; the adoption of a new specialised product, usually from one of the new companies specially set up to be an early exploiter of a technology gap, or to wait for the relational vendors to enhance their products to support OO.

Currently, many of the specialist products have been targeted to support the use of graphical user interface (GUI) technology. The development of GUIs was one of the driving forces behind the original development of OO technology. A GUI is easier to develop and modify when it is built with OO technology, since the behaviour of the objects which appear on the screen can be separated from their actual presentation on the screen so that the presentation form of the objects can be extensively reused. All the leading GUI products, such as Microsoft's Windows/3, Hewlett Packard's New Wave and OSF's Motif, have been developed with OO technology and provide an OO style of interface to the users of the products. The products have also been designed to run in operating environments for the small computer, typically of the client type, the operating environment being primarily the MS.DOS, OS2 and UNIX type operating systems. There are currently no operating systems for the middle and mainframe type computers that support OO products. It is strange that OO is still not yet supported for the big, complex and corporate applications, since that is exactly where the main long term benefits of OO will be obtained.

If an installation already uses relational technology for the major applications in the company then there is a major argument, given the above and the fact that the new specialist vendors are small and lack financial and human resources, for waiting until the relational vendors enhance their products to support OO in the near term. This enhancement is already happening. For example, Ingres Inc. have already made the GUI application development software (Windows 4GL) object-based in that messages are sent to stored procedures in the object tables; the stored procedures contain SQL calls to the object table to access the data properties, the logic for any processing required and to produce the return response. The technology with this product is thus based on, and supports, abstract data types as a precursor to being fully OO. The stored procedure facility can be used as a public method, as a private method to apply the database rules and the sending of messages can be used to support property inheritance; the technology enables "Do It Yourself" OO without polymorphism.

It is essential that the product selected to support the adoption of object orientation is able to provide, preferably, all the OO features; the minimum facilities being class, property inheritance, dynamic binding (polymorphism) and encapsulation (through the use of methods). If a product does not make available all of these four facilities then it should not be used to support object oriented development.

There is little doubt that the C++ programming language is the leading OO language by a substantial margin. This language should be adopted unless there is a strong case otherwise; for example, if it cannot be integrated into the development and runtime environment of an application. It is likely that the major contenders to C++ will be the 4GL programming languages of the relational file handlers, which are almost certain to be upgraded to support OO, rather than any other OO language. It would be extraordinary if the widespread use of 4GL languages was to "wither on the vine" through the advancement of object orientation. It is possible that new 5GLs will be developed with C++ so that they automatically provide object oriented facilities. These new 5GLs would exploit the ability, with C++, to seamlessly incorporate facilities which model a particular problem domain which, in this case, would be the domain of general application frameworks.

7.2.2   Types of applications

As has been explained, OO is a technology that is able to support complexity and change; the former by generalised abstraction and the latter by specialised refinement within class hierarchies. The size and volatility of application systems become an irrelevancy. *Object orientation is therefore tailor made to support large application systems involving fast changing business scenarios.* And given that access to the data is via methods, which does not require knowledge of the structure of the data in the database, it is also able to provide genuinely non-procedural access to data. The limitations of relational procedural access to data (notwithstanding the claims of the relational vendors) are removed.

A common characteristic of large applications is the impossibility of knowing the entire application in detail. With traditional database and 4GL programming technology there is the need to know the format and structure of the data and the logic at the event level in order to know how the application works. Such is not the case with object orientation. An object oriented application program is made up of:

- the event level logic,

- a series of messages to the methods within the class objects which represent the user data,

- other methods containing common procedures and system processing.

The only thing the programmer needs to know is:

- the logic at the event level,

- the methods that need to be invoked with the class objects for the remainder of the business requirement processing,

- the key/search argument of the object instances to be accessed,

- the format of the response to the message.

and that is all. The logic within the methods is completely transparent to the sender of the message, as is the representation of the object instances being accessed. The scope of the learning curve of the developer is therefore much less, being limited to the above four characteristics of the application environment.

7.3 New Development Opportunities

7.3.1 New programming styles

Object oriented technology has created a new software development environment composed of source code, code editors and debuggers, browsers and inspectors[1], and has created at least three new programming styles:

7.3.1.1 *Programming by exploration*

This involves the incremental development of a program from an incomplete specification. Such an incomplete specification could be a rough textual description rather than a full Jackson model with operations or an Action Diagram. The programmer creates a partial solution, as a prototype, and allows this to dictate the direction of further development as the result of feedback from early design reviews, feasibility analyses and early testing by the target users. This approach is perfect for GUI development, particularly if products, like Windows 4/GL from Ingres, are used. The development and evolution of prototype implementations is much more productive under OO than with traditional databases and programming technology because of its ability to encapsulate changes behind a well defined interface. The behaviour of a prototype can be incrementally changed by replacing the logic within the methods without having to disturb any other parts of the prototype.

7.3.1.2 *Programming by refinement*

This is the ability to reuse existing software by allowing exceptions to the behaviour of existing classes to be implemented as subclasses of the general case. The new subclass method contains the exceptional logic. Through inheritance and polymorphism this additional exceptional behaviour, encapsulated in a subclass, can be added into existing software without any

---

[1] The set of tools provided to support program design, coding and testing in this new development environment are often referred to as an IPSE (Integrated Program Support Environment) or CASE (Computer Aided Software Environment) Toolsets. These environments typically provide a graphical and interactive (point and click) interface.

changes to the existing software. This approach can also be used for prototyping.

7.3.1.3 *Programming by factoring*

This is the handling of complexity by creating a superclass to encapsulate properties that reflect common behaviour of more than one subclass object. An example of this is that Persons and Employees both have a Birth Date.

The purpose of these programming styles, which are not mutually exclusive, is to:

- get results quickly,

- involve the target user or technical team in reviewing the result,

- throw away the result if it does not meet the evolving objectives.

The approach is intended to increase confidence that the final result will solve the targeted problem as a consequence of submitting the partial solutions to early design reviews and feasibility analyses. The approach also reinforces a process driven approach to system development rather than a data driven approach.

7.3.2 Large complex systems

To understand how object oriented technology affects the organisation, it is important to understand the characteristics of the systems being built using object oriented technology.

Organisations undertake the construction of large software systems which require the use of diverse teams of collaborating individuals and often incur high development costs. These costs could be reduced if some components of the system were reused from previously developed systems.

Large systems are often too complicated for one individual to comprehend, so that it becomes extremely difficult for users to understand and specify exactly what they want in the context of the whole application system. This can result in an incomplete and inaccurate system specification. And some structured design methods do not help in this regard, particularly in the important area of the HCI. For example, SSADM has no screen design method, and most methods provide no support for windows technology. A prototype can help the users and system analysts to identify the real user requirements in terms of the data needed to support the business requirements, how it should be presented, what HCI features are most effective, and so on. It can also assist, during the design phase, in achieving architectural clarity.

Large, complex, high cost systems employing large teams are also usually long lived. Such systems will, almost certainly during their lifetimes, have to accommodate changes to their original specification. An effective system building technology must recognise that adaptation to change, even during system building process, is a fundamental necessity and that system evolution is inevitable.

To be effective in building such systems, object oriented technology must provide explicit support for:

- leveraging reusable designs and components,

- prototyping,

- structuring teams so that systems can be designed to be easily changed over their lifetimes, even during the design and construction stages.

7.4 OO DEVELOPMENT MODEL

The traditional development model, often called the "Waterfall" Model, is not well suited to object oriented development. The Waterfall Model, as illustrated in figure 7.1, accommodates iteration within a stage but expects each stage to flow from the previous one so that, once completed, a stage is not revisited. Each stage progressively refines, rather than reuses, the information modelled in the previous stage. There is no concept of reuse built into the top down Waterfall approach. *This encourages management to equate the completion of a stage to a project milestone and to associate formal project deliverables with them.*

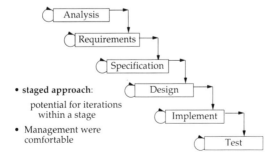

Figure 7.1 Traditional life cycle: waterfall

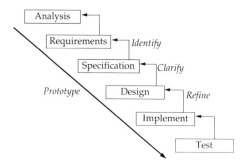

Figure 7.2   Evolutionary life cycle: iterate

With traditional development these clearly delineated project stages will break down when rework and changes become necessary. Such rework is often due to the size and complexity of the system producing an inaccurate and incomplete specification. For long lived projects there is also the need to accommodate changes to the original specification during the project's lifetime. When earlier "completed" stages have to be revisited for these pragmatic reasons the need to also rework the formal procedures associated with its completion can significantly add to the total effort involved.

A different development lifecycle model is needed to support the facilities offered by object oriented technology which accommodates change, maximises reuse of the objects already in place and supports the new programming styles of exploration, refinement and factoring. *The development lifecycle needs to allow iterations between the project stages as shown in Figure 7.2, where each iteration increasingly applies reuse to build from the bottom up in the later physical design and construction phases.*

With an iterative approach to development, each iteration can be used to clarify the system specification, to identify the real user requirements and to achieving architectural clarity in the design and implementation. Prototyping is the method used to achieve these objectives.

7.4.1   Prototyping

A prototype contributes to the process of building the full-scale system by creating an intentionally incomplete or scaled-down version of a system that can:

● refine and clarify the system specification,

● clarify the architectural design,

- address HCI and usability issues,

- support performance testing.

In this context, a prototype is not sufficiently engineered for delivery as a robust product, but it provides evidence that the full product can be developed. *The building of prototypes and bottom up construction are key differences in the structure of an OO project.*

Rapid prototyping refers to the process of quickly building and evaluating a series of functional prototypes which become feasible in an OO project because of the richness of the available repository of reusable components. These prototypes become more robust, as a consequence of being constructed from software components shared and tested by many programmers, which enhances the credibility of the prototype to the target users who can then provide better feedback.

Functional prototyping usually occurs during the early stages of a software project. When starting a project an analysis prototype is created to clarify the formal requirements specification by allowing users to interact with an executable but partial mock-up of the expected product to solicit user reaction and ideas. Once agreement is reached, a formal requirements specification can be documented from the analysis prototype. The outcome of an OO analysis is the set of objects and their initial relationships that represent the required functionality. Analysis prototypes should typically be regarded as throwaway; the goal is to agree on the requirements, not to produce elegant or optimal solutions. This is the SSADM approach to prototyping. Analysis prototypers must be prepared to compromise and be pragmatic.

Following functional prototyping a design prototype is developed to:

- create and verify the system's architecture,

- check for redundancies or inconsistencies in the design,

- determine whether complete functionality can be integrated,

- form the basis for performance and space evaluation.

The resulting architectural clarity of the design prototype provides the basis for coding the actual application software, perhaps using parts of the prototype. Whether the design prototype is thrown away or evolved into the actual application depends primarily upon the results of its performance and space evaluation. It will at least provide an excellent design document for the application development team.

If the prototype is being restricted to the development of the user screens and the supporting screen logic (the HCI is being animated) the prototyping will be limited to an analysis role of the user requirements. The animation is only for the front-end processing of the application, and once the users are able to confirm their satisfaction with the HCI the prototype can be thrown away. If, however, the HCI prototyping environment provides appropriate "hooks" by which the back-end, or "non interactive core", of the application can be attached to it then it becomes feasible to evolve the HCI prototype into the real application's production user interface. Such evolution of a HCI prototype into a complete application is most feasible when the application is primarily externally driven by its end users; the application being composed of components which respond to events triggered by its users.

If the prototyping is to exercise the processing of the user data in the objectbase then it can be used for transaction performance, disk space evaluation and ascertaining whether the full functional requirements of the application are being achieved. Such prototypes have a much better chance of being upgraded into production systems. It can only be achieved where the class library is well developed, so that the scope for software reuse during the prototyping is considerable and the classes support the addition of exceptional cases and new functionality by class derivation and refinement. This approach can also be used to "customise" existing applications for the new business functionality.

It must be recognised that developing and evaluating prototypes leads to improved quality and "fitness for purpose" rather than a reduction in time and effort. Prototyping improves a team's understanding of the design and ensures that the users, who have been involved in early reviews, contribute to achieving an acceptable result. Extensive use will have to be made of existing reusable components in order to produce usable prototypes effectively. New reusable components should be generated during the prototyping activity, thereby enhancing the collection of reusable components for later reuse.

The Human Engineering and usability aspects of the application are areas where significant improvements in "fitness for purpose" can be achieved through prototyping, particularly when graphical user interfaces are being used. The development of the user interface for an application typically accounts for at least 50% of an application's development effort, and requires a thorough understanding of the roles and tasks to be performed by the target users. Usability and user customisation of the HCI are as much components of information systems design as performance. Early participation of the users in evaluating the usability of a prototype user interface can clarify the required roles and tasks, and help to contain the development effort needed to produce acceptable user interfaces. *The reasons that led to the initial development of OO technology for building graphical user interfaces are still applicable today.*

The much increased role of prototyping in OO design and development

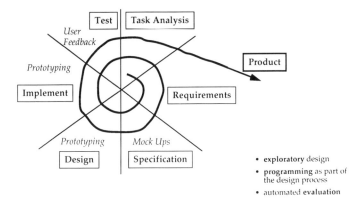

Figure 7.3   Evolutionary life cycle: spiral

encourages the "Spiral" development project lifecycle shown in figure 7.3. The reason for this is that change to the data and, above all, to the logic is so much easier to support—merely add the change required as a sub-class object to the general case, and if the results are still not adequate add yet another subclass. In this way an incomplete prototype can have functionality and behaviour added incrementally on the next iteration round the spiral. New class objects only need to be created where there is no class object in the existing class model with data and logic properties that are suitable for derivation.

The role of OO prototyping depends on the maturity of the class object model as represented in the class library. If the library is large and the methods are suitable for the application being prototyped then the prototyping can be rapid. What is more, because the prototyping is able to use existing class objects the prototype will be largely robust and tested; only the added subclasses contain new code that has to be developed and tested.

7.4.1.1 Benefits

Carefully planned and controlled prototyping during the analysis and design phases of a software development can provide a number of benefits to management.

The prototype evaluation results can contribute to "go/nogo" decision making. If the project proceeds the management knows that the target users were intimately involved in the requirements decision.

Constructing prototypes develops synergy between the teams involved in an OO development lifecycle. As will be seen in Section 7.5, OO development benefits from having two development teams; one responsible for the framework of reusable classes and the other responsible for delivering business applications. Prototyping in the framework context will explore the framework's ability to support many applications. This requires an understanding of the needs of many potential applications. Prototyping in the application context will explore the user's needs and specific requirements of an application. To develop these prototypes rapidly requires an understanding of the capabilities and functionality of the existing framework of reusable classes.

Both the framework and the application teams can benefit from analysis and design prototypes. The analyst prototyper in the framework team is a domain analyst responsible for providing a detailed analysis of a specific domain, such as insurance, radar or expert systems. From this analysis the design prototyper constructs a prototype framework with sufficient breadth to support many applications in that domain. The analyst prototyper in the application team involves the user in creating an executable version of the application. The design prototyper uses this analysis and the framework to satisfy the user's needs.

7.4.1.2 Pitfalls

The demonstration of an OO prototype which appears to show that the anticipated application is actually working can raise expectations of reducing the "time to market" for the real product. Commercial pressures can tempt managers to deliver the prototype to enter a market before the competition.

The tendency to refine and enhance a prototype continuously can blur the distinction between prototype development and product system development, particularly if the same small development team is responsible for both activities. Larger companies should ensure that these two teams are different so that the prototyping activity delivers good design documents.

7.4.2 Evolutionary development

Even when the teams are separate the prototyping activity may seem to be unending—there is always just one more feature to be prototyped! This spiral type of applications development, shown in figure 7.3, has its dangers as a consequence of using OO technology to evolve solutions from prototypes. The user sees the animated HCI and, knowing that change is now much easier to support with OO technology, requests yet another change. Technically, it will be easy to incorporate changes requested during the OO development of an application—it will often simply involve just adding another subclass into the class hierarchy and refining its methods. It is necessary to put a limit on the number of iterations within prototyping and for management to establish, quite clearly before a prototype is started, exactly its purpose and how it is to be evaluated. Iterating over a prototype three times is usually sufficient to reduce the risks associated with production development and to obtain most of the benefits cost effectively.

Evolutionary development will expand the class hierarchies quite extensively by adding more and more subclasses and this itself can become difficult to manage. It is wise, when the prototyping is complete to review the class hierarchies with the objective of rationalising them before use during production. Long chains of subclasses should be merged and unnecessary classes removed; the hierarchies should be pruned and the "deadwood" removed in much the same way as a living tree has to be trained and controlled.

7.4.3 Reuse

The purpose of reuse is to achieve rapid development of robust systems by using what already exists to satisfy a new requirement. To be able to use what already exists it must have been developed into class hierarchies which provide a set of abstractions, or generalisations, that are not limited to a single software development effort. When such class hierarchies exist they will already have been used and will therefore enhance the quality and productivity of any future systems development into which they are incorporated. Many aspects of an OO software development can be reused such as analyses, designs, implementations, test cases, and documentation.

There are five common categories of reuse:

- *algorithms*
  - The same algorithm can be reused on different data structures by using the data abstraction facilities supported by OO technology. An algorithm implemented in a base class is automatically inherited and available to any derived subclasses. For example, the algorithms which allows objects to be written to, and retrieved from a file store can be inherited by any class whose objects need to be persistent, that is, the objects need to exist beyond the termination of the program that created them.

- *classes and instances*
  - Objects can be reused in two ways. Deriving a new class by inheritance reuses its implementation and its methods by modelling the *is*

a relationship. Including an instance of an existing class in the composition of a new class just reuses its methods and models the *has a* relationship. The reuse of the Vehicle class as a Car and as part of a Garage in Section 5.2.9 is an example of these forms of reuse.

- *application frameworks*
  — An application framework consists of abstract classes and the signatures (message formats) of their methods with the expectation that derived subclasses will provide concrete code for these methods which specialises the framework for particular applications. By supporting a variety of subclasses a framework can be reused across many applications. A number of graphical user interface builders provide such frameworks by incorporating a predefined execution model for an application which is usually driven by events arising from the actions of the user of the graphical interface.

- *complete applications*
  — Complete applications, such as file and network managers, text and picture editors and data base managers can be embedded into other applications. If such applications are object oriented the objects they contain can be refined and specialised and the application itself becomes a form of framework.

- *interface specifications*
  — An object oriented interface specification consists of a set of methods that encapsulate a coordinated set of behaviours. Classes whose instances perform the role implied by these behaviours must implement these behaviours and can reuse the existing interface specification to ensure that the role is consistently supported. The use of an abstract class which supports iteration over its members, described in Section 5.2.10.1, is an example of the reuse of an interface specification.

7.4.3.1   Managing reuse

To achieve reuse and reap its benefits a company has to encourage the design and development of reusable components and *then ensure that they are utilised*. This requires managerial and technical support, as well as mutual cooperation between the development teams and the team members. In particular, managers need to adjust the manner in which they supervise, review and compensate software developers for their change in roles in order to encourage the development and reuse of software components. In addition, the development staff have to learn how to develop and utilise reusable components and overcome their personal biases against reusing components which they did not develop; the common "Not Invented Here" syndrome has to be replaced by a recognition that existing components can be refined and specialised.

Managers need to encourage these changes in attitude by modifying the reward structures for the developers so that reuse becomes a requirement; writing new code when an appropriate reusable component exists should be regarded as unacceptable. A librarian should monitor the level of reuse achieved by a component that has been accepted into the corporate library. When the level of reuse is high the developer of that component has made just as significant contribution to the company's bottom line as a salesperson meeting a quota; the reusable component developer has saved the company both time and money. This can be counted, for example, as the number of lines of reused code times the number of objects, and a proportion of the saving given as a bonus to the developer. These savings will accrue over several years and need a long term organisational commitment to be realised.

7.4.3.2 Creating assets

There are several ways to build up a company's library of reusable components. Some internal startup costs can be avoided by buying a commercially available library, but this may not meet a company's own documentation and coding conventions. Reusable components should be shared between projects within a company. This will be more effective if common standards for software formatting and documentation are applied. commercial libraries will be easier to refine and adapt to suit your company's needs if they are purchased in source code form.

To date the approach that has been adopted is to buy software packages that have been designed for complete applications areas, such as payroll, accounting and stock control. With the increasing use of object orientation this is changing and packages, or class libraries, are available at a much lower level of functional granularity. Examples are graphical interface classes and data base interface classes, which provide components from which to construct parts of applications rather than entire applications.

If software development is contracted out with the expectation of obtaining reusable components as a result, ensure that the ownership of these reusable assets is clearly defined in the contract. If the contractor has already developed reusable components this should be reflected in the competitiveness of the contract.

7.5   OO PROJECT STRUCTURE

The structure and roles that have evolved for the design and development of computer applications reflect the capabilities and limitations of existing technology, as discussed in Chapter 1. The classic example is the clear separation of the database and the application programmer. It therefore follows that as the technology changes so must the structure and roles of the organisation that uses the new technology.

An effective approach to the use of OO technology is to structure development projects into a business team and an enterprise, or infrastructure, team. The business team is responsible for the design and development of a specific application that fulfils a contractual obligation with a client. This team interacts with the client to determine the information requirements, either through the formal application of the analysis techniques of a structured method and/or through prototyping, and focuses on reusing existing components, during development, to meet deadlines in a timely fashion.

The enterprise team focuses on developing a basic generic structure, or framework, that can be customised, by the business team, for different business applications in the same domain. Examples of such frameworks are an enterprise framework, that is, a framework which models the normal (generic) business of a company, such as a manufacturing framework or an invoicing framework. Customisation means that optional existing components are selected by the business team and attached to their application framework. For instance, the customisation of an invoicing framework could involve selecting specific local and fiscal tax requirements and debt collection procedures.

The interaction between the enterprise team and the business team is shown in figure 7.4. The enterprise team are the guardians of the generic

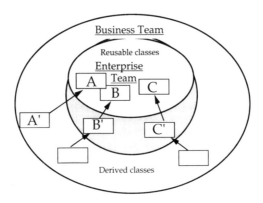

Figure 7.4   Enterprise and business domains

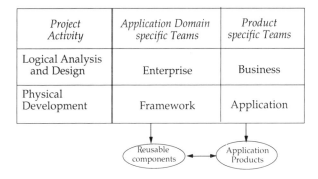

Project Activity	Application Domain specific Teams	Product specific Teams
Logical Analysis and Design	Enterprise	Business
Physical Development	Framework	Application

Figure 7.5   OO development teams

enterprise model encapsulated in a set of general purpose, reusable classes. For a specific application the business team base their application on these classes, as much as possible, and derive more specific ones where the current classes are inadequate. Some of these new derived classes will remain particular to an application whilst others, depicted by A', B' and C' in figure 7.4, are sufficiently general, and tested in operational use, to be included back into the enterprise framework for use by other application projects. In this way the enterprise framework progressively grows, bit by bit, to provide additional capabilities that have the potential for reuse by other business applications.

Part of the motivation for a two-team approach is to exploit the fact that companies develop expertise in their own business domain. The enterprise team focuses attention on the design and development of a specific environment that can be used by business teams to develop different applications within the same application domain.

Although the enterprise and business teams have fundamentally different roles they use the same overall OO processes to achieve their goals. These processes are object oriented logical analysis and physical design, implementation, testing, maintenance and extensions. The way in which each team applies these processes will be influenced by the need to prototype and achieve reuse.

7.5.1   Team structures

The proposed structure for an OO project is suggested in figure 7.5. It is different from that currently practiced in that, during both the analysis and design stages and the development stages, two teams are established which work in parallel. One set of teams address the construction and development of a generic framework which is tailored to the needs of applications of interest to the business with the objective of providing reusable components. The other set of teams focus on the development of specific applications (products) for the business.

7.5.1.1   The logical analysis and design teams

The structure for the analysis and design stages consists of a Business Team and an Enterprise Team.

The Business Team   This team analyses the business requirements of the users using traditional information modelling techniques, such as entity modelling, dataflow diagramming, entity life history analysis, dialogue design and action diagrams, which have long been practiced by such methods as Information Engineering, SSADM and Merise. There is no change in the initial stages of the information design process. The analysis and design teams already in operation can be used for this task without retraining since they can continue to use familiar techniques. The Business Team does not need to know that the implementation of the design will be object oriented; *no new skills are required by the Business Team.*

The Enterprise Team   They are specialists in the OO logical modelling of applications and in the construction of a generic model of an enterprise which is customisable to different business applications. They develop and maintain a Model of the Enterprise which consists of reusable and extensible design models and components from which specific applications can be derived and into which specific application requirements can be incorporated by generalisation.

They take a logical design specification model of the application, developed by the Business Team, and convert it into an OO Logical Design Specification. This requires them to:

- identify class hierarchies in the entity model and conduct any class abstractions of common behaviour into super-class objects and exceptional behaviour into sub-class objects,

- classify the OO relationships between class objects on the basis of inheritance (the *is a* semantic), composition (the *has a* semantic) and business (free form semantic as with traditional data modelling),

- normalise the logic of the business requirements/events as methods to the class objects. It is suggested that this be modelled with the Jackson technique as this has the benefit that the logic operations are added to the objects and the events as appropriate; the technique is already object based,

- add the system class objects to the business model so far constructed,

- map the access paths of the business requirements against the class object model.

The techniques for these tasks have been detailed in Chapter 6.

7.5.1.2   *The physical development teams*

The physical development stages of the project are also structured into two teams known as the Application Team and the Framework Team.

The Application Team   This team produces the physical design of the application. However, this is not an isolated task. The design of an OO system starts from the basis of what has been designed previously, and whether it can be reused or requires abstraction to provide additional generalisations and specialisations to support the requirements of a new application. The ability to reuse and the need for abstraction cannot be ascertained without reference to the Framework Team. In a sense the Application Team is negotiating a "contract" with the Framework Team to provide software (the methods) that will support the behaviour expected for the messages that are sent to Framework Team's objects from the Application Team's objects. The required behaviour has to be established as the two teams liaise as part of the reuse process.

Where the behaviour of the Framework class objects is deficient it is the responsibility of the Framework Team to refine the existing general case class objects into appropriate sub- or super-class objects. If the required behaviour is at the event level, it is the responsibility of the Application Team to do the development. If the development is via the creation of a sub-class object in the class object model, it can be done either via the Application or the Framework Team. If it is done by the Application Team it must be under the supervision of the Framework Team. The division of responsibility is such that the Application Team deals with the 20% of the logic that is event specific or application dependent whilst the Framework Team are the custodians of the 100% of the data and 80% of the logic that is generic to the business.

The Framework Team   The Framework team is the guardian of the OO design. It is responsible for creating and maintaining the generic structure of the class object model and the maintenance of the class library of the business and system class objects.

As the Framework Team liaises with the Application Team it will:

- identify new and derived business and system class objects that are needed to support the additional functionality of the new business system,

- "customise" the generic class object model for individual applications,

- decide when application specific class objects become common to more than one application and thereby need to be migrated into the generic class object model. There is no redesign in the overall class object model, merely a transfer of ownership of the class objects from the Application Team to the Framework Team.

The Framework Team maintains the set of System and Application Domain classes from which an Application Team can construct a particular application. As illustrated in figure 7.6 the Application Team is able to concentrate on developing the event level objects that characterise their application to "glue" together a set of Framework class objects that provide most of the required behaviour for the application.

7.5.2   New roles in an OO project

Developer issues in an OO development are primarily concerned with culture changes; convincing software engineers that reuse is a worthwhile endeavour is achieved through an appropriate review and reward structure. The key participants in an OO development team and the criteria for evaluating their effectiveness are:

- *Domain analyser*   The generality of the domain specification produced.

- *Framework designer*   The general reusability of the framework structure.

- *Framework tester*   Testing the variability and generalness of a framework. This is done by creating new appropriate components to establish whether the framework can support them.

- *Component tester*   Testing for the applicability of reusable components in different contexts.

- *Reuse librarian*   Provides effective and consistent management of libraries of reusable assets by assessing the quality and breadth of additions, communicating what is available and coordinating the use of reusable components in designs.

The two tester roles are testing for reusability by establishing whether software components have been designed for broader applicability. The component tester should collaborate with the design prototyper to recommend the design of abstractions that could be added to the library for use in other applications. The design prototyper is responsible for creating

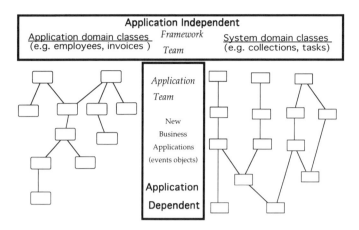

Figure 7.6 Framework and application domains

reusable components within a project, but the real benefits of OO technology are achieved when reuse extends across projects; hence the need for more general abstractions.

7.5.2.1 Reuse librarian

A new and and significant role in leveraging OO technology is that of the librarian who must:

- constantly review software for inclusion into the corporate library,
- consult with the analyst prototypers on the reusable artefacts that could be leveraged,
- participate in the design prototype reviews to ensure that reuse is properly anticipated,
- identify which elements of a design prototype could be reusable,
- propose to R&D management ideas for generalising applications into frameworks.

This role is the most important addition to the development team. It needs to be undertaken by a skilled programmer with a keen ability to recognise potential abstractions and specialisations, but also with an understanding of the abstraction rules for generalisation and specialisation described in Chapter 6. The librarian also needs to be a skilled communicator expected to participate in every review in order to identify where reuse can be leveraged. The librarian must also consider acquiring reusable components from commercial sources. The value of this role to a company's exploitation of OO technology should be reflected in the status and compensation accorded to the reuse librarian.

7.6   COSTS AND BENEFITS

The typical profile of the costs and risks during the lifecycle of a conventionally developed application system is illustrated in figure 7.7. It is a purely illustrative chart without a scale, since actual costs can be influenced by the experience and expertise of the staff involved and other factors, such as the effectiveness of the CASE tools. It shows the profile of the design and development of an application on the basis of a structured method with CASE support. The costs/risks are low during the analysis and logical and physical design stages, but increase substantially during development of the database and program code.

The costs/risks are low during operational running until the system needs upgrading to support new business requirements (adaptive and perfective changes) and to remove errors in the program (corrective maintenance). Adaptive maintenance is concerned with adapting an application to external changes, such as upgrades to the system's execution environment or changes to the business' environment. Perfective maintenance is the incorporation of new functionality to meet new business

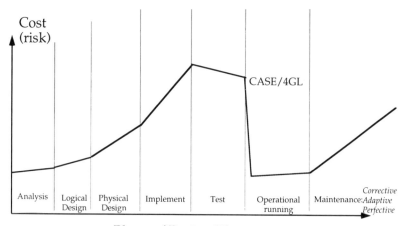

Figure 7.7   Traditional project cost profile

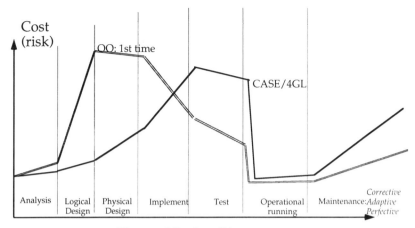

Phase of Project life

Figure 7.8 Lost profile of first OO project

or user needs. Corrective maintenance is the normal task of bug fixing, that is making the application meet its original requirements and specification.

It has long been accepted that some 60% of the software development effort that is spent today by the IT department is on the maintenance of existing systems. *These maintenance costs significantly exceed the business benefit obtained by a company, as any additional functionality is usually quite small compared with the effort expended.*

This cost/risk profile remains constant for each iteration of the development of applications using the existing structured methods, CASE tools and 3/4GL programming languages. The reason for this lack of improvement is that each iteration starts from the same point and is unable to exploit much, if any, of the earlier developments.

By contrast, the profile of an object oriented project, illustrated in figure 7.8, is very different and also changes for each subsequent project development and enhancement. These changes in the cost/risk profile occur as the objectbase matures and the portfolio of reusable objects grows. The design stages are initially more costly than the conventional approach, particularly when the objectbase and class libraries are being initially designed. This is because:

- there are more class objects to identify and model through abstraction. In addition to the classes needed to model the user data and the business methods there are the system classes needed to support the implementation of the design,

- the logic needs to be normalised and defined as methods,

- the class hierarchies need to be identified and the class properties abstracted to the appropriate level of generality and specialisation,

- consideration has to be given to reusing any existing classes, by speciali- sation if necessary, and to designing new classes to maximise their poten- tial for future reuse.

The cost/risk profile reduces during implementation because of the struc- ture and encapsulation imposed by object orientation. *However, the real sig- nificant benefit comes during the maintenance and upgrading of the applications, and during the development of new applications.* Because object oriented devel- opment is designed to support change, by the technique of creating derived classes to support specialisations and exceptions to the existing class objects and by encapsulation, the changes identified during maintenance and upgrading can be added to the existing application design without modify- ing it. Object orientation's support for polymorphism allows the new sub- classes to be gracefully integrated into an existing application without having to change the existing application in any way; objects of these new sub-classes will appear to be instances of their parent classes to the existing application. *Maintenance and functional enhancement is by addition instead of by modification.* The risks and the cost of software maintenance is thereby reduced. Object orientation therefore provides a substantial benefit to a business during the later phases of an application's design and development life cycle.

The other real benefit of object orientation is that as further applications are designed they are able to reuse the well tested existing application and system classes and interfaces during the design and implementation phases of their development life cycles. If the existing methods are not quite what is required they do not have to be changed. New derived classes can be added to encapsulate the additional logic in refined methods which can use the existing methods, as appropriate, to satisfy the new business require- ments. *The approach is the same as that used during maintenance to add sub- classes rather than modify existing classes.* The class object model is added to and also becomes progressively more and more mature and robust as the volume of reuse increases. The opportunity to reuse classes, their interfaces and, above all, the logic encapsulated in their methods increases as new applications are added to the objectbase. This means that the need to design new applications from scratch is progressively reduced; *there is a virtuous cir- cle of increasing reusability.* This can be seen in figure 7.9 where the cost/risk profile of the second object oriented applications is much lower during the design stages than the first application; the cost/risk profile for the design stages becomes lower with each new application.

The benefits of object orientation continue to increase the more that object

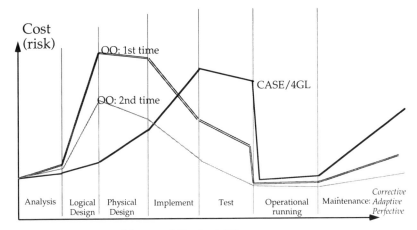

Phase of Project life

Figure 7.9   OO projects cost profile

orientation is used. The more stable and mature the objectbase the bigger the benefit. The initial biggest benefit is in maintenance but the benefit progressively accrues during enhancement.

7.6.1   The benefits of reuse

Statistics released by AT&T, the developers of the C++ programming language, show that lines of code can be saved from reusability by the adoption of object orientation. Three versions of an application are shown, in figure 7.10, with the lines of code that were reused from the previous version of the application during the development of the new version. The saving of code by adding new classes where the existing general case method is not quite adequate starts by being only 25%—itself a high figure—and gets better as later versions are developed; the increase representing the fact that that there is more to reuse in the later version. Without that additional reuse of classes the fifth version would have been bigger by 35,741 lines of code. The same trend can be seen in the reuse, through property inheritance, of the existing classes when the method does not provide all the functionality for the new, or changed, business requirement. This figure starts at 15% and improves to 19% after two more versions have been developed. Without the additional property inheritance the fifth version would have been bigger by 14,670 lines of code. The total lines of code in the fifth version would have been 182,534 without the reuse of classes and through inheritance from the third version; an overall saving of 27% was achieved. The savings in coding

Reused lines of code (between subsystems)		
Version total code	reused classes	saving
3	94591	31201	25%
4	128944	61809	32%
5	132123	66942	33%

- without class reuse

66942 - 31201 = 35741

Reused lines of code (by inheritance)		
Version total code	reused classes	saving
3	94591	16555	15%
4	128944	27392	17%
5	132123	31225	19%

- without inheritance reuse

31225 - 16555 = 14670

Vesion 5 code would have been 182534 = **93%** increase

instead of **40%** increase

Figure 7.10   Savings by reuse (AT &T Bell Laboratories)

provided by object orientation can be substantial—and it must be remembered that the code that is reused is code that is stable and tested. *The risk of the reused code is zero.*

There is also a real safety factor in that the logic within a method, and the data properties of a class, can be modified without affecting applications that use the class to which they belong so long as the interface to the class, that is, the signatures of its methods that respond to messages, does not change. Alternative implementations of a method can be plugged in, to provide different performance trade-offs between space and speed, for instance, without the risk of there being any unexpected side effects. Similarly, the data properties in a class may be modified without the risk of any knock-on effect to the applications, or other classes, that use the class.

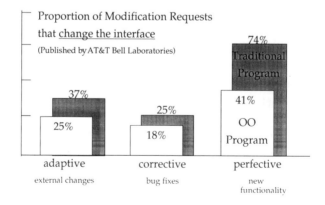

Figure 7.11   Maintenance benefits of OO

This is the major benefit of the total encapsulation provided by object orientation which removes a major risk that is always present when conventionally developed applications are modified. The statistics released by AT&T show that the benefits of relying on the complete encapsulation of detail behind the interface to a class are real. They compared the percentage of maintenance changes that required modifications to the existing interfaces in a conventional application with those an object oriented application on the basis that it was only changes to the interface that could involve any risk. The statistics indicate that the proportion of changes to the interface, that is to the method signatures, in an object oriented systems is substantially smaller than changes to the interface, that is, to the procedure call signatures, within a conventionally developed application.

The magnitude of this reduction is depicted in figure 7.11, analysed by the type of maintenance activity (adaptive, perfective and corrective as defined in Section 7.6). The most significant reduction (from 74% to 41%) in changes to the interface occurs with perfective maintenance. This indicates that object oriented applications are much more able to be adapted to meet changing requirements in functionality than traditionally developed applications.

7.6.2 Project evaluation

The introduction of OO technology changes the evaluation criteria for a successful project to include:

- was the library of reusable objects exploited?
- were new artefacts added to the library?
- is the design that solved the current problem extensible?
- is the implementation understandable?

One of the major benefits of OO implementation is that the vocabulary used in the implementation of the information model is the same as that used in the real world problem domain; this significantly contributes to the understandability of the implementation.

OO projects may incur higher start-up costs than normal due to the need for training and new languages and tools, but it should be the reduction in recurring costs that are most significant. Developing prototypes is only more costly if they are not managed to ensure convergence in a timely manner. Measuring source lines of code is inappropriate for OO programmers; reusing code increases productivity by reducing the amount of code to be written but the cost per line of that which is written, measured against the overall project, will increase.

The short-term benefits of a strategic approach to OO technology are in delivering more robust and acceptable software solutions that are modifiable. The longer term benefits occur when a rapid response to change requests become feasible and the reusable library contains a set of truly significant reusable assets.

7.7 SUMMARY

The realisation of the benefits of an OO approach to application development can only be achieved with the long term commitment of management to adopt and nuture a different approach and attitude to the development of software systems. The major issues of concern to management when considering such a change are:

- *Solution space closer to problem space*   Increases the transparency of the implementation and reduces development effort, although it can discourage formal analysis and design.

- *Prototyping*   Achieves architectural clarity and involves the user but the prototype may be treated as the Product and prototyping is difficult to stop.

- *Use of evolutionary development*   Enables cost effective prototyping and staged decision making which can raise expectations and be difficult to manage and control.

- *Reuse*   Improves quality, productivity and modularity but needs investment and a different management approach.

8

MIGRATING TO AN OBJECT ORIENTED ENVIRONMENT

There are four strategies for migrating current application systems to an object oriented design. The strategies are described, with advice as to when and what to migrate to object orientation. There is the "wrapper" facility for interfacing between the objectbase and the current database files as the current systems are being migrated. Advice is also given as minimising the effort involved in the migration process.

There are a large number of questions that confront a manager who is planning to migrate current applications to object oriented technology. The list of the major questions include:

- should the strategy be a single "big bang" step migration of all the applications or a gradual migration of individual applications one at a time?

- should one leave the existing applications to run on the existing technology until they die a "natural death" or migrate them at a forced pace?

- which applications should one migrate first to object orientation?

- when should one migrate?

The important point at this stage is that it must be appreciated that all these questions are intertwined and occur simultaneously. They must therefore all be addressed as a job lot and not one at a time.

8.1   INFORMATION REDESIGN—YOU HAVE TO CROSS YOUR "RUBICON"

Although it has been said that object orientation does not require one to be "born again" and throw away one existing information design and development skills and technology architectures, there is no doubt that object orientation does require some change in the modelling of information and hence to the design of application systems. Information is currently modelled on key based tables of data and event based programs of logic, whereas with object orientation the data is modelled on the class and aggregation facilities, albeit on top of keys and the logic normalised to the object class, albeit grouped/messaged by event level processing. There are thus many more classes in an object oriented design than there are entities/tables in a relational design and more methods than program procedures.

There are four main changes in the way that information is modelled:

- The data has to reflect the class and aggregation facilities "sitting" on top of the key based tables of data.

    There is abstraction of the source entities/classes through class generalisation and specialisation: generalisation for the common and specialisation for the uncommon behaviour in the source classes, and aggregation generalisation of the data and related logic properties of complex objects.

- The event level logic is normalised to the business classes.

    The logic normalisation follows the same principles as that for the data, but with the addition that it must also reflect the class and aggregation abstractions. The result of logic normalisation is that some 80% of the logic is now spread across object calsses in the same manner as data. *Only 20% of the logic remains unchanged from a relational design when converted to an OO design—and that 20% is the event level logic. All the other information—100% of the data and 80% of the logic may be different.* It now reflects class and aggregation as well as key.

- Generalisation of common operations in the application class methods to form super-class method only common procedures.

- Generalisation of polymorphic methods.

    There will be occasions where different classes will contain methods that have similar business purposes with the same name. Polymorphism enables common functionality to be generalised as a "shadow" super-class method of the class model. The polymorphic software will know which "version" of the source base methods to invoke from the class of the object instances being accessed.

All of the above object oriented changes in the way that information is modelled from the traditional relational model means that the information in the existing application systems will likewise require redesign at some stage. There is no avoiding this. The only question is when to undertake the redesign, how difficult will it be, and what is the man effort required for it?

8.2   THE OBJECT ORIENTED "WRAPPERS"

Unless one adopts the "big bang" approach to object orientation migration some of a company's existing data will be in the corporate database, some of the migrated data will be in the new objectbase, and application programs will require to access data in both data modelling paradigms. They should be able to do so in a transparent manner, so that the application programmer is not aware of the two technology paradigms.

While this is the case it will be necessary for application programs communicating between the database and the objectbase to use a "wrapper" mechanism of some kind, a facility that provides a two-way isolation of the database from the objectbase and the objectbase from the database. An object oriented application program sends messages irrespective of whether the data to be accessed is stored in the objectbase or the database and a relational type application program sends database file handler calls irrespective of whether the data is stored in the database or the objectbase. A two way translation mechanism is required—object oriented to database for the object oriented application program and vice versa for the database application program. Unless this is done each application program that accesses the database from the objectbase and the objectbase from the database will require tailored bespoking of the access to a "foreign" data modelling paradigm.

The wrapper "translates" the database access calls/objectbase messages from the application program into a form the file handler of the "other" type" recognises. This involves not only converting file handler calls to the database into messages to the methods in the objectbase and vice versa but also a data mapping facility.

If the application program is written to access the database (that is the application program itself has not been migrated to object orientation) then the file handler calls to what the program "thinks" is a traditional database record need to be converted into one or more message calls if the data to be accessed is in the objectbase—if the record in the database has been subject to abstraction when migrated to the objectbase then what was one file handler call to a database single record type will be converted into several objectbase messages, one to the source classes and n to the abstracted classes

And the reverse is true. If a method requires to access a record that it "thinks" is a class but is actually a database record/table then the wrapper

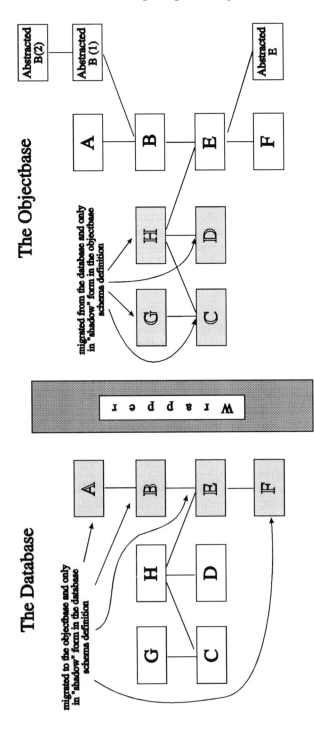

Figure 8.1   Database–objectbase interface

The Database

The Objectbase

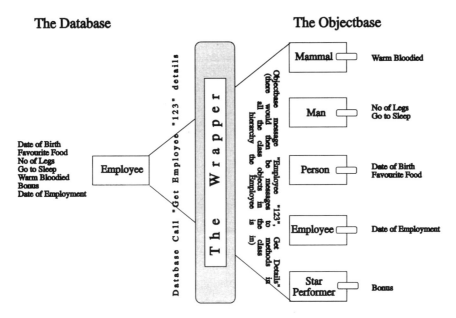

Figure 8.2 Database–objectbase wrapper

must convert the message to a file handler call. And if there has been abstraction then all the data to be accessed for the business requirement in the class or aggregation hierarchy requires to be concatenated into a database record. Any abstraction in the class model requires to be reversed before the database can accept a file handler call from the object oriented application program.

Figure 8.1 illustrates the general problem. The original database is on the left hand side with some of the tables already migrated across to the objectbase as shown. Some of the tables, B and E, have been abstracted, the B being generalised and the E specialised.

If the access requirement is "For a specified H access its Ds, Es and Fs" and the application program is written to access the database then the call to access the H and the Ds would be standard calls to the database file handler and of no concern to the wrapper, but the wrapper would be required to convert the accesses to the E into messages to the E and its specialised Abstracted E and a message to the F classes. Likewise if, the access requirement is "For a specified E access its related H and its Ds" and the application program is written to access the objectbase then the messages to the class object E would remain unaffected and of no concern to the wrapper but the messages to H and its D would require to be converted into database file handler calls.

A specific example of the problem is illustrated in figure 8.2 where there has been substantial abstraction of the table Employee into the class model.

The situation is that some of the employees are stored in the current database and some are in the new objectbase. The database call is to access Employee 123. It may be that Employee 123 is in the objectbase. Where there was one call to the database there has to be messages to 5 classes to access the now abstracted data properties. The fact that the data is most probably stored in concatenated form, illustrated in figure 3.1, means that much of the migration is in fact as one-for-one transfer of the database table rows to objectbase class instances, with the redesign being one of class schema definition. This does not alter the fact that 5 class based messages are still required to invoke 5 methods to access the data properties defined in the 5 classes. *The application program "sees" the objectbase as defined in the objectbase schema, not as stored on disk.* The compilation of the application program undertakes the concatenation of the schema definition to the format of the object instance on disk. The reverse would be required when accessing from the objectbase to the database.

The wrapper needs to have the following facilities.

- Common components
  - A two-way map of the database and objectbase designs with a cross referencing of the placement of the data in the database to the object-base and the objectbase to the database. This map is required even if the data is held either in the database or the objectbase, but not in both. The user needs to be able to specify access to data without knowing whether the data is in the database or the objectbase. If the query is posed against the database then the map of the database to the objectbase is required and vice versa.
  - A two phase commit mechanism if the program is updating data in both the existing database and the objectbase in order to ensure synchronisation of the updates. Where there has been class abstrac-tion the two phase commit cannot be the same facility as in distributed database as that works on the basis that the two database models are the same. A "home grown" version to handle any abstractions in the objectbase will need to be constructed.

- Database design to objectbase design
  - the replacement of file handler calls by messages to the methods. Where there has been class abstraction of the tables of data a single file handler call may be replaced by several messages. The messages need to reflect that fact that the "access path" to the classes must take into account the need to use property inheritance. Where this occurs the target class may well be different from the original table and the routine may need to reconstruct the individual message responses back into the single file handler call. This may require some final processing before sending the response.

— the replacement of procedure calls by messages to the methods. If the code of a former program module is now split amongst several methods then the single call needs to be split into several messages. The responses of the messages need to be reconstructed back into the form of the procedure call. This may require some final processing before sending the response.

- Objectbase Design to Database Design
  — The messages require to be broken down into file handler calls. Where there is class or aggregation abstraction of the data the n messages to the class and its super and sub classes will become merged to possibly one file handler call. The results from the file handler call need to be reconstructed back into the message response(s). This may require some final processing.

8.3 MIGRATION STRATEGIES

8.3.1 "Big Bang"

Having decided to adopt object orientation, the bold manager moves from the relational design (assumed) directly to an object design in a single move. This is the high risk, "big bang" approach.

There is a single migration from the technology of the relationally based design, with all the data based on keys in tables and application programs stored and designed separately at the event level, to the class and aggregation based data and logic design of object orientation. The high risks are clear—a single leap from one information technology paradigm to another, from keys and events to class and aggregation on top of keys and events with the normalisation of logic—so that much of the information, particularly the logic, will require redesign. New object oriented design facilities need to be learned, with class and aggregation, abstraction, property inheritance and message passing being just some of the new facilities.

For the data designer there is the need to redesign the data according to class and composition as well as to key, this requiring the:

- class and aggregation abstractions of the data properties to super and sub classes as appropriate;

- the definition of the relationships between the classes according to their type, class "is a", aggregation "has a" and business free form, and from this the class and aggregation hierarchies for property inheritance;

- reallocation of the data properties as appropriate to the abstracted class and aggregation objects in the objectbase schema definition;

- instantiation of abstract class generic date property values as appropriate.

For the logic designer there is the need to:

- normalise the logic of the business requirements to the business and abstracted class and aggregation objects in the class model;
- generalise the common operations in the methods into common procedures;
- identify and model polymorphic methods;
- define the messages to the methods.

For the physical programmer there are the added facilities of dynamic binding and the other facilities of genericity and function name and operator overloading.

The above is a substantial learning curve.

The impact of object orientation on an existing design and the single step migration to full object orientation can be seen in figure 8.3.

The logic redesign will be much simplified and the migration risk reduced if the logic of the existing application programs has been well structured, whereby the process logic is related to and grouped with the access logic, as illustrated in figure 8.4. If the application program has been written so that one table of data is accessed and then processed and then another is accessed and processed, then the migration to object orientation will be easier, as the blocks of code relating to the tables can be abstracted and

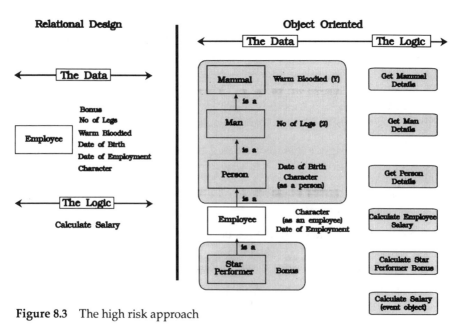

Figure 8.3   The high risk approach

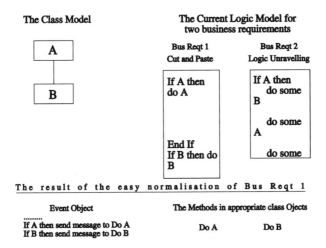

The result of the easy normalisation of Bus Reqt 1

Event Object	The Methods in appropriate class Ojects	
....		
If A then send message to Do A	Do A	Do B
If B then send message to Do B		

Figure 8.4 The normalisation of logic—easy and difficult

converted directly into methods in the matching classes. This is the case with business requirement 1, where the accessing of table A is followed by the processing of the data of A followed by the accessing and processing of the data of B. The accessing and processing of A becomes a method in the class of A ,and the accessing and processing of B becomes a method in the class of B. *Conversion to an object oriented application program design should be a matter of cut and paste, one of rearranging code and not rewriting it.* If the processing of A and B are intermingled then it will have to be a matter of unravelling the code and normalising it to the classes to which it belongs. This is the case with business requirement 2.

The problem of migrating and abstracting the data in the database to the objectbase is much less than for the application programs on the basis that there is only one objectbase migration/take-on application program to write. Bearing in mind that the data in the object instances are mostly the same as in the tables in the database, the conversion of the database into an objectbase is mostly a matter of a one-for-one transfer of the table data to the class data, further simplifying the task. Figure 8.1 shows the extent of the one-for-one transfer for a typical example—there only being abstractions of B and E.

Where there is a rearrangement of the data through abstraction of common data properties, then the migration program must move the abstracted table data properties into the appropriate class objects. This is the case with the Person and Star Performer classes in figure 3.1, if, and it is an if, that is the way in which the object oriented file handler works.

If the product is an extended relational file handler then the tables and their table rows become the classes and their instances on disk on a one-for-one

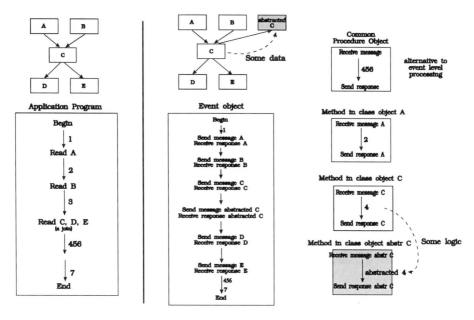

Figure 8.5   Conventional program   OO program

basis, with the sub-class object properties held as properties in the source table. In the case of the Employee table, 50 of the 500 Employees would have a value for the Bonus data property and the other 450 would have a null value. The only redefinition would be to the database schema in the dictionary to reflect the abstracted data properties into super and sub classes. Any abstract class would be defined and stored only in the schema with the appropriate data property instantiation. With the pure object oriented approach there would be two tables, one for the base table/object Employee and one for the sub-class Star Performer. Thus, with the extended relational approach there would be no need to recreate the database, only to redefine the schema. With the pure object oriented approach the relational database table rows would have to be "cut and pasted" from one relational table to two object files, as well as the schema being redefined.

Figure 8.5 shows the conversion of a conventional application program into an object oriented application program and the allocation of the normalised logic to methods in the application classes. *The whole process of converting conventional application programs to object oriented application programs is, of course, the normalisation of the logic.* With this particular application program there is some initialisation of the variables (1), a read access statement to access table A, then do some processing (2), then access table B and do some processing (3), then access tables C, D and E and do some processing to the returned joined data (456) before completing (7). For the first two accesses the processing (2 and 3) is a simple transfer directly to the objectbase as two methods to classes A and B is all that is required. For this part of the existing application program it is a simple case of cut from the old and paste to the new. This part of the current application program is already normalised.

There is a problem with the logic to the tables C, D and E. First, entity C has had some data properties generalised into a super class. There is thus a need to normalise some of the logic relating to the source class C to the Abstracted C. The logic number 4 to table C needs to be unravelled with some of the processing being moved to an abstracted method in the abstracted super class to C, the Abstracted C, with some of the logic remaining appropriate to the new method in class C, and then to issue messages from C to Abstracted C to support class property inheritance. The rules of logic normalisation will show which logic needs to be abstracted as a method in the super class Abstracted C. Also, the logic 5 to table D and logic 6 to table E need to be extracted and moved to methods for the classes D and E. An alternative to this is to create a common procedure of the logic 456, this also being illustrated in figure 8.5.

There are benefits to the high risk approach to the migration to object orientation. The benefits from object orientation are obtained at the earliest opportunity, and the problems of having two simultaneous information modelling and technical paradigms, one relational for the current applications and one object oriented for the new applications, is avoided. There is no need for a wrapper.

Clearly, there are dangers, not least the fact that there is a need to learn a major new technology and information design approach as quickly as possible. There is also the need to redesign the data that is abstracted and to normalise 100% of the existing logic—potentially no mean task if the current application is badly designed.

The danger is more apparent than real. If the objectbase is a problem when first installed one can always revert back to the existing system while the problems are sorted out. It need not be a case of migrating without an opt out capability.

8.3.2 Staged strategies

It is more than likely that the migration to object orientation will be in stages, particularly for large installations. There can be n variations of the proposed strategies. The strategies, which are not mutually exclusive, are:

- *Forced pace strategies*
  - An object-based design without class and aggregation abstraction as the first step, followed by a full conversion to object orientation. This is strategy 1.

— An object-based design with class and aggregation abstraction, followed by a full conversion to object orientation. This is Strategy 2.

- *Replacement strategy*
  Create a permanent wrapper mask between the existing applications and the object oriented applications, adopting object orientation only with new applications.

The strategies are considered in detail below.

8.3.3   Common option

There is a technical operating environment that is most suitable for object orientation, and hence is applicable for any of the above strategies. This environment is client-server, which has been designed to take advantage of the processing power of PC and workstation computers, and has enabled installations to distribute processing to the users on the client and away from the centralised server processor. The human/computer processing is done on the client, this typically being the use of windows technology and personal processing such as spreadsheets and word processing, as well as the more traditional processing of the menu and dialogue screens of the application systems. The server processor supports database processing, the access to the central database, and any processing of the data prior to transmission to the appropriate client.

Client-server technology matches exactly the object oriented philosophy of normalising some 80% of the application logic to methods in the application objects in the objectbase (to be placed on the server) and the residue of the logic in the event class objects (to be placed in the client).

8.3.4 Strategy 1

This is a two stage approach—the first stage is to make the application design object based without class and aggregation, and the second and more difficult stage is to migrate from the object based design to full object orientation.

An object-based design is still based solely on the concept of keys, so that the "class model" does not support the class and aggregation facilities. There are no class and aggregation hierarchies and hence no property inheritance. The logical data model becomes the class model on a one-for-one basis. The objects in the objectbase are the same as the entities. The "class model" is the same as for a relational entity model.

This approach requires in stage 1 that:

- the data tables in the database to remain unchanged in the objectbase as business classes;

- the logic to be normalised as appropriate. An example could be that the logic of the Calculate Salary business requirement is normalised to the event class and to the Employee;

- the elimination of relational joins when accessing multiple tables/classes as part of the move to an object-based design. Calls in the format of messages are sent from the event class to the application methods in each of the business classes to be accessed. The joins to be undertaken by the event class when responses have been received from the invoked application object-based methods;

- the placement of SQL calls in the methods defined for the business classes. This enforces encapsulation. There is no issuing of SQL calls in the event class;

- conversion of procedure calls to message formats.

The above can be seen in figure 8.6.

The main benefit to be obtained from object orientation in stage one—the reuse of data and logic—is not possible. This is the big disadvantage of stage 1.

The main advantage that the designers of the application information, while continuing to use their current database and programming technology, are learning some important object oriented facilities using technology they are familiar with, facilities such as encapsulation, logic normalisation, methods and messaging. *One is taking a design risk, not an implementation technology risk.*

But even here the design risk is small. The design techniques of some of the structured design methods, especially SSADM version 4, are tailor-made for producing object based logical designs. The logical data modelling techniques, of course, remain unchanged in stage 1. Logical data modelling can be used for the "class model". The other techniques also remain unchanged. The traditional techniques of entity life history, event processing and dialogue design remain unchanged. It is the interpretation of the deliverables that is slightly different. For example, the processes at the bottom of the Jackson process model diagrams are methods rather then potential modules of application programs with single table SQL DML access calls. The Action Diagrams logic for each table becomes a method. *One can model an object-based design using standard design techniques in operation today.*

And some of the relational vendors have enhanced their products so that they can also support object-based application systems. Ingres is a perfect example of this, with the sending of messages to stored procedures that are related to the tables, with the stored procedures containing SQL calls to

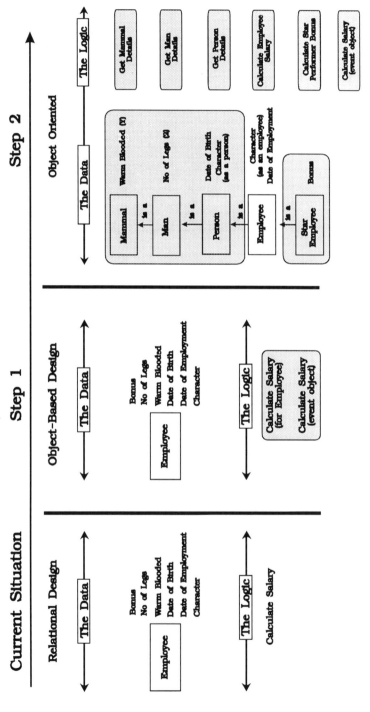

Figure 8.6   The low risk approach 1: object based migration

access the data properties. Relational joins in SQL have been abandoned, and the sending of messages to the procedures provides encapsulation. One is gaining some of the benefits of object orientation with today's techniques and technologies.

And the fact that you are doing a DIY approach to object orientation is no worse that what you are already doing with object oriented programming languages. Most of the current object oriented programming languages, such as C++, require the programmer to do this anyway. These languages are back to the days of pre-database technology, so that the relationships and any property inheritance between tables/class objects are supported in the application program DML logic and not in the file handler DDL. It is up to you to send messages to the super classes to obtain property inheritance. *Object orientation is still very much DIY.* This can be seen in the messaging example to support the example of the Test method in figures 2.7–2.9.

Step 1 of this migration strategy has much to recommend it—if one is using a relational file handler with stored procedures and triggers. The stored procedures "play the role" of public methods and the triggers "play the role" of private methods. Step 1 is an excellent way for preparing for object orientation before the relational vendors release object oriented upgrades of their products. The method of processes to class A in figure 8.7 could be a stored procedure.

The problem with stage 1 is that the logic has been normalised, possibly at considerable effort, to what are not class and aggregation classes. The normalisation of information is only to key-based business classes. One is therefore essentially "playing" at being object oriented. There has still not been the redesign of the data and the normalisation of the logic to reflect the class and aggregation facilities. One can see this in figure 8.7. The blocks of application program code are cut and pasted to the entity based objects, relational joins have been abandoned, the logic 4,5,6 has been separated on the basis of the objects accessed, and the file handler calls have been changed to become procedure calls (in the form of messages) to the methods in the objects. But there is no redesign to reflect class and aggregation—there is thus no property inheritance and therefore no data or software reuse. *The only benefits of object orientation being obtained are logic normalisation and encapsulation.*

The main step is step 2, the migration from an object-based design to an object oriented design. This requires the:

- creation of class and aggregation-based objects through generalisation and specialisation, as appropriate;

- definition of the semantic descriptions and construction of the class and aggregation hierarchies and their property inheritance;

- abstraction of the data properties as appropriate to the class and aggregation objects.

322

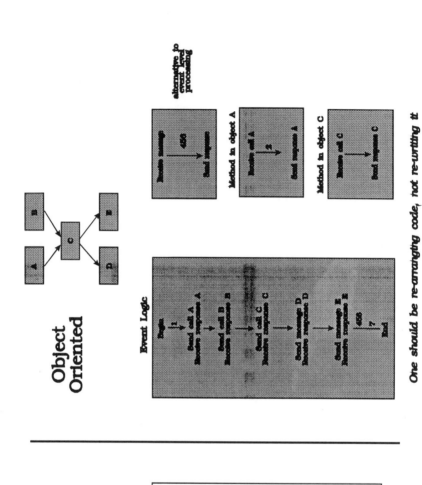

Figure 8.7   Step 1 of object oriented migration

Given that the actual storage of the object oriented data on disk remains unchanged from the relational model (certainly for the extended relational database products that will be object oriented in the next few years[1]), there is no requirement to restructure the database into an object-base. It is more a case of redefining the objectbase structure in the schema definition than a redesign of the objectbase data;

- allocation of generic class values to the data properties of abstract classes as appropriate;

- normalisation of logic to reflect the class and aggregation abstractions. The logic is therefore abstracted in the same way as the data. In figure 8.8 the logic 4 in the method for class C would require abstraction to reflect that part of the data properties of class C which have been generalised to a super class "Abstracted C", with the need to send a message to the Abstracted C class to access the abstracted C's data.

It is the introduction of the class and aggregation facilities into the design of information that requires the redesign of the data and the logic. There will thus need to be the same redesign of the data as described for the high risk strategy, and a second tranch at the redesign of the logic. The entity-based logic from stage one will require redesign to reflect any class and aggregation abstractions—access calls will need to be moved from the entity-based objects to the abstracted classes with the abstracted data properties. And this redesign would be for all application programs accessing the abstracted classes. Again, no minor task.

There is, nevertheless, a statement of comfort whichever approach is used—as with the first strategy, one is not rewriting code when one converts from existing application programs to object-based or oriented programs. What one should only have to do is to *rearrange the code and data*, from 100% event level code to 20% event level code and to class and aggregation-based data sitting on top of the key-based classes.

If the current application program code is badly designed and is not grouped according to the tables being accessed, then there is a genuine need to redesign the code, to the extent that it may have to be rewritten. The need to rerite code is a sign of bad original design.

8.3.5 Strategy 2

This would be the same as the object-based strategy, but with the objects in stage 1 being designed on the basis of class and property inheritance from the outset.

---

[1] Two of the leading relational vendors have confirmed that the storage of data on an objectbase will be exactly the same as that of the relational database. This is illustrated in figure 3.1. The class hierarchy is stored on disk as a union of all the classes in the class hierarchy.

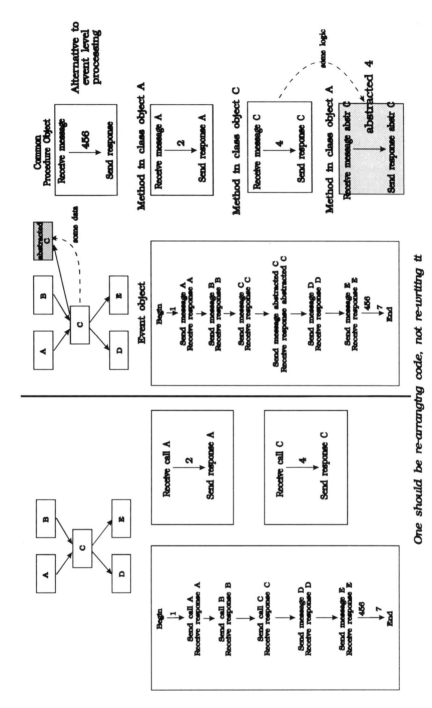

Figure 8.8   Step 2 of object-base migration

The entities in the logical data model would be redesigned to reflect the class and aggregation facilities from the outset, the data properties abstracted through generalisation or specialisation as appropriate, the class hierarchies defined and the property inheritance supported through explicit messages from the sub classes to the super classes. The technology used would remain relational, so that any abstractions would still be regarded as relational tables with keys allocated (pseudo key to the abstract classes). The physical database design would thus be the same as a class model, but the class and aggregation property inheritance would be by DIY in the application programs.

The logic of the application programs would be normalised to the class and aggregation based objects, with the abstraction of the logic matching the data abstractions—as can be seen in figure 8.9 with the logic of the abstracted 4 method matching the Abstracted C class.

The rationale of this strategy is that one does not have to wait for object oriented technology to become available before you start designing object oriented applications. The vast bulk of object oriented information modelling can be achieved with relational technology where it has stored procedures and triggers. The relational facilities that can be used are:

- the tables can be used as classes. If they have been abstracted and are abstract classes then the tables can be defined with a pseudo object ID key (as required), so that the table is a single row table;

- the stored procedures can be used for:
  — the public methods in the classes. The link between the methods and the tables is established in that relational joins are abandoned in the SQL statements—the SQL statements being single table access only. These are in the stored procedures and only to a single table at a time, the table that the stored procedure is "related to";
  — the event level processing. This process is concerned with sending messages to the stored procedure "methods" of the classes, receiving their responses, joining the data from the various class tables that have been accessed, and conducting any final processing;

- the triggers can be used for the private methods in the classes. These are triggered when a certain condition occurs, and are thus system triggered. They can also be triggered by the receipt of a message from a class-based stored procedure method;

- the procedure calls can be formatted to be in the form of messages;

- *Data inheritance can be simulated through the relational view;*

- *Logic* property inheritance can be achieved by the sending of messages from the sub-class methods to the super-class methods, as required.

The only object oriented modelling facility that cannot be supported is polymorphism; this because of the need for dynamic binding.

This has the advantage that applications which need to be developed can be so designed that when they are eventually migrated to an object oriented solution it is not a case, as it would be with strategy 1, of redesigning the applications. When the relational vendors release their own object oriented solutions, the migration will be a simple case of:

- a redefinition of the database schema to an objectbase schema. There is no need to restructure the database as it is converted into an objectbase. As indicated in figure 8.1, the generalisation and specialisation of the relational data model to an object oriented class hierarchy is modelled in the objectbase schema definition, not the objectbase data storage. The objectbase data storage remains the same as relational storage—the object instances in the objectbase being a union of the class schema model definition;

- one-for-one translation from the an object oriented-like database to an objectbase. There will be no need for an objectbase take-on exercise;

- messages to methods rather then calls to "method like" procedures.

There is also the added advantage that object oriented design techniques and almost all the implementation technology[1] would be learnt from the beginning of the strategy.

8.3.6   Replacement strategy

This strategy is, in a sense, a course of action for not migrating the existing applications to object orientation, but letting them continue to function to the end of their natural business and technical lives. Any migration to object orientation will not be at a "forced pace", and will only occur as current applications "die".

The wrapper will be the interface between the slowly forming objectbase and the slowly ageing database. Its role and mechanism is described in Section 8.2.

---

[1]   Facilities such as genericity and function name overloading would not be used until full object orientation is installed.

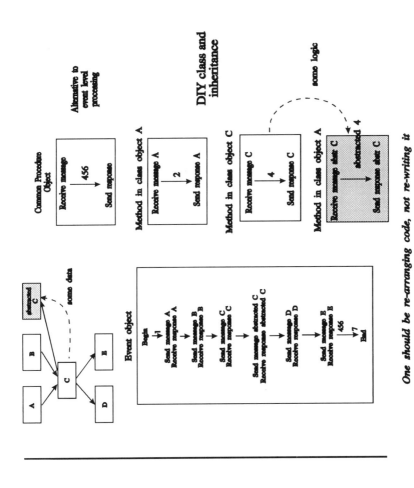

OO-based program

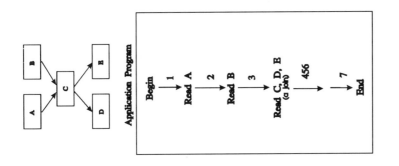

Figure 8.9   Conventional program

The advantage of this strategy is that maximum use is made of current application systems. They are migrated to object orientation only when there is a pressing technical or business need to replace them.

The disadvantage of this strategy is that there will be a longer time that two information design and implementation paradigms are in place at a company, with two sets of design skills and two sets of implementation technologies. This will need two sets of designers and programmers and careful liaison between two sets of teams that "see" information design and development in potentiality very different ways. And all of this is of no technical or business benefit to the company. Problem is being added to problem. The "hassle" of migration will be prolonged.

8.3.7   The client/server option

The beauty of adopting a client/server approach to the design of object oriented applications is that the object oriented information modelling paradigm matches exactly the hardware strategy—that is the "separation of powers".

Object orientation separates the event level "what" from the application object "how". The event classes with the 20% logic contain the logic that defines what information is required for a business requirement. It does this by sending messages to the appropriate methods in the business classes in the objectbase. The messages are the "what is required" aspect. This can be seen in figure 2.17 with the "what is required" being the Unload Vessel Cell S17 with Container Crane 12 and Add an object instance of Container Crane 13. The how it is to be achieved is with the methods Unload and Add. It is the invoked methods in the application objects that contain the logic that accesses the data properties and manipulates the data accessed on the basis of "how it is to be achieved" prior to sending a response to the event level class for any final processing. Figure 2.18 shows the "how it is to be achieved" with the method Unload checking the Lift Capacity of the Container Crane and sending a response that the lift capacity has or has not been broken.

And so it is with client/server technology. The client processor is a workstation/PC type processor designed to process the human/computer interface logic and send data access "what is required" messages to the server processor. The server then accesses the database/objectbase and issues a "I have now achieved it" response of the processed data back to the client for it, the client, to present the response to the screen. There is thus a clear separation of the user processing from the objectbase processing. The client undertakes the "what is required" and the server the "how it is to be achieved".

One can nicely blend the client/server and the object oriented information modelling paradigms with the client processor supporting the event "what"

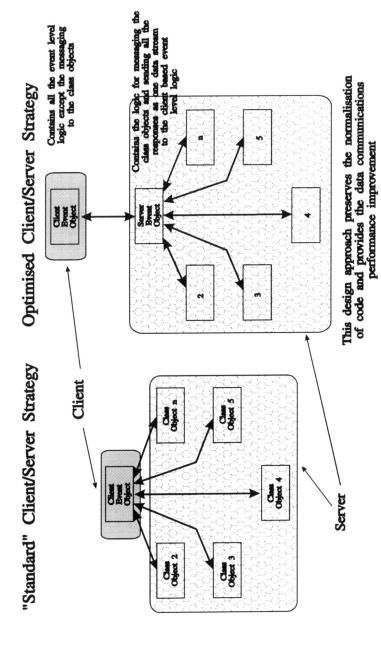

Figure 8.10 Client/server strategies with object orientation

processing and the server the application object "how" processing—the 20% of logic on the client and 100% of the data and 80% of the logic on the server.

There is a potential problem of performance. On a recent project there was a need to pass a large number of responses between the server and the clients. The messages were over a wide area network (WAN) and the overheads were such that the overheads of sending a data communication were a large part of the data transmission time. Sending a message from the clients to each class on the server and getting a response was a highly inefficient approach. This was what was called the "standard" client-server model, and can be seen in the left part of figure 8.10. The access strategy to the objectbase is Central Policeman, with the event class being solely responsible for the sending and receiving of messages. The problem with Central Policeman is the sending of these messages back and forth between the client and the server over the WAN, with the high overhead of WAN transmission, as well as the slow data transmission speeds of the lines. The solution was to split the event class process into two parts. The client part of the event process was limited to receiving the message from the input screen, sending a single event level message to the server part of the event process with the concatenated access path search parameters, receiving the single response and conducting any local processing as appropriate. The part that was concerned with the sending of messages to the methods and synchronising the responses from the methods was placed on the server. The process received the event messages from the client, the messages detailing all the classes to be accessed for the business requirement, sent a message to the appropriate classes, received the responses in return, and then sent a single concatenated reply back to the client. This approach enabled only a single message to be sent from the client to the server and a single response to be received in return. This can be seen on the right side of figure 8.10.

The client/server option can be used for any of the migration strategies defined above.

8.4   WHAT TO MIGRATE?

Not all information is ideally suited to be moved to an object oriented environment; some is more suited then others. And not all the facilities of object orientation are applicable all of the time. There are times when, for example, the crucial facility of class abstraction is not appropriate.

There are certain distinct components of computer systems and types of business applications that are particularly suited for development under object oriented technology. They include:

- *The Technical Sectors*
  The sectors of the market that are being addressed most earnestly by the new entrant vendors of object oriented products include:

  — the graphical user interface (GUI). The human/computer interface (HCI) part of application systems design is currently the "hottest" part most suited to OO, particularly if it is using windows technology. The windows are full of objects, such as buttons, menus, canvass areas and so forth, with logic that is distinct and normalisable to the objects. Class libraries of these object-based functions can be purchased and added to the class model as part of the system objects in the objectbase.

  — embedded software systems, such as robotics, and control systems such as signalling systems (on the railways for example) and telecommunication systems. The code that is embedded in the robots is logic that is normalised to the class Robot, and which therefore can be regarded as a client type processor to the server objectbase.

  — realtime systems, such as operational military systems.

- *Complex Applications*
  Applications with a large amount of class and aggregation information, where there can be substantial abstraction from the source class, and from this the ability to use class and aggregation property inheritance. This has the advantage that the full benefits of object orientation can be obtained.

- *Changing Applications*
  Applications that are highly volatile in business terms, with frequent changes required of the objectbase. This is particularly the case of the methods, as the logic is more volatile than the data, supporting as it does the business requirements. As explained in Chapters 1 and 2, object orientation provides facilities specifically suited for the management of change, that is specialisation of the changes into sub classes and the facility of encapsulation.

- *Low Risk Applications*
  Clearly, the adoption of object orientation involves a certain risk—it is new technology that requires a redesign of both the existing data and logic. It is commonsense not to migrate applications central to the running of the business until the learning curves have been completed and the DP department feels confident with the technology.

8.5   WHEN TO MIGRATE

The answer to this question is simple—now, even if there is not a suitable pure object oriented product. This is very much the situation with those who use relational technology and are waiting for the relational vendors to release object oriented versions of their products. Don't wait, get on with it.

It needs to be remembered that current object oriented programming languages and file handlers very must require the DIY approach, with the programmer being responsible for the sending of messages to the super classes, for the sending of messages to the methods and then methods accessing the data properties of the class objects and so on. Certain of the object oriented programming languages, such as C++, allow the by-passing of object oriented facilities, such as encapsulation. This flexibility is a double edged weapon. The downside is that it is up to the programmer to enforce object orientation. The result is that object orientation is DIY. *Object orientation is still in large measure do it yourself, even today.* So why not DIY object orientation with the current relational technology? There is much already in the leading relational products that supports the DIY of object orientation. The ability to define rules, triggers and database procedures goes some way to supporting methods, one can enforce encapsulation by issuing calls from the event method to stored procedures attached to tables, and the stored procedures to issue a single table/object SQL access call to the data attributes. These procedures play the role of methods in the application classes. And there is no reason why one cannot build class into the database design. If the class is an abstract data type then give it a pseudo key and instantiate the data properties with the CHECK facility. And property inheritance is quite feasible, with explicit calls to "super-class" procedures for the logic properties and the view facility for the data properties. Why not?

Before object orientation adoption is undertaken there are a number of issues that should be considered. They include:

* *The relational extensions*
  The fact is that the major vendors of relational database technology have not released object oriented upgrades to their products, and will not do so for a few years yet.

  The vendors are moving towards adding a layer of software on top of the relational architecture that will enable the underlying tables of data to become classes, with the methods stored separately as variable length records and chained to the related class either as pointers or symbolic references. The methods will contain the SQL calls to the data properties, but the calls will be to the single table only. Relational joins in the methods will be abandoned. They will have to be done at the event level either:

— explicitly in the programming as in pre-relational database technology

— passing the results of the method responses to the relational optimiser

— using the view facility

The problem of the object oriented relational join is a major subject and beyond the scope of this book.

If you have a large investment in relational technology then it is worth waiting for the product to be enhanced to support object orientation, and not adopt the specialist object oriented programming languages and file handlers to today's technology. It is quite unnecessary to move to these specialist object oriented products.

- *The new players versus the "old timers"*
  The dangers of adopting an object oriented product from the new entrant specialist companies entering the object oriented marketplace prior to the current relational vendors and hoping to "make it big" before the existing database vendors respond. The problem here is that many of these new companies are small and of limited financial resources—and when the relational vendors respond they will be under even greater pressure. The long-term survival of some of them must be open to some doubt. If you are a large commercial operation the above characteristics need to be addressed if the adoption of specialist products is being considered.

- *The speed of migration.*
  Migrate at your own pace and time. The existing database and programming technology works and is well understood. *Object orientation is a risk technology, offering a benefit only in the long term*. There is a large amount of up-front investment to be made with object orientation.

- *Once migration has started don't dally*
  If you are going to migrate then don't dally. Do a trial first, and when confidence has been obtained then migrate with speed. The problems of the wrapper and the integration of two information modelling paradigms has already been highlighted, and are not minor. And it is likely that there will be tensions between the teams supporting what is inevitably regarded as a dying technology, database technology, and the "rising star" technology of object orientation—one team with a dwindling role and the other with an expanding one.

8.6   SUMMARY

The chapter shows that:

- the most viable strategies are those of unforced migration with the wrapper facility between the database and the objectbase and strategy 2, converting direct to an objectbase design from the current applications. Half way house migrations to an object-based design prior to full object orientation merely postpones the day of information redesign that object orientation requires;

- client/server technology is in line with object orientation—the 20% of logic at the event level on the client and the 80% of logic normalised to the classes on the server;

- the fact that migration of a relational database data to an objectbase is a case of redefining the database schema definition to reflect the abstractions of the objectbase, and not a case of reorganising the data on disk;

- migrating code to object orientation should be a matter of rearrangement, not rewriting;

- start to migrate to object orientation now, even with a relational product in use.

REFERENCES

G Booch *Object Oriented Design with Applications* Benjamin/Cummings, New York, 1991.

P Coad and E Yourdon *Object Oriented Analysis* Prentice-Hall, Englewood Cliffs, NJ, 1990.

M Ellis and B Stroustrup *The Annotated C++ Reference Manual* Addison-Wesley, Reading MA, 1990.

J S Hares *SSADM for the Advanced Practitioner* Wiley, Chichester, 1990.

J S Hares *Information Engineering for the Advanced Practitioner* Wiley, Chichester, 1992.

J D Ichbiah *et al Reference Manual for the Add Programming Language, ANSI/MIL-STD-1815-A-1983* Castle House Publications, Tunbridge Wells, 1983.

S Khoshafian and R Abnous *Object Orientation: Concepts, Languages, Database, User Interfaces* Wiley, Chichester, 1990.

B Meyer *Object-Oriented Software Construction* Prentice-Hall, Englewood Cliffs, NJ, 1988.

J Rumbaugh *et al. Object Oriented Modelling and Design* Prentice-Hall, Englewood Cliffs, NJ, 1991.

S Shlaer and S J Mellor *Object Life Cycles: Modelling the World in States* Yourdon Press, New York, 1992.

B Stroustrup *The C++ Programming Language Second Edition* Addison-Wesley, Reading MA, 1991.

D Taylor *Object Oriented Information Systems* Wiley, Chichester, 1992.

INDEX

TITLES IN THIS SERIES

Fletcher J. Buckley ● Implementing Software Engineering Practices

John J. Marciniak and Donald J. Reifer ● Software Acquisition Management

John S. Hares ● SSADM for the Advanced Practitioner

Martyn A. Ould ● Strategies for Software Engineering
The Management of Risk and Quality

David P. Youll ● Making Software Development Visible
Effective Project Control

Charles P. Hollocker ● Software Review and Audits Handbook

Robert L. Baber ● Error-free Software
Know-how and Know-why of Program Correctness

Charles R. Symons ● Software Sizing and Estimating
Mk II FPA (Function Point Analysis)

Robert Berlack ● Software Configuration Management

David Whitgift ● Methods and Tools for Software Configuration Management

John S. Hares ● Information Engineering for the Advanced Practitioner

Lowell Jay Arthur ● Rapid Evolutionary Development
Requirements, Prototyping and Software Creation

K.C. Shumate and M.M. Keller ● Software Specification and Design
A Disciplined Approach for Real-Time Systems

Michael Dyer ● The Cleanroom Approach to Quality Software Development

Jean Paul Calvez ● Embedded Real-time Systems
A Specification and Design Methodology

Lowell Jay Arthur ● Improving Software Quality
An Insider's Guide to TQM

John S. Hares ● SSADM Version 4
The Advanced Practitioner's Guide

Keith Edwards ● Real-Time Structured Methods
Systems Analysis

John S. Hares and John D. Smart ● Object Orientation
Technology, Techniques, Management and Migration